The Wake of the Gods

The Wake

STANFORD UNIVERSITY PRESS

STANFORD, CALIFORNIA · 1963

H. Bruce Franklin

of the Gods

MELVILLE'S MYTHOLOGY

Stanford University Press
Stanford, California

© 1963 by the Board of Trustees of the
Leland Stanford Junior University

Library of Congress Catalog Card Number: 63-10733

Printed in the United States of America

To
Yvor Winters

PREFACE

Since all myth is by definition fictional, no one should be surprised to find that literary fiction is mythic. Literary fiction does essentially the same thing as primitive mythic fiction: both tell made-up stories about the human and natural worlds and both implicitly assign a high order of truth to these made-up stories. Their subjects and methods often seem almost indistinguishable. We can, of course, make an infinite number of theoretical distinctions between what we choose to call myth and what we choose to call fiction. But theoretical distinctions themselves are by and large fables. Perhaps it may seem more meaningful to make the distinction between what we call primitive myth and literary fiction. But any attempt to distinguish between literary and mythic fiction on the basis of its source rather than its form must face two simple facts: the myths with which we are most familiar come to us from the literature of highly developed civilizations; modern psychology has given everybody, no matter how civilized or how literate, his own share of the mythopoeic faculty. Where, how, or by whom a particular story was told will not tell us whether it "is" a myth any more than its subject and method will. Perhaps the best answer is to say that literary fiction is a kind of written mythmaking.

The problem grows more complicated when we realize that "myths" in the broadest sense form the subject of all fiction. Literary fiction must use the myths which surround its conception; it may embrace or dissect, assume or assault, but it cannot keep them from its pages. Literary fiction by definition is a myth maker and by nature a myth user. Only a gross act of simplification can order these problems into the terms of this study. This act will be to call myths the parts of a mythology and to call a mythology the collection of stories told about some particular set of gods which we do not worship.

What can the writer of fiction do with a mythology, the stories of someone else's gods? He can surreptitiously appropriate one or more of these stories, thus taking advantage of unconscious psychological values, if any, inherent in mythic patterns, whatever those may be. He can use that old literary standby, the mythological simile or metaphor, to extend or define meaning or emotion. He can retell stories from mythology, in idioms as different and with purposes as divergent as Shakespeare's *Venus and Adonis,* Shelley's *Prometheus Unbound,* Hawthorne's *Wonder Book for Boys and Girls,* and Shaw's *Pygmalion.* Or he can do what this study claims Melville did—make mythologies themselves, as well as myths, part of his subject. This poses another problem: how can we define Melville's knowledge of mythology?

The stories told about gods take innumerable forms, and the origin and ultimate truth of all myths are inscrutable. Different ages accept different forms as well as different explanations of the same myths. As a profound student of mythography has recently put it:

Like the clouds of Hamlet or the somewhat more stable inkblots, myths are such vague and amorphous configurations that an epoch invariably tends to project itself into them. . . . The primitive mythic mind is lost forever; but every century has fantasies about its unknowable ancestors, and these are closer to our understanding. The long array of mythographers of the past twenty-five hundred years, from Democritus and Hecataeus of Miletus through Jung, all bear the distinctive physiognomies of their age. Present-day inquiries into the few remaining primitive societies have revealed the investigators more often than the savages. The contemporary who describes the primordial function of the myth in either a sociological or a psychic context often says more about his own attitude toward moral problems, toward progress, God and the devil, toward reason and the uses of the imagination than he does about the mind of aboriginal man. (Frank E. Manuel, *The Eighteenth Century Confronts the Gods,* pp. 11–12.)

Thus arise two more problems for a study such as the present one. The first is exorcising the demonic ghost of the psychological tautology, trying one's best to read something other than oneself in both Melville's fiction and the mythology with which it is concerned. The second is determining which period of mythological study helps most in understanding Melville's work. I have chosen the period which I shall refer to throughout this work as contemporaneous—roughly from the mastering of Sanskrit by Sir Charles Wilkins and Sir William Jones in the 1780's to just before Sir James Frazer began to displace astronomical gods in favor of vegetation gods in 1890.

Few of the comparative mythologists of this period are now known by name and even fewer are read or written about. Therefore, I have had to go directly to their work wherever I could find it—in magazines, newspapers, learned journals, travel books, encyclopedias, and treatises on philosophy, theology, ancient history, archeology, and mythology proper. In order to understand the comparative mythology of this period, I found it necessary to compose my own history of it. No doubt adequate secondary material would have helped both my history and the uses to which I put it. But the lack of secondary material is not altogether a disadvantage, at least to understanding Melville's mythology. For what I know about contemporaneous mythology cannot exceed what Melville could have known.

Just how much was Melville interested in the mythology of this period and just how much did he know about it? A work to which this book pays little attention most clearly answers both parts of the question. *Clarel,* very largely nothing but a study of comparative religion and mythology, evinces a wide and deep knowledge of its subject and shows the impact which that knowledge could have on nineteenth-century faith. A book could easily be written directly on Melville's interest in and knowledge of mythology.

This study, rather than tracing Melville's knowledge of mythology, tries to show how Melville consciously used myths, mythologies, comparative mythology, and mythological theories in his major works—*Mardi, Moby-Dick, Pierre, Bartleby, Benito Cereno, The Confidence-Man,* and *Billy Budd.* My central thesis is that Melville's mythology determines and defines large parts of the structure and meaning of these works. This brings us to a final caveat.

I believe that mythology in each of these works is important both to structure and to meaning. Even when pagan myth is more or less

ACKNOWLEDGMENTS

It is hardly news to any serious student of Melville that he was profoundly interested in mythography and mythology. The scholarship and criticism of the last forty years have shown in detail and in general Melville's continual use of mythology. In fact, there is hardly a major study of Melville which has not at some point dealt with this use, and the number of articles at least touching on Melville's mythology is rapidly becoming countless. It is impossible for me to acknowledge my full debts to Melville scholars and critics.

There are, however, a few works dealing with aspects of Melville's mythology which should receive at least a brief mention. There are the important annotations found in these recent editions: Henry Murray's *Pierre*, Walter Bezanson's *Clarel*, Howard Horsford's *Journal of a Visit to Europe and the Levant*, and, most important, Howard Vincent and Luther Mansfield's *Moby-Dick*. There are the source materials found in Howard Vincent's *The Trying-Out of Moby-Dick*, Charles R. Anderson's *Melville in the South Seas*, Merrell Davis's *Melville's Mardi*, and, of course, Merton Sealts, Jr.'s *Melville's Reading*, which, even without the forthcoming supplement of information gathered in the last decade, is still the sharpest source-digging tool. And there are the major works which have focused on Melville's literary reactions to various religions and mythologies: William Braswell's *Melville's Religious Thought*, Nathalia Wright's *Melville's Use of the Bible*, Lawrance Thompson's *Melville's Quarrel with God*, Dorothée Finkelstein's *Melville's Orienda*, Richard Chase's *Herman Melville*, Charles Olson's *Call Me Ishmael*, and James Baird's *Ishmael*. Although I disagree with the arguments advanced by a few of these works, each has contributed to this work.

I wish to thank the Government of India Tourist Office in San Francisco for the picture of the Trimurti on the jacket and the *New*

England Quarterly, which published part of Chapter 5 as " 'Apparent Symbol of Despotic Command': Melville's *Benito Cereno*" (December 1961). I am deeply indebted to Professors David Levin, Thomas Moser, and Lawrance Thompson, who read the manuscript and furnished many valuable suggestions; to the staff of the Stanford University Press, particularly Mrs. Shirley Taylor, who was an understanding and incisive editor; to Miss Nadia Jacobowsky, who checked many of the quotations; to Mrs. Linda Brownrigg, who prepared the Index; and to Professor Yvor Winters, who first inspired my study of Melville and who has encouraged and aided me at every stage. To the one who has given most no debts are due, for she is my partner in the enterprise.

H. B. F.

CONTENTS

The Wake of the Gods

I then went on, beginning with the rise and progress of the primitive religions, and coming down to the various religions of the present time.—MOBY-DICK

MELVILLE AND THE GODS

PAGAN GODS IN THE WORLD OF MELVILLE

For pagan gods the Renaissance was indeed the time of resurrection. While the gods of Greece and Rome, freed from the bonds of Christianized allegory, were again becoming living forces in European literature, the ancestors of the Greek and Roman gods were being brought back from the east and gods unheard of by the ancients were coming in Spanish, Portuguese, and English ships from the west. Through the sixteenth century, European literature was content to use the old European gods for traditional literary purposes—decoration, drama, allegory, and eroticism. The seventeenth century inquired more and more into the ancestry and meaning of all the pagan gods. From the old euhemerism of Ralegh's *History of the World* and the remodeled allegorism of Bacon's *De Sapienta Veterum* through the new fear theories of Hobbes and Spinoza, the ponderous etymologies of the polyhistors, and the diffusionism of Athanasius Kircher's *Oedipus Aegyptiacus* to the part psychological, part euhemerist, part diffusionist, part allegorical, part mystical *True Intellectual System of the Universe* of Ralph Cudworth, the question, "Where, when, how, and why were the gods born?" became more persistent and more troublesome, while the answers became more complicated and more confusing. As Europeans learned from their voyages to the Americas, India, China, and Africa that there really were heathen societies which really did worship heathen deities in heathen rituals, they slowly began to realize that the ancient gods were not mere literary conventions or moral abstractions. Even the old pagan gods of the Bible took on substantial form. Bracketing Cudworth's tomes in time were two landmarks which pointed the way to the past and the future roles of the pagan gods in Western thought. Eleven years before had come *Paradise Lost*; nineteen years after was to come Pierre Bayle's *Dictionnaire historique et critique*. For Milton the pagan gods were still captives of Christianity: Moloch, Chemos, Baal, Astarte, Thammuz, Dagon, Rimmon, Osiris, Isis, Horus, the Ionian gods, and even old Titan with his brood dutifully performed their substantial but allegorical functions in the great Christian epic. But Bayle took the pagan gods only slightly less seriously than he took the Christian God. His *Dictionnaire* was to prove much more than a passing whimsical attack on the Judaic-Christian God; it was to prove the forebear of many eighteenth-century investigations of religion and carefully worked out theories of religious belief. These investigations and theories have had in turn a vast and influential progeny.

The theories themselves strongly influenced most of later Western thought, including Melville's ideas and the ideas of modern commentators on Melville. Confronted with more and more irrational myths and uncivilized rituals, the eighteenth-century *philosophes* constructed systematic psychological theories to explain religious belief. Constructing these theories led them into formulating for the first time the systematic notion of a distinctly primitive mind, a mind distinguished as sharply as possible from the ideal philosophic mind of the eighteenth century.[1] To the primitive mind they allocated the mythopoeic faculty. The later history of these theories and this notion is now a familiar story. The eighteenth-century faith in common sense gave to the Romantics a rational justification for holding up the primitive mind as the lamp of truth; to the savage, the peasant, the child, even to the idiot and the lunatic, they went for revelation. Almost deified by the Romantics, the primitive mind became increasingly an object of study as well as of worship in the nineteenth century. The eighteenth century first had located the primitive mind

---

[1] Numbered notes will be found at the back of the book, pp. 209–20.

in remote times and places, then located it also in the uncivilized individual living in familiar times and places (the child, peasant, lunatic, idiot), and finally located it as well in the collective popular mind. The nineteenth and twentieth centuries have located the primitive mind below the conscious part of each mind and in the collective unconscious of all minds. This location has made possible a systematic aesthetic of the primitive. The idea of a distinctly primitive mind, first developed by the eighteenth-century mythologists to explain to civilized minds the myths of barbarous times and places, is now used to explain and exalt primitive and mythic elements in what had once been thought some of civilization's most distinguishing products. The myth critics have already reaped a bountiful harvest of archetypical mythic patterns from Melville's work. This study will not, like some recent Melville studies, show how Melville's works demonstrate theories advanced by Freud, Jung, and their followers. But it will try to show the contexts which gave rise to the mythological theories not only of Freud and Jung but also of the myth critics themselves. For it was eighteenth- and nineteenth-century comparative mythology which produced and defined the notion of archetypical mythic patterns and provided the means for exploring the human mind in terms of its myths.

The investigations spawned by Bayle have had in some ways a more irreversible influence than the theories. Investigations of religions and mythologies joined closely with the contemporaneous investigations of biology and geology, but they were much more shocking to the orthodox. Layers of rock far older than the Biblical date of the Creation, species of animals extinct eons before Noah, and evidence that man was a relative newcomer to the earth were upsetting, but they could not upset as much as the Christ-like saviors which were found from India and Egypt to Peru and Polynesia, and the festivals, discovered all around the Northern Hemisphere, corresponding both to Christmas and the winter solstice, both to Easter and the vernal equinox. These investigations turned much of Western Scripture from historical fact into metaphorical or psychological fact—or, perhaps, mere fancy.

Bayle had helped make the sands of mythology a playground for skeptical investigations and a plantbed for psychological theories of religious belief. As the sea of faith receded, this enlarged playground and plantbed became, for nearly two centuries, one of the major intellectual battlegrounds of the Western world. As Western Europe began to question its own God, the philosophical, etymological, polemic games it played with the other gods became increasingly serious. It was in the first half of the nineteenth century that these games became most serious and most deadly and the grounds upon which they were played became most large and most important. Only after the war to preserve Scripture as literal Revelation was lost did the battles of mythology become again mere alarms and skirmishes. While the battles were hottest, while new discoveries were daily shaping new weapons, while the outcome of the war was for the last time in doubt, Melville composed all the prose fiction published in his lifetime, from *Typee* in 1845 to *The Confidence-Man* in 1857. Nineteen years later he published a two-volume poem which refights the major battles of the skeptic and Christian comparative mythologists; but the Christian apologist in *Clarel,* an Anglican priest named Derwent (from *derw,* the widely discussed root of *Druid*), can never defend the mythological barricades he is forever building.

Because it was shaped in the heat of the most violent polemics, the comparative mythology known to Melville may seem to lack some of the so-called "objectivity" of some present-day anthropology. Perhaps it does, and one may well ask how "true" this comparative mythology was. It is a question that deserves an answer, particularly because it is central to many of Melville's works, but it is inherently unanswerable. Melville focused so intensely on this question because the truth of comparative mythology depends on the "truth" of myth, and all truth available to man appears finally to be mythic. Each age of Western thought has had its own mythological theories, and each age has tended to judge harshly the theories of every other age. Most of the mythology known to Melville lies now in oblivion; most of the rest is looked upon as merely curious. Perhaps this is the fate it deserves. Yet many of the ancient mythologists, many of the mythologists of Melville's day, and even Melville himself were peculiarly well qualified, in one way or another, to study, compare, and theorize about the myths of man.

The ancient mythologists had the great advantage of being close in time and place to the birth of many gods. Herodotus, for instance, saw the rituals and heard the stories and theology of the entire Mediterranean world and beyond in the fifth century before Christ. He visited and talked with priests and peoples from Thrace and Scythia to Babylon, Ecbatana, Susa, and Elephantine. A few centuries later the mythologists had a vast corpus of mythological literature, much of which is no longer extant, and they still enjoyed some of the ancient travel privileges. All that the ancient comparative mythologists lacked was access to some remote parts of the world such as Polynesia and the Americas.

The comparative mythologists of Melville's day could visit virtually the entire world. Although they were ignorant of many languages known today, they learned many other languages well at an early age. Before they became mythologists—indeed before they became men—they studied in the original language the comparative mythology and the travel literature of the Greeks and the Romans. Sir William Jones, perhaps the most important of the late eighteenth-century mythologists, was only twenty-one when he wrote learned disquisitions on hitherto untranslated Asiatic poetry, and according to Melville, he eventually mastered thirty languages. Of the less extraordinary mythologists, many were clergymen who brought to their later work an early knowledge of Hebrew and an intimacy with the pagan gods of the Bible. Many of these clergymen learned Coptic, Syriac, and Chaldean in their seminaries, and, after 1800, some began serious work with Sanskrit. Their knowledge of contemporary Western languages was, of course, wide and often deep, and they had a double professional interest in all contemporary travel literature, particularly that of the missionaries, the missionaries' helpers (such as the Royal Society of Bengal and Calcutta), and the missionaries' critics (such as Herman Melville).

Two great linguistic events of the late eighteenth century were to

change the course of all Western comparative mythology: in the
1780's Europeans first mastered Sanskrit; in 1799 Europeans found
the Rosetta stone in Egypt. In 1822 these two events had their cli-
maxes. While the explorers were combing Egypt, Champollion un-
locked the Egyptian hieroglyphics. While the mysteries of ancient
Hindustan were pouring into Europe, Jacob Grimm (in the second
edition of *Deutsche Grammatik*) systematically explained the correspondence of consonants among all the Indo-European languages.
With Grimm's Law of Indo-European consonants came the concept
of an Indo-European mythology.

All this happened before Melville was three years old. Mountains
of comparative mythology had been piling up for centuries; and even
before Melville learned to read, these mountains were being discovered by the popular media of the day. By the time he began
writing fiction, these old mountains were being explored, mined, and
sold in chunks by a real intellectual infant—the popular periodical.
Poole's *Index to Periodical Literature* lists hundreds of articles before
1860, a fair sign that there were thousands. The casual reader could
now find mythology not only in the plays and poems of his favorite
authors, in travel books, in the Bible, in Biblical encyclopedias (such
as Kitto's *Cyclopedia of Biblical Knowledge*), and in the popular
mythological dictionaries (such as Bell's *New Pantheon*) which explained to him literary references to pagan gods, but also in his weekly
and monthly magazines. Popular educational aids such as *Hogg's
Instructor* colorfully recounted Hindu as well as Greek myths; the
Christian magazines scornfully derided each newly found god and
gave precise instructions to the young missionary preparing for polemics with learned Brahmans and terrifyingly ascetic Yogis and
Saniassin; the major reviews looked over the outpouring mass of
mythological explorations and comparisons six and eight books at
a time.

Although Melville read great numbers of these periodicals, his
favorite reading was ancient and modern travel literature, which
heavily influenced his fiction.[2] Some of these travel books set out to
compare religions and mythologies; others seemed incapable of avoid-

ing comparative mythology and religion. Of the travel books which we know Melville used as sources, some, such as William Ellis's four-volume *Polynesian Researches* (a source for *Typee, Omoo,* and *Mardi*), were scholarly investigations into other societies and their religions. Others, such as Amasa Delano's *Narrative of Voyages and Travels* (a major source for *Benito Cereno*), deal almost entirely with unscholarly, worldly, and practical matters. But even Delano does more than simply comment on Polynesian and Asiatic religions; he constructs his own theories of mythology. After describing with the aid of the Edinburgh Encyclopedia the idols of the Hindu Trimurti which he had seen in the Caves of Elephanta, the usually shrewd but simple-minded Captain Delano unintentionally reveals to us a great deal about the popular state of comparative mythology in the early nineteenth century:

This account gives us three attributes personified by three heads. We might be inclined to trace an analogy between these and the cherubic figures described in our sacred books, which so many christians consider as representing the Deity, were it not that Seva seems to be too nearly the same with Satan to be introduced among the emblems of the God described in the Bible. Another difficulty also might be supposed to arise from the variation in the numbers, the cherub of Ezekiel having *four* heads, and the figure of the cave having but *three*. Where numbers are fundamental, a personification which is *fourfold,* and another which is *threefold,* must be somewhat uncomfortable to the mythologist in his attempts at reconciliation. It is our own opinion however that the difficulty is not insurmountable when the true philosophy of the mythology of all nations is understood. It is not necessary to consider Seva as a distinct deity, and answering to Satan, but he may be taken as a personification of avenging justice, the right or the disposition to punish the obstinately guilty, as this attribute exists in the true God. The personification of one attribute more, or one less, does not alter the theory of the explanation, or prevent us from using it as an illustration of the same great truths.[3]

Literature took up the discoveries of the traveling scholars and sea captains as fast as they were made. Seven years before Delano's theory of the Hindu Trimurti, Southey published *The Curse of Kehama,* a long and involved versification of many of the fine points of

Hindu mythology. Although none of the other Romantics plunged so deeply as Southey into exotic mythologies, they made many strange myths familiar and many better-known myths commonplace. The voguish literary Orientalism of the eighteenth century, decorated by new discoveries, became an undercurrent of nineteenth-century literature from Coleridge to Kipling.

Melville read widely in the popular sources of mythology—modern periodicals and ancient and modern poetry, fiction, drama, and travel literature. He also read deeply in the central documents of post-Renaissance mythology—the ponderous polemical tomes of learned heretics and divines. It has been shown that Melville used as sources, for instance, an English translation of Bayle's *Dictionnaire* and the Reverend Thomas Maurice's *Indian Antiquities*.[4] But these were not simply sources. Melville's works make many significant connections between these two examples, the first great modern psychological analysis of mythology and the last major Christian defense against psychological theories of mythology. Melville knew well and used carefully the theories of Maurice and his nineteenth-century followers—that pagan myths were merely Revelation spread by man's travels and distorted by man's mind—and those of Bayle and his eighteenth-century followers—that all man's myths and gods were merely products of man's mind. As this study will show, Melville uses the language, the theories, the knowledge, and the techniques of both the Christian and the skeptical mythologists to explore the relations between man and his gods.

Whether they came originally, as the skeptics suggested, from man's conceptions of what his senses reveal, or, as the apologists maintained, from man's misconceptions of what God revealed, the gods of strange lands poured from many directions and in many channels into the America of Melville's early life. From Africa, Asia, and Oceania, from South America, Central America, and the center of North America they came in the works of European translators, mythologists, and poets, the tales of American sailors, settlers, and missionaries, and the accounts of explorers, archeologists, and historians of all nations. A few of Melville's contemporaries welcomed some of these gods with open arms. The Transcendentalists in fact made the American East into another home for religions of the Orient.[5]

In 1841, at the age of twenty-one, Melville left Massachusetts in a whaleship. The following July, while in Massachusetts Emerson and Thoreau were beginning the series called "Ethnical Scriptures" in *The Dial,* Melville, as a captive of the Typee savages, was beginning a field study of Polynesian mythology.

MELVILLE IN A WORLD OF PAGAN GODS

Melville's knowledge of Polynesian religion has remained a matter of debate ever since the publication of *Typee.* He has been considered everything from a major authority to a mere literary pretender to a downright liar. Charles Anderson has pointed out that "Melville is cited as an authority in such studies as those of Sir James George Frazer, Robert Wood Williamson, and Louis Rollin," and Frazer alone "quotes *Typee* with approval more than a score of times."[6] But Anderson has also shown Melville's heavy reliance on literary sources, and he therefore tends to suspect the accuracy of Melville's knowledge, preferring to rely on the findings of modern anthropological expeditions, even if they in turn were forced to rely on the memories of the surviving natives. Melville did have probably the most intimate contact of any Westerner with the Marquesan tribal civilization, but, as Anderson observes, "Melville was the first to confess his lack of any real understanding of the theology of the Typees."[7] Melville's confession of ignorance is not, however, a simple one.

When Melville, after spending several weeks as a captive of the Typees and after later reading almost every available account of the Marquesas, confesses ignorance, he is making a statement more about knowledge than about the Typee valley. He saw in the Typee mythology and theology the fundamental enigmas of all mythology and all theology; that is, he saw the fundamental enigmas in all human knowledge. He saw all knowledge as more or less mythic. For almost half a century, beginning in *Typee* and not ending until his death, Melville explored these enigmas with the tools, methods, and vocabulary of comparative mythology.

When Delano recalls the gigantic three-headed stone figure of the Hindu Trimurti in the Cave of Elephanta, he thinks of Satan, cherubim, and the attributes of his own God. When Melville recalls the gigantic stone terraces of Typee, he thinks "of Stonehenge and the architectural labours of the Druid"[8] and of "the mighty base of the Pyramid of Cheops." Melville receives the islanders' explanation of the stones perhaps as astutely as some more recent Polynesian investigators:

These structures bear every indication of a very high antiquity, and Kory-Kory, who was my authority in all matters of scientific research, gave me to understand that they were coeval with the creation of the world; that the great gods themselves were the builders; and that they would endure until time shall be no more. Kory-Kory's prompt explanation, and his attributing the work to a divine origin, at once convinced me that neither he nor the rest of his countrymen knew anything about them. (P. 658)

When Melville generalizes on the stones, he implicitly opposes the usual orthodox theory of comparative religion and mythology:

These remains naturally suggest many interesting reflections. They establish the great age of the island, an opinion which the builders of theories concerning the creation of the various groups in the South Seas are not always inclined to admit. For my own part, I think it just as probable that human beings were living in the valleys of the Marquesas three thousand years ago as that they were inhabiting the land of Egypt.
(P. 659)

Orthodox Christians were explaining the similarities among the world's religions with the theory of geographical diffusion and were insisting that this diffusion began in the Near East. The prior antiquity of Near Eastern religion depended upon the prior antiquity of the Near Eastern peoples. When Melville claims that the people of the Marquesas may have been coeval with the people of Egypt, he implicitly allies himself with those who were finding the travel of religions across half the world (mostly water either way they went) not necessarily the most plausible theory.

The lines of diffusionist and anti-diffusionist theories crisscross in complicated patterns throughout the nineteenth century at large and throughout Melville's work in particular. In the mid-eighteenth century the Christian apologists, hard pressed by the psychological theories of deists and skeptics, fortified themselves behind simple diffusionist theories, usually constructed from the Genesis account of Ham, Shem, and Japheth. Although the main attacks against this position continued to come from the skeptics' psychological and astronomical theories of religious belief, toward the close of the eighteenth century a new major assault began. The new discoveries in India, brought about by the Asiatic Society's pioneering work in Sanskrit, threatened to turn diffusionism itself against the apologists. For many of the Hindu Vedas seemed to be at least as old as the Old Testament and embarrassingly similar to the New. Sir William Jones, the Society's first president, advanced the rather desperate hypothesis that spurious gospels must have circulated in ancient Hindustan. Upon this hypothesis was built a major restatement of diffusionism, the seven quarto volumes of *Indian Antiquities* and three folio volumes of *The History of Hindostan* by the Reverend Thomas Maurice. Maurice's efforts to explain away the apparently prior antiquity of Hindu mythology were foredoomed. The diffusionist barricades built by the apologists were gradually taken over by the skeptics and heretics, who mounted upon them some of their most dangerous weapons. By the time Melville abandoned prose and turned to poetry, the revolution was practically complete. In *Clarel* (1876), it is Derwent the Anglican priest who offers mild psychological theories and Rolfe the heretic who darkly hints of diffusionism.

> [Derwent:] "Why question me?
> Why pound the text? Ah, modern be,
> And share the truth's munificence.
> Look now, one reasons thus: Immense

> Is tropic India; hence she breeds
> Brahma tremendous, gods like seeds.
> The genial clime of Hellas gay
> Begat Apollo. Take that way;
> Nor query—Ramayana true?
> The Iliad?"⁹

Rolfe does suggest one kind of psychological theory, one as old as the
fear theory of Democritus and the gratitude theory of Proclus:

> Yea, long as children feel affright
> In darkness, men shall fear a God;
> And long as daisies yield delight
> Shall see His footprints in the sod.
> (I, xxxi, 191–94)

But as he goes on, Rolfe shows that for him, unlike Derwent, the
history and geography of religion may make its truth equivocal. Although psychology may be the basis for the idea of God, geographical
neighbors may do more to shape that idea than geographical structure
or climate. Rolfe darkly hints that the proximity of the Osiris myth
may have shaped the story of Christ:

> "Hint you," here asked Vine,
> "In Christ Osiris met decline
> Anew?"—[Rolfe:] "Nay, nay; and yet, past doubt,
> Strange is that text St. Matthew won
> From gray Hosea in sentence: *Out*
> *Of Egypt have I called my son.*"
> (I, xxxi, 223–28)

In the last year of his life, Melville in his own voice speaks of the
geographical diffusion of the gods. In "The New Zealot to the Sun"
(published in *Timoleon*, 1891) he addresses as "Arch type" a Persian
who rises "aflame from climes of sacrifice" amidst "rites whose tenor
trace all worship hitherto":

> Mid terrors dinned
> Gods too came conquerors from your Ind,
> The brood of Brahma throve;
> They came like to the scythed car,
> Westward they rolled their empire far,
> Of night their purple wove.

Chemist, you breed
In orient climes each sorcerous weed
That energizes dream—
Transmitted, spread in myths and creeds,
Houris and hells, delirious screeds
And Calvin's last extreme.[10]

After a lifetime of comparing religions, Melville sees Calvinism as only an extreme development of Persian sacrifice. He distinguishes neither religion from a sorcerous opiate.

Typee and *Omoo* represent the first definable probings of Melville's ever widening and ever deepening exploration of comparative religion. In both books Melville apparently weighs primitive religious beliefs and practices against those of the Christianity practiced in Polynesia, and the scales seem very nearly level. Although some of the islanders' beliefs may be childishly simple and others incomprehensibly obscure and complicated, although some of their practices may be absurd and others dangerous, Melville's attitude toward these beliefs and practices more nearly resembles Rousseau's than a Christian missionary's. The narrators of *Typee* and *Omoo* profess an orthodox Christianity, but they weigh the beauty, happiness, health, and childish simplicity of the natives before Christianity comes to the islands against their deformities, misery, disease, and hypocrisy after. Still professing orthodox Christianity, the narrators seem to weigh jolly old fraudulent native priests, who possibly are cannibals, against viciously deceptive Christian priests, who certainly are rapacious predators. But the pagan and Christian religions described by the narrators are not in reality weighed against each other. They are both weighed against a persistently assumed religion which might be called anything from deism to a primitive Christianity. The weighing of each results in clearly writing out its *mene, mene, tekel, upharsin*. The strange mythology of the Typee valley is found no more wanting than the sermon of the Tahitian missionary, with its myths of the "Wee-wees" (the French) and their wicked priests. In *Typee* Melville discovers that these two inadequate religions may be weighed by indicating their essential identity. The temples, myths, rituals, and priests of Typee therefore are metaphorically equated with those of the reader.

The Typee temples make the narrator think of Christian as well as Egyptian and Druidic temples:

> Here were situated the Taboo groves of the valley—the scene of many a prolonged feast, of many a horrid rite. Beneath the dark shadows of the consecrated bread-fruit trees there reigned a solemn twilight—a cathedral-like gloom. The frightful genius of pagan worship seemed to brood in silence over the place, breathing its spell upon every object around. Here and there, in the depths of these awful shades, half screened from sight by masses of overhanging foliage, rose the idolatrous altars of the savages, built of enormous blocks of black and polished stone, placed one upon another, without cement, to the height of twelve or fifteen feet, and surmounted by a rustic open temple, enclosed with a low picket of canes, within which might be seen, in various stages of decay, offerings of bread-fruit and cocoa-nuts, and the putrefying relics of some recent sacrifice. (P. 578)

When the narrator of *Typee* wishes to reach beyond the Typee valley for a comparison adequate to its ominous gloom, apparently by chance he seizes upon a cathedral. The narrator of "The Two Temples" sees the same relationship from the other side; imprisoned in a New York cathedral, he reaches back to the primitive wilderness for a comparison adequate to its ominous gloom:

> A strange trepidation of gloom and loneliness gradually stole over me. Hardly conscious of what I did, I reascended the stone steps: higher and higher still, and only paused, when once more I felt the hot-air blast from the wire-woven screen. Snatching another peep down into the vast arena, I started at its hushed desertness. The long ranges of grouped columns down the nave, and clusterings of them into copses about the corners of the transept; together with the subdued, dim-streaming light from the autumnal glasses; all assumed a secluded and deep-wooded air.[11]

The "cathedral-like gloom" of the secluded and deep-wooded Typee grove surrounds what Melville calls the "pulpits" of its priests:

> In the midst of the wood was the hallowed "hoolah hoolah" ground— set apart for the celebration of the fantastic religious ritual of these people —comprising an extensive oblong pi-pi, terminating at either end in a

lofty terraced altar, guarded by ranks of hideous wooden idols . . . Vast trees, standing in the middle of this space, and throwing over it an umbrageous shade, had their massive trunks built round with slight stages, elevated a few feet above the ground, and railed in with canes, forming so many rustic pulpits, from which the priests harangued their devotees.

(P. 578)

Melville made his metaphorical comparisons of primitive pagan priests and civilized Christian priests into a theme upon which he played many later variations. In *Mardi,* much of the religious satire centers upon the Holy Island of Maramma, literally a Polynesian island replete with fetishistic idols, allegorically both the Vatican and Palestine. In *Moby-Dick,* the mincer, functioning as a primitive phallic priest, is offered as a candidate for an "archbishoprick" or Pope. In *Benito Cereno,* the African slaves, embodying savage terror and naked evil, persistently seem to the naïve narrator "monks" and "friars" in a monastery; they are in fact, as we shall see, the allegorical incarnation of the Catholic Church. In *Clarel,* "the Druid priest Melchizedeck" (I, iii, 41) of Genesis 14 creates what Walter Bezanson's note calls "a 'primeval' scene of Druidic rites to set the tone for contemporary rituals"; he foreshadows the Anglican priest, Derwent, etymologically and symbolically the descendant of the Druids. Daniel Orme, the title character of an unpublished sketch at first subtitled "A Druid," dies on Easter while musing on the crucifix cut into his chest. *Billy Budd,* as we shall see, finally resolves pagan and Christian priests into a complicated order. In *Typee* and *Omoo* the theme is more simple and conventional: pagan priests like Kolory, the "Lord Primate of Typee," play their "episcopal part" with good-natured, unconcerned, primitive humbuggery; Christian priests not only deceive the natives, but humiliate and enslave them while hypocritically deceiving the folks back home about the native religion and the progress of Christianity in Polynesia. The narrator of *Omoo* hears the malicious and self-seeking sermon of a Tahitian missionary; the narrator of *Typee* sees the line of wagons parked on Sunday before the elegant chapel of Christianity, each wagon drawn by two naked natives.

In *Typee,* Melville compares not only Christian and pagan temples, priests, and practices but also Christians' descriptions of paganism with his own observations. He is fascinated with three aspects of the Typee religion: its fetishism, the careless abandon with which the natives treat their fetish gods, and the complete inscrutability of the Typee "theology." Moa Artua, the most important god, who "could take the whole island of Nukuheva in his mouth and dive down to the bottom of the sea with it," is only a bandaged piece of wood which is abused and threatened. Mystified by Moa Artua's helpless omnipotence, by the generally inferior position of gods to worshipers, and by intricate rituals and explanations, Melville concludes not only that he "hardly knew what to make of the religion of the valley," but that he is "inclined to believe, that the islanders in the Pacific have no fixed and definite ideas whatever on the subject of religion." He sharply criticizes other Polynesian investigators, deriding as "a vast deal of unintentional humbuggery" the "scientific" accounts of Polynesian religion and implying that the missionaries' accounts are humbuggery which is anything but unintentional. Melville says that the writer of the typical treatise on Polynesian religion "enters into a very circumstantial and learned narrative of certain unaccountable superstitions and practices, about which he knows as little as the islanders themselves . . . were the book thus produced to be translated into the tongue of the people of whom it purports to give the history, it would appear quite as wonderful to them as it does to the American public, and much more improbable." When, four years later, Melville offered *Mardi* as his own learned treatise on Polynesian societies and religions, he wrote it in the language of the natives, who did indeed find it highly improbable. For *Mardi* presents all lands as a world of pagan gods.

CHAPTER 2

MARDI
A Study of Myths and Mythmaking

The Polynesia of *Mardi* is the many islands of this world, and *Mardi* surveys their many religious, political, social, sexual, economic, literary, and philosophical idols as well as the wooden idols carved by the Mardian Pope's official idol maker. Although each of these idols depends from a myth in the most general sense of myth, some of them depend from myths in the most restricted sense. To the extent that these myths are a theme of *Mardi*—and this is a vast extent— *Mardi* is a study of mythology. To the extent that these myths are evaluated in terms of one another—and this also is vast—*Mardi* is a textbook of comparative mythology. *Typee* and *Omoo* had assumed an ideal religion which could brand the idolatrous theologies of pagans and Christians as mere mythology. *Mardi* is the first of Melville's works which does not assume an ideal religion but which quests for it and questions all that the quest discovers. Because there is no assumed religion in *Mardi,* any theology may or may not be mythology and any myth may or may not be divine.

Mardi draws upon the mythologies of the Hindus, the Polynesians, the Incas, the Hebrews, the Greeks, the Christians, the Romans, and the Norse, and compares them to one another and to man's other myths and his idols. In this survey *Mardi* quests through these myths and idols for a truth behind and beyond them.

The quest begins in the westward voyage of the ship *Arcturion.* When it veers north, the narrator leaves it. He takes with him Jarl, a modern Viking, and continues west in the whaleboat *Chamois*. From the *Chamois* he and Jarl board the mysterious brig *Parki,* and after the *Parki* sinks they resume their westward voyage in the *Chamois,* taking with them the last survivor of the *Parki*'s crew, Samoa, "master of Gog and Magog, expounder of all things heathenish and obscure." The narrator then finds Yillah, a mysterious maiden who seems to be the consummation of his quest, on a sacred Polynesian ark. He kills the priest who worships and is about to sacrifice Yillah, carries her to the *Chamois,* and sails westward with her, Jarl, and Samoa to Mardi. When Yillah mysteriously disappears, the quest resumes as an allegorical voyage through Mardi. Jarl and Samoa are soon killed, and the narrator's last links with extra-Mardian lands are thus snapped. He now shares his quest with four others, each as interested as himself in its outcome. Each of the other four consummates his quest, but the narrator is damned to never ending his.

Of the five questors who sail on the allegorical voyage, each has a peculiar mythological function: Mohi the historian narrates historical mythology; Yoomy the poet warbles poetical mythology; Babbalanja the philosopher babbles philosophical mythology. As these three mythologize in the background, King Media acts the role of a euhemerized demigod, and "Taji," the name assumed by the narrator, acts the role of an astronomical avatar. These five functions must be seen in the context of contemporaneous mythology.

The great eighteenth-century Sanskrit research put comparative mythology and religion as well as ethnology, prehistory, and philology permanently on a new path. In 1856 Max Müller, the follower of the eighteenth-century philological mythologists, pointed back along the path: "If Hegel calls the discovery of the common origin of Greek and Sanskrit the discovery of a new world, the same may be said with regard to the common origin of Greek and Sanskrit mythology."[2] The man who led the discoverers of both new worlds was Sir William Jones.

Melville seemed to consider Jones what he may very well have been—the greatest linguist of all time.[3] Jones and Sir Charles Wilkins, working together, became in the early 1780's the first Europeans to master Sanskrit. Although Wilkins went on to translate the *Bhagavad-Gita* and *Hitopadesa,* Jones exerted much the stronger influence on contemporary mythology. He was for a time undoubtedly the most influential of all mythologists.

In 1784 Jones helped organize the Royal Society of Bengal and Calcutta. Under his leadership, the Society published its extremely important *Asiatick Researches* and promoted scholarship in Asiatic history, geography, geology, botany, philology, philosophy, ethnology, and, most especially, comparative religion and mythology. Jones himself was the chief contributor to this last concern. As a fearless Protestant apologist, he industriously translated Asiatic sacred, legendary, and profane writings into the language of most Protestant missionaries. His relating of Hindu scripture to Christian scripture and his hints to future Christian missionaries in India were reiterated and amplified by dozens of early nineteenth-century periodicals; his studies of Hindu gods were quoted and paraphrased in hundreds of books and magazines; he became an almost legendary learned champion of the Judaic-Christian revelation.

Jones's most important single work was an essay entitled "On the Gods of Greece, Italy, and India," published in the first volume of *Asiatick Researches.* In this essay, he displayed the two new worlds he had discovered—the common origin of Greek and Sanskrit and the common origin of their mythologies.

Jones's theories, his techniques, his facts, his symbolic stature, and almost the entire essay "On the Gods of Greece, Italy, and India" were all included and enlarged upon by Maurice's *Indian Antiquities* and *History of Hindostan,* works familiar to Melville. Whether Jones's essay was a direct source for *Mardi* is unimportant. "On the Gods of Greece, Italy, and India" deals with some of the central concerns of *Mardi,* treating them in strikingly similar terms; it precisely locates *Mardi*'s mythology in its chronological and intellectual setting, and thus defines what is perhaps the most important structural principle of the book.

As Jones witnessed and abetted the discovery of Sanskrit literature, he realized the dangers of what he was finding. If previous knowledge of pagan religions had made possible a Bayle, a Voltaire, and a Hume, what monstrous generation of skeptics would this new discovery breed? Sanskrit literature contained striking similarities to the Bible, evinced as high a degree of civilization, and appeared to be more ancient. If the similarities between the Hebrew and Egyptian religions had caused skeptics to suspect that the Mosaic cosmogony was merely a product of Moses' exposure to the Egyptian court, what would they say about the striking similarities between ancient Hinduism and the Hebrew, Egyptian, Greek, Roman, and Christian religions? And at the same time, archeology, astronomy, and geology were casting doubt on some of the dates and other details of the Bible. With both the uniqueness and the accuracy of the Judaic-Christian revelation daily becoming more equivocal, Jones attempted in "On the Gods of Greece, Italy, and India" to wrest the weapons of comparative mythology from the hands of the skeptics, deists, free-thinkers, and atheists, to appropriate for orthodox Christian apologetics what was later to be called Higher Criticism.

Jones begins by denying the theory developed throughout the eighteenth century—the psychological explanation of similar mythologies:

We cannot justly conclude, by arguments preceding the proof of facts, that one idolatrous people must have borrowed their deities, rites, and tenets from another; since Gods of all shapes and dimensions may be framed by the boundless powers of imagination, or by the frauds and follies of men, in countries never connected; but when features of resemblance, too strong to have been accidental, are observable in different systems of polytheism, without fancy or prejudice to color them, and improve the likeness, we can scarce help believing, that some connection has immemorially subsisted between the several nations who have adopted them. It is my design, in this Essay, to point out such a resemblance between the popular worship of the old *Greeks* and *Italians* and that of the *Hindus*. Nor can there be room to doubt of a great similarity between their strange religions and that of *Egypt, China, Persia, Phrygia, Phoenicia, Syria*; to which, perhaps, we may safely add, some of the southern kingdoms, and even islands of *America*: while the *Gothic* system, which prevailed in the northern regions of *Europe*, was not merely similar to those of *Greece* and *Italy*, but almost the same, in another dress, with an embroidery of images apparently *Asiatick*. From all this, if it be satisfactorily proved, we may infer a general union or affinity between the most distinguished inhabitants of the primitive world, at the time when they deviated, as they did too early deviate, from the rational adoration of the only true GOD.[4]

After outlining his own theory of the sources of mythology, which we shall later examine in detail, Jones passes on to the importance of comparative mythology "in an age when sane intelligent and virtuous persons are inclined to doubt the authenticity of the accounts delivered by *Moses* concerning the primitive world." He then defines the lines of battle:

Either the first eleven chapters of *Genesis* (all due allowances being made for a figurative eastern style) are true, or the whole fabric of our national religion is false; a conclusion which none of us, I trust, would wish to be drawn. I, who cannot help believing the divinity of the *Messiah,* from the undisputed antiquity and manifest completion of many prophecies, especially those of *Isaiah,* in the only person recorded by history to whom they are applicable, am obliged, of course, to believe the sanctity of the venerable books to which that sacred person refers as genuine: but it is not the truth of our national religion, as such, that I have at heart; it is truth itself; and if any cool, unbiassed reasoner will clearly convince me, that *Moses* drew his narrative through *Egyptian* conduits from the primeval fountains of *Indian* literature, I shall esteem him as a friend for having weaned my mind from a capital error, and promise to stand among the foremost in assisting to circulate the truth which he has ascertained. (P. 225)

After the central part of the essay—a detailed comparison of Roman, Greek, and Hindu gods—Jones returns to his more vexing problems: "Since *Egypt* appears to have been the grand source of knowledge for the *western,* and *India* for the more *eastern,* parts of the globe, it may seem a material question, whether the *Egyptians* communicated their Mythology and Philosophy to the *Hindus,* or conversely." Then, after giving some tenuous evidence suggesting the prior antiquity of the Egyptians, he maneuvers around the entire significance of prior antiquities: "Be all this as it may, I am persuaded that a connection subsisted between the old idolatrous nations of *Egypt, India, Greece,* and *Italy,* long before they emigrated to their several settlements, and consequently before the birth of *Moses*: but the proof of this proposition will in no degree affect the truth and sanctity of the *Mosaick* History, which, if confirmation were necessary, it would rather tend to confirm." In his next sentence Jones shows how the greater antiquity of other religions confirms "the sanctity of the *Mosaick* History": "The *Divine Legate,* educated by the daughter of a king, and in all respects highly accomplished, could not but know the mythological system of *Egypt*; but he must have condemned the superstitions of that people, and despised the speculative absurdities of their priests, though some of their traditions concerning the creation and the flood were grounded on truth." After rhetorically enlarging this point, Jones concludes: "There is no shadow then of a foundation for an opinion, that *Moses* borrowed the first nine or ten chapters of *Genesis* from the literature of *Egypt*: still less can the adamantine pillars of our *Christian* faith be moved by the result of any debates on the comparative antiquity of the *Hindus* and *Egyptians,* or of any inquiries into the *Indian* theology." Melville examines the same problem, but his conclusion differs from Jones's: "I shudder at the idea of ancient Egyptians. It was in these pyramids that was conceived the idea of Jehovah. Terrible mixture of the cunning and awful. Moses learned in all the lore of the Egyptians. The idea of Jehovah born here."[5]

In the decades immediately following the publication of Jones's essay, Pacific voyages brought the problem full circle around the world. One of the known sources of *Mardi,* William Ellis's *Polynesian Researches,* tries to stretch the ever thinning line of diffusionism eastward from India to Polynesia, or, alternately, from India to America and westward to Polynesia.[6] Ellis has the task of showing simultaneously the ultimate Hebrew and more recent Hindu origin of the Polynesians:

One of their accounts of creation . . . and the very circumstantial tradition they have of the deluge, if they do not, as some have supposed, (when taken in connexion with many customs, and analogies in language,) warrant the inference that the Polynesians have an Hebrew origin; they show that the nation, whence they emigrated, was acquainted with some of the leading facts recorded in the Mosaic history of the primitive ages of mankind. Others appear to have a striking resemblance to several conspicuous features of the more modern Hindoo, or Braminical mythology.[7]

In his attempts to identify Hindu and Polynesian mythology and to account geographically for Polynesian history, Ellis continually returns to the "great mystery" which surrounds Polynesian origins. *Mardi* defines the identity of Asiatic, Pacific, and Mediterranean gods—Brami (Brahma), Manko (Manco Capac), and Alma (Christ) —in terms which steer clear of the perilously strained diffusionism of Jones and Ellis.

The concluding steps in Jones's argument bring us to this central mythological concept of *Mardi*. He accounts for the striking similarities between the stories of Krishna (an avatar of Vishnu) and Christ by postulating that "the spurious Gospels, which abounded in the first age of *Christianity,* had been brought to *India,* and the wildest parts of them repeated to the *Hindus,* who ingrafted them on the fable of *Cesava,* the *Apollo* of *Greece.*" These very similarities will be, Jones concludes, the most difficult obstacle in the way of a mass conversion of the Hindus:

The *Hindus* . . . would readily admit the truth of the Gospel; but they contend, that it is perfectly consistent with their *Sastras.* The Deity, they say, has appeared innumerable times, in many parts of this world, and of all worlds, for the salvation of his creatures; and though we adore him in one appearance, and they in others, yet we adore, they say, the same God, to whom our several worships, though different in form, are equally acceptable, if they be sincere in substance. (P. 274)

If this obstacle proves insurmountable, then, says Jones in his final words, "we could only lament more than ever the strength of prejudice, and the weakness of unassisted reason."

The same prejudice and same unassisted reason seem to victimize the official chronicles of Mardi, for these chronicles use both the Hindu concept and word *avatar* to describe Christ (Alma):

Alma, it seems, was an illustrious prophet, and teacher divine; who, ages ago, at long intervals, and in various islands, had appeared to the Mardians under the different titles of Brami, Manko, and Alma. Many thousands of moons had elapsed since his last and most memorable avatar, as Alma on the isle of Maramma. Each of his advents had taken place in a comparatively dark and benighted age. Hence, it was devoutly believed, that he came to redeem the Mardians from their heathenish thrall; to instruct them in the ways of truth, virtue, and happiness; to allure them to good by promises of beatitude hereafter; and to restrain them from evil by denunciations of woe. Separated from the impurities and corruptions, which in a long series of centuries had become attached to every thing originally uttered by the prophet, the maxims, which as Brami he had taught, seemed similar to those inculcated by Manko. But as Alma, adapting his lessons to the improved condition of humanity, the divine prophet had more completely unfolded his scheme; as Alma, he had made his last revelation. (II, 38–39)

The Mardian chronicles, like Jones's Hindus, identify Brahma and Christ. These chronicles are the official statements of Mardian history, narrated by Mohi, the official chronicler. To understand why this Western heresy is Mardian orthodoxy, to understand the relation between the Mardian mythology and the narrative framework of *Mardi*, and to understand the relation of *Mardi* to contemporaneous mythological theory, we may turn to Jones's theory of mythology. For this theory coherently orders *Mardi*'s mythology.

Jones's theory assumes "four principal sources of all mythology" —the distortion of natural and human history, the adoration of astronomical events, poetic invention, and metaphysical invention. His analysis distinguishes among various kinds of mythological producers and their products. Historians and the kings they serve produce one kind of myth; astronomical worship produces another kind; poets and philosophers produce still other kinds. The gods created by royal policy, by astronomical awe, by poetic conceits, by philosophic hypotheses substantially differ from one another. On the Mardian quest sail both producers of myth—Mohi the historian, Yoomy the poet, Babbalanja the philosopher—and products of myth—Media the royal deity, Taji the astronomical deity, and Azzageddi the metaphysical devil. The quest seeks Yillah, who combines elements of historical, astronomical, poetic, and metaphysical mythologizing. Some of the questors end with Alma, who also combines elements of the four kinds of mythologizing. Let us now look carefully at the producers of myth and their mythic products, comparing Jones's theoretical mythology with the mythology Melville dramatizes.

THE MYTHS OF HUMAN AND NATURAL HISTORY

I. Historical or natural truth has been perverted into fable by ignorance, imagination, flattery, or stupidity; as a king of Crete, *whose tomb had been discovered in that island, was conceived to have been the God of* Olympus . . . *hence beacons or volcanos became one-eyed giants, and monsters vomiting flames; and two rocks, from their appearance to mariners in certain positions, were supposed to crush all vessels attempting to pass between them; of which idle fictions many other instances might be collected from the* Odyssey, *and the various* Argonautick *poems. The less we say of* Julian *stars, deifications of princes or warriors, altars raised, with those of* Apollo, *to the basest of men, and divine titles bestowed on such wretches as* Caius Octavianus, *the less we shall expose the infamy of grave senators and fine poets, or the brutal folly of the low multitude: but we may be assured, that the mad apotheosis of truly great men, or of little men falsely called great, has been the origin of gross idolatrous errors in every part of the Pagan world.*

"ON THE GODS OF GREECE, ITALY, AND INDIA," p. 222

The chronicles of Mohi, the official historian, exemplify point by point Jones's first source of mythology. The fact that Mohi, rather than Yoomy, narrates the traditional perversions of Mardian natural truth may perhaps suggest that Melville is consciously maintaining Jones's categories. Be that as it may, strict euhemerism forms the larger part of Jones's first category and an extremely large part of the voyage through Mardi. Indeed, by focusing narrowly on royal myths, one can perceive a careful structure and a consistent purpose in what otherwise may seem a chartless voyage.

After the royal entourage leaves Media's kingdom, the first four visits trace four stages of kinghood, from King Peepi the puny boy, to King Donjalolo the thin debauched youth, to King Uhia the vigorous muscular man who has forsaken debauchery, to fat jolly old Borabolla. The stages are chronological, physical, moral, and spiritual, and each stage but the last has an appropriate myth to support it. The myth of Peepi the boy king says that he inherits the souls of many of his subjects; Borabolla, who has no myth, is also supposed to have no soul. The first three kings are victims of myths who victimize their subjects because of these myths; the last is a victim of no myth who victimizes his subjects because he has no myth. While Peepi's subjects live in terror of the boy with many souls, Borabolla's subjects die to support the gluttonous old man with no soul. Donjalolo the debauched youth and Uhia the reclaimed man rule entirely in terms of their myths. Donjalolo's myth tells him that, because of a legendary ancestral battle and vow, he can live only in the secluded glen at the heart of his kingdom. Uhia's myth tells him that when an island moves he will rule all of Mardi. A mythic legend from the past deceives one; a mythic prophecy deceives the other. Entirely because of these myths, Donjalolo retreats from the world, Uhia tries to conquer the world, Donjalolo abandons himself to his harem, Uhia disbands his harem, Donjalolo dissipates his manhood in ultrarefined pleasures, Uhia nurtures his manhood and eschews all pleasures, both envy the most miserable of their subjects, and both add to the misery of their subjects. The myths in which they have transcendental faith, like the myth of King Peepi and the divine Mardian avatars, are presented to us, most significantly, as part of the chronicles of Mohi, the chronicles which also include the Mardian Bible. Perhaps this Bible will prove not only as fallacious but also as dangerous as the other myths of Mardi.

Indeed, the slavery of these Mardian kings and their subjects to royal myth foreshadows the slavery of the priests, pilgrims, and people of Maramma to Biblical myth. The chronicles which support these kings are distinguished in no way from the chronicles which represent sacred writ in general and the Judaic-Christian Bible in particular. What the voyagers find on Maramma, the Holy Island, is merely an intensification of what they have found on the royal islands of Mardi.

There are numerous connections between the island kingdoms and the Holy Island—such as the fat priest on Borabolla's island who seems to be "another Borabolla," the priest on Donjalolo's island who invests the king in his sacred girdle, the priests on Media's island who torture the king's subjects for heresy, the priests on Uhia's island who present the spear of the god Keevi to persuade the most recalcitrant recusant. But none of these connections is as important as Mohi's chronicles, and Mohi's chronicles most rigidly connect the courts of Mardi to its churches.

Mohi himself is introduced as "a venerable teller of stories and legends, one of the Keepers of the Chronicles of the Kings of Mardi." This designation of "Kings" includes all the gods of Mardi; Mohi gives the official story and legend not only of each demigod king, but of every Mardian god, including Alma. It is important to note that, although Mohi is an "historian," none of Mohi's stories gives unequivocated historical truth. When Mohi, "the teller of legends," is compared with particular historians, it is with Diodorus and Herodotus, whose pages abound in the fabulous, the mysterious, and the mythical. Mohi's history is fabulous and, because of his position, title, and role, official.

Mohi tells first of King Peepi and a strange rock. In the course of his stories, he illustrates in detail Jones's first source of mythology, the perversion of human and natural history. When he describes the divinity and mythical powers of Peepi the boy king, he dramatizes quite literally what Jones called "the mad apotheosis of little men falsely called great." Jones had thus illustrated the perversion of natural truth: "beacons or volcanos became one-eyed giants, and monsters vomiting flames; and two rocks, from their appearance to mariners in certain positions, were supposed to crush all vessels attempting to pass between them." Mohi illustrates the perversion of natural truth with legends about a rock, which appears to mariners in certain positions as "the open, upper jaw of a whale." He tells how the water which drips from it cures ambition "because of its passing through the ashes of ten kings, of yore buried in a sepulcher, hewn in the heart of the rock." Mohi's last legend of the rock will prove worth remembering:

"Mohi," said Media, "methinks there is another tradition concerning that rock: let us have it."
"In old times of genii and giants, there dwelt in barren lands not very

remote from our outer reef, but since submerged, a band of evil-minded, envious goblins, furlongs in stature, and with immeasurable arms; who from time to time cast covetous glances upon our blooming isles. Long they lusted; till at last, they waded through the sea, strode over the reef, and seizing the nearest islet, rolled it over and over, toward an adjoining outlet.

"But the task was hard; and day-break surprised them in the midst of their audacious thieving; while in the very act of giving the devoted land another doughty surge and somerset. Leaving it bottom upward and midway poised, gardens under water, its foundations in air, they precipitately fled; in their great haste, deserting a comrade, vainly struggling to liberate his foot caught beneath the overturned land.

"This poor fellow now raised such an outcry, as to awaken the god Upi, or the Archer, stretched out on a long cloud in the East; who forthwith resolved to make an example of the unwilling lingerer. Snatching his bow, he let fly an arrow. But overshooting its mark, it pierced through and through, the lofty promontory of a neighbouring island; making an arch in it, which remaineth even unto this day. A second arrow, however, accomplishing its errand: the slain giant sinking prone to the bottom."

"And now," added Mohi, "glance over the gunwale, and you will see his remains petrified into white ribs of coral."

"Ay, there they are," said Yoomy, looking down into the water where they gleamed. "A fanciful legend, Braid-Beard."

"Very entertaining," said Media.   (I, 248–49)

Mohi next gives the legend to which King Donjalolo and his subjects are enslaved. The narrator introduces this recital by saying, "Braid-Beard unrolled his old chronicles" and "regaled us with the history." Thus this legend, like the "very entertaining" legend which immediately preceded it, may be only entertainment to the travelers. But the "sacred oracle" of the legend, propagated by priests, imprisons King Donjalolo in a rocky glen and leaves his subjects to be ruled by irresponsible and cruel viceroys. Babbalanja asks the all-important question to which there is no answer: "Is it a fable, or a verity . . . ?" In the same paragraph, Babbalanja comments on another legend from Mohi's chronicles: "Touching the life of Alma, in Mohi's chronicles, 'tis related, that a man was once raised from the tomb. But rubbed he not his eyes, and stared he not most vacantly? Not one revelation did he make." Is, then, the raising of Lazarus like the legend of Donjalolo in more ways than that of being known only from Mohi's equivocal chronicles? After Mohi's next legends about Donjalolo's island, the narrator remarks, "traditions like these ever seem dubious."

Before landing on the Holy Island of Maramma, Mohi tells not only myths of three demigod kings (Peepi, Donjalolo, and Uhia), but also myths of three gods—Vivo, Keevi, and Roo. He describes the ascent of the god Vivo and the descents of the gods Keevi and Roo. The myth of each of these gods reduces elements of Alma's myth to absurdity:

> Approached from the northward, Ohonoo, midway cloven down to the sea, one half a level plain; the other, three mountain terraces—Ohonoo looks like the first steps of a gigantic way to the sun. And such, if Braid-Beard spoke truth, it had formerly been.
> "Ere Mardi was made," said that true old chronicler, "Vivo, one of the genii, built a ladder of mountains whereby to go up and go down. And of this ladder, the island of Ohonoo was the base. But wandering here and there, incognito in a vapor, so much wickedness did Vivo spy out, that in high dudgeon he hurried up his ladder, knocking the mountains from under him as he went. These here and there fell into the lagoon, forming many isles, now green and luxuriant; which, with those sprouting from seeds dropped by a bird from the moon, comprise all the groups in the reef."   (I, 314)

One object of interest in Ohonoo was the original image of Keevi the god of Thieves; hence, from time immemorial, the tutelar deity of the isle.

His shrine was a natural niche in a cliff, walling in the valley of Monlova. And here stood Keevi, with his five eyes, ten hands, and three pair of legs, equipped at all points for the vocation over which he presided. Of mighty girth, his arms terminated in hands, every finger a limb, spreading in multiplied digits: palms twice five, and fifty fingers.

According to the legend, Keevi fell from a golden cloud, burying himself to the thighs in the earth, tearing up the soil all round. Three meditative mortals, strolling by at the time, had a narrow escape. (I, 319)

Mohi's account of Keevi's absurd descent precedes by a few pages his account of another absurd descent linked more directly to Alma:

> "It was by this same peak," said Mohi, "that the nimble god Roo, a great sinner above, came down from the skies, a very long time ago. Three skips and a jump, and he landed on the plain. But alas, poor Roo! though easy the descent, there was no climbing back." (II, 9)

According to Ellis, Roo was one of "the most benevolent" Polynesian gods. Melville plays on Roo's name, likening him to a kangaroo, calls him a great sinner, and, six paragraphs later, identifies the mountain of his descent with the legendary mount of Alma's ascent. Alma, who both descends and ascends, links Vivo, Keevi, and Roo into the mythological chain of Maramma. They in turn make equivocally absurd the scripture which tells the Mardians of Alma.

Mohi's chronicles include the Old Testament as well as the New. The allegory occasionally thins sufficiently for explicit citations:

> "However that may be," said Mohi, "certain it is, those events did assuredly come to pass:—Compare the ruins of Babbelona with book ninth, chapter tenth, of the chronicles. Yea, yea, the owl inhabits where the seers predicted; the jackals yell in the tombs of the kings." (II, 125)

Some contemporary research had found the ruins prophesied in Isaiah 13:21 and 34:13 and Jeremiah 50:39. But other contemporary research had made more important parts of Mohi's scripture clearly mythical.

Babbalanja vows that Nature, Oro's* book, "gives the grim lie to Mohi's gossipings." He bases his vow on the latest geological theories, which he then recounts at length. To these theories, Media blandly responds: "Mohi tells us that Mardi was made in six days; but you, Babbalanja, have built it up from the bottom in less than six minutes." The quarrel between Babbalanja's scientific truth and Mohi's chronicled truth, in a world apparently without knowable truth, places both the cosmology of the Old Testament and the Saviour of the New beyond human knowledge.

In a world filled with similar gods, Babbalanja and Mohi must wage their disputes about Alma in the absurd context of Vivo's ascent and the descents of Keevi and Roo:

> "But, my lord, you well know, that there are those in Mardi, who secretly regard all stories connected with this peak, as inventions of the people of Maramma. They deny that any thing is to be gained by making

---

* Melville makes Oro, the name of the great Polynesian god, the Mardian equivalent of the Judaic-Christian "God."

a pilgrimage thereto. And for warranty, they appeal to the sayings of the great prophet Alma."

Cried Mohi, "But Alma is also quoted by others, in vindication of the pilgrimage to Ofo. They declare that the prophet himself was the first pilgrim that thitherward journeyed: that from thence he departed to the skies."   (II, 10)

Without divine revelation, all scripture becomes myth. By 1849 it had become clear that the Judaic-Christian scripture was not entirely literal revelation.

Although all these legends come before we learn that Brami, Manko, and Alma are avatars, they come after we have learned of another deity who descended like Keevi, who voyaged from the sun like Vivo, and who, like Brami, Manko, and Alma, is an "Avatar" —"white Taji, a sort of half-and-half deity, now and then an Avatar among them"; "a gentleman from the sun." Taji, the narrator of *Mardi* and an auditor of Mohi's stories, produces Jones's second kind of myth. But since he himself is also the product—an astronomical demigod—he can be considered more profitably with the other products. Another of the questors produces Jones's third kind of myth.

POETIC MYTH

III. Numberless divinities have been created solely by the magick of poetry, whose essential business it is to personify the most abstract notions, and to place a Nymph or a Genius in every grove, and almost in every flower.

"On the Gods of Greece, Italy, and India," p. 223

Jones sharply distinguishes between myths created by poetry and myths created by versified history, dividing them between two of his four categories. Melville divides the two sources of these myths along precisely the same lines, but he then shows these lines to be equivocal. The legends of Yoomy the poet are often indistinguishable from Mohi's official legends. Yoomy's legends obviously come from the fancy and obviously are meant to entertain; but many of Mohi's legends are just as fanciful and entertaining. The relation between Yoomy and Mohi, between poetic and historical mythology, between, indeed, Mardian poetry and Mardian history, is made most clear in Chapter 93, "Babbalanja Steps in Between Mohi and Yoomy; and Yoomy Relates a Legend." This chapter immediately follows the chapter in which Mohi recites the legends of Keevi descending from a golden cloud and of the souls of fifty warriors ascending from a "fatal leap," and it begins with Mohi ready to relate another legend. With Mohi about to turn over his chronicles, Yoomy interposes to ask that he be permitted to narrate. Mohi, "highly offended," mutters "something invidious about frippery young poetasters being too full of silly imaginings to tell a plain tale." Yoomy's answer is the age-old answer, familiar in English since Sidney's *Defense of Poesy*:

Said Yoomy, in reply, adjusting his turban, "Old Mohi, let us not clash. I honor your calling; but, with submission, your chronicles are more wild than my cantos. I deal in pure conceits of my own; which have a shapeliness and a unity, however unsubstantial; but you, Braid-Beard, deal in mangled realities. In all your chapters, you yourself grope in the dark. Much truth is not in thee, historian. Besides, Mohi; my songs perpetuate many things which you sage scribes entirely overlook. Have you not oftentimes come to me, and my ever dewy ballads for information, in which you and your musty old chronicles were deficient? In much that is precious, Mohi, we poets are the true historians; we embalm; you corrode." (I, 322–23)

In another context, this answer might be no more than a well-stated commonplace. But here it is a dead end, not the end sought, of a long and involved epistemological quest. Babbalanja the philosopher attacks both the poet and the historian: "Peace, rivals. As Bardianna has it, like all who dispute upon pretensions of their own, you are each nearest the right, when you speak of the other; and furthest therefrom, when you speak of yourselves."

Jones had said that part of the "essential business" of poetry was "to place a Nymph or Genius in every grove, and almost in every flower." Yoomy's legend betters Jones's description by placing a manikin or nymph in *every* flower, and making manikins and nymphs grow into vines and flowers. Yoomy's "little nymphs" not only "haunted the lilies," but also "toiled all night long at braiding the moonbeams together, and entangling the plaited end to a bough; so that at night, the poor planet had much ado to set." When Mohi interposes to ask, "Pause you to invent as you go on?" Yoomy responds by parodying Mohi's usual language: "Little or nothing more, my masters, is extant of the legend." After Yoomy adds a few more whimsical details, the argument of philosopher, poet, and historian resumes:

> "Now, I appeal to you, royal Media; to you, noble Taji; to you, Babbalanja," said the chronicler, with an impressive gesture, "whether this seems a credible history: Yoomy has invented."
> "But perhaps he has entertained, old Mohi," said Babbalanja.
> "He has not spoken the truth," persisted the chronicler.
> "Mohi," said Babbalanja, "truth is in things, and not in words: truth is voiceless; so at least saith old Bardianna. And I, Babbalanja, assert, that what are vulgarly called fictions are as much realities as the gross mattock of Dididi, the digger of trenches; for things visible are but conceits of the eye: things imaginative, conceits of the fancy. If duped by one, we are equally duped by the other." (I, 326)

Babbalanja decides that the poetic legend of Yoomy's nymphs and manikins has no more nor less of reality than, say, Mohi's legend of a goblin slain by the god Upi, though verified by Mohi's pointing to "his remains petrified into white ribs of coral." Mohi reasonably turns on Babbalanja: "But come now, thou oracle, if all things are deceptive, tell us what is truth?" Although, as Babbalanja promptly admits, "that question is more final than any answer," Babbalanja himself has some tentative answers.

METAPHYSICAL MYTH

IV. The metaphors and allegories of moralists and metaphysicians, have been also very fertile in deities; of which a thousand examples might be adduced from Plato, Cicero, *and the inventive commentators on* Homer, *in their pedigrees of the Gods, and their fabulous lessons of morality.*

"ON THE GODS OF GREECE, ITALY, AND INDIA," p. 223

As mythologizer, Babbalanja the philosopher has much in common with both Mohi the historian and Yoomy the poet. Babbalanja tends to align and identify himself with Yoomy; he too is a "poet," a propounder of conceits of the fancy rather than conceits of the eye:

"Yoomy: poets both, we differ but in seeming; thy airiest conceits are as the shadows of my deepest ponderings; though Yoomy soars, and Babbalanja dives, both meet at last. Not a song you sing, but I have thought its thoughts; and where dull Mardi sees but your rose, I unfold its petals, and disclose a pearl. Poets are we, Yoomy, in that we dwell without us; we live in grottoes, palms, and brooks; we ride the sea, we ride the sky; poets are omnipresent." (II, 139)

But Babbalanja is also interested in Mohi's legends, finding in them metaphors and allegories for his metaphysics.

Babbalanja is expected to object to Mohi's "silly conceit," his legend of the Plujii, little demons who cause all the minor annoyances on Quelquo. As "arrant little knaves as ever gulped moonshine," the Plujii seem quite as fanciful as Yoomy's manikins and moonbeam-weaving nymphs. But Babbalanja instead shows in detail to what use moralists and metaphysicians may put such legendary conceits:

"I have been thinking, my lord," said Babbalanja, "that though the people of that island may at times err, in imputing their calamities to the Plujii; that, nevertheless, upon the whole, they indulge in a reasonable belief. For, Plujii or no Plujii, it is undeniable, that in ten thousand ways, as if by a malicious agency, we mortals are woefully put out and tormented; and that, too, by things in themselves so exceedingly trivial, that it would seem almost impiety to ascribe them to the august gods. No; there must exist some greatly inferior spirits; so insignificant, comparatively, as to be overlooked by the supernal powers; and through them it must be, that we are thus grievously annoyed. At any rate, such a theory would supply a hiatus in my system of metaphysics." (I, 306)

Here Babbalanja uses only the subjunctive "would supply." But soon he is demonstrating just how materially a legend may supply a metaphysical hiatus. Babbalanja's transmutation of the legend of the Plujii takes two steps beyond Mohi's narrative. The first is the construction and proof of a mythical theory in Chapter 104, "Wherein Babbalanja Broaches a Diabolical Theory, and in His Own Person Proves it." The second is the creation of Azzageddi, a real devil who, at least metaphorically and allegorically, possesses Babbalanja.

The Plujii were described in the same language and present the same moral and metaphysical problems as the devils later invented and embodied by Babbalanja. The Plujii apparently sprang from the fancies of the people of Quelquo and from their wish to be irresponsible: "In short, from whatever evil, the cause of which the Islanders could not directly impute to their gods, or in their own opinion was not referable to themselves,—of that very thing must the invisible Plujii be guilty. . . . All things they bedeviled." Media, sensing the dangers of this myth of moral irresponsibility, deflated it with hard "facts." After Mohi had described an old lady being abdominally tormented by the Plujii, Media said that he had seen her eat twenty unripe bananas just before these torments.

Babbalanja propounds his diabolical theory also to absolve man from responsibility, and Media reacts as he did to Mohi's myth. The Plujii bedeviled all things; Babbalanja claims that "all men who knowingly do evil are bedeviled." Media threw the hard facts of twenty unripe bananas at Mohi's myth of irresponsibility; he throws ropes and gags at Babbalanja's myth of irresponsibility, roping the devil in him and gagging his devilish doctrine. But shortly the company of questors receives its third allegedly supernatural being, the mythical and invisible devil Azzageddi, who apparently possesses Babbalanja. When released from his ropes and gag, Babbalanja had said, "the strong arm, my lord, is no argument, though it overcomes all logic." Now Azzageddi, though no argument, overcomes the strong arm. He appears, taunts Media with impunity, and is pushed back down by Babbalanja only when the philosopher wishes to assume responsibility for the words coming from his mouth.

The historian, the poet, and the philosopher—each produces myths. Only the different purposes of the historical, poetic, and philosophic myths distinguish them from one another. When Mohi's official myths are not obviously propping up royal or ecclesiastical pretensions, they are hard to distinguish from Yoomy's myths, aimed at entertainment and poetic truth. Poetic truth shades off into philosophic truth, which also can take mythical form, whether filling metaphysical gaps, illustrating abstractions, or protecting the philosopher. Historical and philosophic myths may be "poetic"; the poet and the philosopher may use historical myths. Although all their myths are most equivocal, each branch of the Mardian mythology creates verbal realities which may materially affect the Mardian world.

As the Mardian mythologists define the myths of Mardi, they sit in a boat with Media the royal demigod and Taji the astronomical demigod, they hunt Yillah the idol of man, and they end the hunt with the god Alma. These four worshiped beings—Media, Taji, Yillah, and Alma—incarnate the major myths of *Mardi*: the State, the Cosmic Role, Romance, and the Church. The true nature of these myths is the subject of *Mardi*.

THE DEMIGOD OF THE STATE: MEDIA

It was not long after 1848; and, somehow, about that time, all round the world, these kings, they had the casting vote, and voted for themselves.

"THE PIAZZA" (1856)

On the map that charts the spheres, Mardi is marked "the World of Kings."

MARDI (1849)

When the first four Mardian visits reveal four stages of kinghood, they indicate that one of the main objects of the search will be to discover what a king is. From the time that Media says, "I myself am interested in this pursuit," until he renounces both his assumed role and the search itself, the changing definition of King Media forms much of the structure of the voyage. Media's progress is an apparent decline which is really a rise, from sitting as a living idol in his own temple in his own kingdom to kneeling on a strange island in order to renounce his demigodship and invoke the blessings of Alma, the "prince divine." From the beginning of the apparent fall, there are hints of the reality behind the appearance. Media's apparent height is the pedestal in his temple; here beside the idol of Media the royal demigod and Taji the astronomical demigod is the idol of a third demigod—a deified maker of plantain pudding. In Media's "endless pedigree," he reckons "deities by decimals." Before they depart, Taji says that they in "due time met with several decayed, broken down demigods: magnificos of no mark in Mardi." Many of the jokes throughout the voyage (particularly recurrent ones, such as the fear of death betrayed by "immortal" demigods) reduce euhemerism to an absurdity.

But euhemerism in Mardi is much more than an absurdity. As we have seen, several of the Mardian kings, themselves enslaved, subject their people to the most extravagant and destructive myths; by use of myths, these kings attain and maintain their supreme earthly power:

> These demi-gods had wherewithal to sustain their lofty pretensions. If need were, could crush out of him the infidelity of a non-conformist. And by this immaculate union of church and state, god and king, in their own proper persons reigned supreme Caesars over the souls and bodies of their subjects. (I, 207)

As a result, the Mardians often "addressed the supreme god Oro, in the very same terms employed in the political adoration of their sublunary rulers." Media is no exception to the rule of Mardian kings; in his kingdom men "shrieked" for denying his divinity: "There, men were scourged; their crime, a heresy; the heresy, that Media was no demigod." Only after Media encounters real divinity does he vow that these groans will no longer be heard in the groves of his kingdom. By this time, however, a revolution has taken the matter out of his hands.

The voyage through Mardi reveals kings on several levels of allegory, and on each level is written the *mene, mene, tekel, upharsin* of all kings. Each kind of allegorical tour ends with the hint or fact of revolution. The revolution against Media comes at the end of the voyage and brings it full circle. Although the outcome of this revolution remains in doubt, Media's name suggests what it will be: the historical empire of Media was submerged when its last king was dethroned by a revolution.

Even before the voyage starts, while Media is basking in the full glories of his state, his name and role hint of the voyage's end. After he has donned his divinity, crowned in "the primitive Eastern style," and looking "very much like a god," Media evokes in Taji's mind the first tour of kings, which foreshadows in detail the allegorical tours of the Mardian voyage. It takes place in the chapter entitled, most significantly (see Daniel 5:28), "Belshazzar on the Bench":

> A king on his throne! Ah, believe me, ye Gracchi, ye Acephali, ye Levelers, it is something worth seeing, be sure; whether beheld at Babylon the Tremendous, when Nebuchadnezzar was crowned; at old Scone in the days of Macbeth; at Rheims, among Oriflammes, at the coronation of Louis le Grand; at Westminster Abbey, when the gentlemanly George doffed his beaver for a diadem; or under the soft shade of palm trees on an isle in the sea.
>
> Man lording it over man, man kneeling to man, is a spectacle that Gabriel might well travel hitherward to behold; for never did he behold it in heaven. But Darius giving laws to the Medes and the Persians, or the conqueror of Bactria with king-cattle yoked to his car, was not a whit more sublime, than Beau Brummel magnificently ringing for his valet.
>
> A king on his throne! It is Jupiter nodding in the councils of Olympus; Satan, seen among the coronets in Hell.
>
> A king on his throne! It is the sun over a mountain; the sun over law-giving Sinai; the sun in our system: planets, duke-like, dancing attendance, and baronial satellites in waiting.   (I, 216)

From Nebuchadnezzar and Macbeth to Jupiter and Satan and thence to the sun is a long way, and a way that suggests what the forthcoming allegorical tours will find.

These tours begin with generalized allegorical kings, pass on to thinly allegorized nineteenth-century political forces and figures, and end by focusing again on King Media. The kings found on each tour range one behind another, each shadowing forth another's most prominent features. Upon King Ludwig (of France) and King Bello (of England) are thrown the shadows of King Piko and King Hello, who prune their excess subjects with murderous games, and of Kings Peepi, Donjalolo, Uhia, and Borabolla, who chain their subjects to destructive myths; upon them all are thrown the shadows of Nebuchadnezzar and Darius, of Louis le Grand and gentlemanly George, of Jupiter and of Satan. And all these shadows pin down Media when, drunk, he reveals that "Peace is War to all kings." The destructive power of all these kings derives, in the words of Sir William Jones, from "historical or natural truth [that] has been perverted into fable by ignorance, imagination, flattery, or stupidity."

The king of all these Mardian kings is Hivohitee, Alma's supreme earthly priest, who "lived and reigned, in mystery, the High Pontiff of the adjoining isles: prince, priest, and god, in his own proper person: great lord paramount over many kings in Mardi; his hands full of sceptres and crosiers." When Hivohitee reveals that the mystery through which he reigns is founded upon "nothing," he reveals that the greatest as well as the least king of Mardi is a mythical fraud. The royal demigods of Mardi are as fraudulent as Taji, the demigod who comes to Mardi by way of the sun, in reality a runaway sailor who steps out of a stolen whaleboat.

THE COSMIC DEMIGOD: TAJI

II. The next source of them [myths] appears to have been a wild admiration of the heavenly bodies, and, after a time, the systems and calculations of astronomers; hence came a considerable portion of Egyptian *and* Grecian *fable; the* Sabian *worship in* Arabia; *the* Persian *types and emblems of* Mihr, *or the Sun; and the far extended adoration of the elements and the powers of nature; and hence, perhaps, all the artificial* Chronology *of the* Chinese *and* Indians, *with the invention of demi-gods and heroes to fill the vacant niches in their extravagant and imaginary periods.*

"On the Gods of Greece, Italy, and India," p. 222

As Merrell Davis has demonstrated, the conception of the sea as space, islands as stars, and the Mardian archipelago as a constellation in the Milky Way was central to the genesis of *Mardi*.[8] The narrator's astronomical role is defined even before he quits "the firmament blue of the open sea," lands on "some new constellation," and proclaims himself an astronomical demigod. He is the perpetual westward voyager who breaks from the *Arcturion* when it veers north, who steers perpetually by Arcturus, who thinks the *Arcturion* may "illustrate the Whistonian theory concerning the damned and the comets."

After he lands on the Mardian constellation, he claims that he came from the sun. Later (II, 271), after envisioning the Mardian isles as clusters of stars, he thinks of himself as a miniature counterpart of the sun: "And, as the sun, by influence divine, wheels through the Ecliptic; threading Cancer, Leo, Pisces, and Aquarius; so, by some mystic impulse am I moved, to this fleet progress, through the groups in white-reefed Mardi's zone." As Taji, he pursues Yillah, "a seraph from the sun" who first instilled in his mind and in the minds of the Mardians the notion that he is a demigod. Taji and Yillah are pursued by the moonlike Hautia, who "glided on: her crescent brow calm as the moon, when most it works its evil influences." A "thousand constellations" cluster about Hautia, who "burned" as a "Glorious queen! with all the radiance, lighting up the equatorial night"; "all space reflects her as a mirror." In some sort of allegorical or metaphorical sense, Taji is a comet, Yillah a sun, and Hautia a moon.

Such curious identities would not be strangers to the comparative mythology of the seventeenth, eighteenth, and nineteenth centuries, in which mythology was habitually related to astronomy. Before the close of the eighteenth century, many skeptics and mystics had reduced all mythology to fictionalized astronomy. The astronomical identifications of Taji, Yillah, and Hautia, although almost frivolous, help to order the structure of *Mardi*. When they are defined as comet, sun, and moon, Taji, Yillah, and Hautia take their places in the mythology of Mardi. It is mere myth which gives them cosmic roles.

But Taji is a comet in another sense, and his voyages dramatize a particular kind of comet, a Whistonian comet. In the first of *Mardi*'s one hundred ninety-five chapters, the narrator learns that the *Arcturion* is about to head from the equator to the pole. He then makes what proves to be a most important suggestion: "We were going, it seemed, to illustrate the Whistonian theory concerning the damned and the comets:—hurried from equinoctial heats to arctic frosts." The source of this suggestion shows what it means in detail:

I observe, that the Sacred Accounts of *Hell,* or of the Place and State of Punishment for wicked Men after the general Resurrection, is agreeable not only to the Remains of ancient profane Tradition, but to the true

System of the World also. This sad State is in Scripture describ'd as a State of *Darkness*, of *outward Darkness*, of *blackness of Darkness*, of *Torment* and *Punishment for Ages, or for Ages of Ages, by Flame,* or *by Fire,* or *by Fire and Brimstone, with Weeping and Gnashing of Teeth*; where *the Smoak of the* Ungodly's *Torment ascends up for ever and ever*; where they are Tormented *in the Presence of the Holy Angels, and in the Presence of the Lamb; when the Holy Angels shall have separated the Wicked from among the Just, and have cast them into a Furnace of Fire.* Now this Description does in every Circumstance, so exactly agree with the Nature of a Comet, ascending from the Hot Regions near the Sun, and going into the Cold Regions beyond *Saturn,* with its long smoking Tail arising up from it, through its several Ages or Periods of revolving, and this in the Sight of all the Inhabitants of our Air, and of the rest of the System; that I cannot but think the Surface or Atmosphere of such a Comet to be that *Place of Torment* so terribly described in Scripture.[9]

Long before the narrator meets Yillah and conceives of passing himself off as a demigod, he is regarded more than once as a supernatural being, as, to be specific, a ghost or goblin. When, at the very end, he claims to be the "spirit's phantom's phantom" of Taji and renounces this "life of dying," he pulls together fragments of a structure that are scattered through the book. The narrator is in fact a Whistonian damned soul, at least to the extent that he is a Whistonian comet. His damnation consists of repeating over and over again an act of moral abdication and being regarded, after each abdication, as a supernatural being. In the first chapter, with something like tragic irony, the narrator brashly proclaims "were I placed in the same situation again, I would repeat the thing I did then."

His first abdication is his midnight leap from the *Arcturion,* "an undertaking which apparently savored of a moral dereliction." Immediately, this abdication makes him feel as though he were a ghost: "For the consciousness of being deemed dead, is next to the presumable unpleasantness of being so in reality. One feels like his own ghost unlawfully tenanting a defunct carcass." As the first illustration of the Whistonian theory, Jarl and the narrator become like lost souls: "What a mere toy we were to the billows, that jeeringly shouldered us from crest to crest, as from hand to hand lost souls may be tossed along by the chain of shades which enfilade the route to Tartarus." Soon "the sun and the Chamois seemed all that was left of life in the universe"; "All became vague and confused; so that westward of the Kingsmill isles and the Radack chain, I fancied there could be naught but an endless sea." Beyond Mardi the narrator will indeed find "an endless sea"; for these very words appear again as the last words of the book.

At this point the narrator not only anticipates his fate but actually experiences it. The mere toy of a boat drifts into a calm, and it seems that the two lost souls have entered the unformed chaos on the edge of the universe:

. . . the two gray firmaments of sky and water seemed collapsed into a vague ellipsis. And alike, the Chamois seemed drifting in the atmosphere as in the sea. Every thing was fused into the calm: sky, air, water, and all. Not a fish was to be seen. The silence was that of a vacuum. No vitality lurked in the air. And this inert blending and brooding of all things seemed gray chaos in conception. (I, 64)

This is the very region to which the narrator, just after his "desire to quit the Arcturion became little short of a frenzy," thought the captain had brought him: "The ignoramus must have lost his way, and drifted into the outer confines of creation, the region of the ever-lasting lull, introductory to a positive vacuity." At that early point the narrator's musings had been prophetic: "Thoughts of eternity thicken. He begins to feel anxious concerning his soul."

When they board the *Parki,* Jarl thinks the ship "purely phantom-like," "a shade of a ship, full of sailors' ghosts" which soon "would dissolve in a supernatural squall," and his "superstitions" are partly borne out when the *Parki* dissolves in a natural squall. His feelings are matched by those of the two survivors of the *Parki*'s crew, Samoa and his mate Annatoo: "For their wild superstitions led them to conclude, that a white man's craft coming upon them so suddenly, upon the open sea, and by night, could be naught but a phantom. Furthermore . . . they fancied us the ghosts of the Cholos." The "Cholos" were the two half-breed pirates who had led the attack on the *Parki* and who had been killed by Samoa. The mistaking of Jarl and the narrator for their avenging ghosts foreshadows the spectral avengers who later haunt the allegorical voyage through Mardi. Samoa and Annatoo next think that Jarl and the narrator are "goblins," which is exactly what Jarl had thought them. Jarl and the narrator had behaved so strangely that they "almost led Samoa to fancy that we were no shades, after all, but a couple of men from the moon." On the other hand, Jarl "to the last" "stoutly maintained that the hobgoblins must have had something or other to do with the Parki," and later the narrator finds that his "suspicions" concerning Samoa's story "returned." In an odd anticipation of the devils which possess Babbalanja and the people of Quelquo, Annatoo is "possessed by some scores of devils." The narrator's moral abdication on the *Parki* is a mere peccadillo, the fraudulent seizing of the ship's command to further his personal quest. When the *Parki* goes down in a squall and Annatoo is swept into the sea, Samoa, Jarl, and the narrator take to the *Chamois*. They soon discover that they look to each other as Jarl and the narrator had looked just after abandoning the *Arcturion*: "a cadaverous gleam" from the sea makes them look "to each other like ghosts."

The narrator attains his next supernatural identity after his most heinous moral abdication, the murder of the priest Aleema. He persuades Yillah, the maiden he has seized from Aleema, "to fancy me some gentle demi-god, that had come over the sea." Yillah becomes an "idol" for the narrator, and Jarl prophetically thinks her "an Ammonite syren, who might lead me astray." In the chapter entitled "The Dream Begins to Fade," the narrator finds that his sexual love of his idol is dissipating his own divinity. "Love" in turn induces him "to prop my failing divinity; though it was I myself who had undermined it": "in the sight of Yillah, I perceived myself thus dwarfing down to a mortal." Meanwhile both Yillah and Jarl think of Samoa as a "goblin," while, significantly like the narrator, Samoa also makes Yillah an "idol." Thus as the *Chamois* draws near Mardi, its occupants include beings who at one time or another have been considered goblins, ghosts, phantoms, wandering shades, a demigod, and a goddess.

The narrator's penultimate abdication comes when he makes his grandest claim, assuming the astronomical half of the Whistonian theory. On the *Arcturion* the narrator had talked to the clouds and developed a "fellow-feeling for the sun." After leaving the *Arcturion,* he had become a "fellow-voyager" of the sun. When he lands on Mardi, he proclaims himself a demigod from the sun: "Men of Mardi, I come from the sun. When this morning it rose and touched the wave, I pushed my shallop from its golden beach, and hither sailed before its level rays. I am Taji."

This penultimate abdication is his penultimate allegorical death, and it signalizes his death as the most important being in *Mardi.* From this point on, ironically and appropriately the Mardians become far more important than the narrator. "Taji" as a Mardian conception becomes more significant than the player of Taji. The three mythologists and their king make Taji's quest their own. Although they finally all disassociate themselves from his quest, realizing that Yillah is but a phantom, they follow until then what they believe to be "white Taji, a sort of half-and-half deity, now and then an Avatar," to the brink of doom. Taji's own quest for Yillah continues after they forsake him, and it ends as it began, with an abdication:

"Now, I am my own soul's emperor; and my first act is abdication! Hail! realm of shades!"—and turning my prow into the racing tide, which seized me like a hand omnipotent, I darted through.

Churned in foam, that outer ocean lashed the clouds; and straight in my white wake, headlong dashed a shallop, three fixed specters leaning o'er its prow: three arrows poising.

And thus, pursuers and pursued flew on, over an endless sea.

Before this abdication he has reduced himself to "the spirit's phantom's phantom" of Taji. His soul has completed its hellish orbit, earlier described: "Thus deeper and deeper into Time's endless tunnel, does the winged soul, like a night-hawk, wend her wild way; and finds eternities before and behind; and her last limit is her everlasting beginning." "Behind and before," are not only eternities, but ever, as in the chapter of that title, the pursuers and the pursued.

THE IDOL OF ROMANCE: YILLAH

As a comet and as a damned soul, the narrator passes through world after world on his circular orbit from the *Arcturion* to the *Chamois* and *Parki* to Odo to Serenia and back to the endless sea beyond Mardi. Yillah is worshiped and sought by inhabitants of each of the worlds in *Mardi*. From the *Arcturion* and the *Parki* come the narrator and Samoa, who slay the Polynesian priest carrying Yillah to the sacrificial rites. Yillah then becomes the idol of the *Chamois,* worshiped both by the narrator and by Samoa, "master of Gog and Magog, expounder of all things heathenish and obscure." When the *Chamois* is beached on Mardi, Yillah becomes a goddess of the Mardians. After she disappears, four symbolic questors come from the allegorical worlds of history, poetry, philosophy, and government to join the narrator's search for her.

Yillah may be, as she has been variously defined, Truth or Happiness or the Absolute or simply the eternal Lure. But whatever else, she is what Babbalanja tells Taji she is, "a phantom that but mocks thee." She is to Taji, Media, Babbalanja, Mohi, and Yoomy what the *Chamois* is to the fish that follow it singing "we care not what is it, this life/that we follow, this phantom unknown." Yillah's history is significant only in so far as the characters misconstrue it, fashioning it into a myth to shape their own quest.

Yillah herself has been wrought upon by the priests whose "pupils almost lose their humanity in the constant indulgence of seraphic imaginings." "Enshrined as a goddess" by the priest of Amma, she is easily passed off by Taji, the new priest who has murdered the old, as a "seraph from the sun." The narrator at first admits that he "might have been tranced into a belief of her mystical legends." Later, he acts as though they were true, rejecting her true and mundane history as coming "too late, too late." Their sexual relations tend toward the "extinguishment of her own spirituality," but when she lands on Mardi she retains enough so that "the adoration of the maiden was extended to myself."

As the search for Yillah continues, philosophy and history have less and less to say about her, and poetry becomes her interpreter. Yoomy begins the search confident that "Yillah will yet be found." His hopes become dimmer and dimmer as his descriptions of Yillah become increasingly enlightened. Toward the end of the quest, he uses the same language to describe Yillah that Taji had used before her disappearance. Taji and Yoomy, using the commonplace romantic hyperbole, equate a romantic idol with the sun. Taji tells how "my Yillah did daily dawn, how she lit up the world"; Yoomy tells how "Yillah now rises and flashes!/Rays shooting from out her long lashes," and how she makes "All the buds blossom" and "leaves turn round." But Taji's and Yoomy's conceit is something more than a hyperbolic cliché. Yillah is the sun in a very real, if only metaphoric and allegoric, sense. She is a false sun, whose pursuit leads to destruction and damnation.

The narrator as Whistonian comet crosses paths first with Yillah, who seems to be the sun, and then with Hautia, who seems to be the moon. Both Yillah and Hautia prove to be Whistonian meteors, "Mock-Suns . . . resembling the Moon or Sun for a while."[10] Yillah, as a mock sun, is the phantom that but mocks Taji; Hautia, addressed by Taji as the moon, is merely a "meteor." *Mardi*'s astronomical mythology consummates in the true Sun.

THE GOD OF CHURCH AND HEART: ALMA THE SUN

Until they reach Serenia, the five questors maintain their mythological roles. Mohi's historical mythology, Yoomy's poetical mythology, and Babbalanja's philosophical mythology provide the background and chorus for Taji the astronomical pseudo-avatar, Media the euhemerized king, and Alma the institutionalized myth of Mardi. But the true Alma of Serenia shatters these roles. The psychological and moral truth of Alma, experienced in Serenia, makes impertinent the historical, philosophical, and poetic truth of all myths, including the official myth of Alma.

Babbalanja is the first to recognize the true sun in "great Oro and his sovereign son": " 'Oh, Alma, Alma! prince divine!' cried Babbalanja, sinking on his knees,—'in *thee,* at last, I find repose. Hope perches in my heart a dove;—a thousand rays illume;—all Heaven's a sun. Gone, gone! are all distracting doubts. Love and Alma now prevail.'" Babbalanja's conversion breaks the demigods' leadership and for all except Taji ends the quest. All now follow Babbalanja's leadership but Taji, Alma's rival avatar, who pursues his destructive chase of Alma's rival absolute—Yillah, a false sun.

For the others, the true sun puts out all false suns. Yoomy sees the summer's dependence not on Yillah but on Alma: "In Alma all my dreams are found, my inner longings for the Love supreme, that prompts my every verse. Summer is in my soul"; Mohi cries out, "I see bright light"; Media renounces his divinity and cries, "Alma, I am thine." When "king, sage, gray hairs, and youth" all kneel, they are bathed in the light of the true sun: "There, as they knelt, and as the old man blessed them, the setting sun burst forth from mists, gilded the island round about, shed rays upon their heads, and went down in a glory—all the East radiant with red burnings, like an altar-fire." The sunset and the night that follows consummate the astronomical images of *Mardi*.

The astronomical level of action received its first extended definition in the first few pages of *Mardi,* where one passage can now be seen as central to the book's astronomical rhetoric and astronomical conceits. *Mardi* dramatizes, clause by clause, the strange rhetoric and fantastic conceits of this passage:

King Noah, God bless him! fathered us all. Then hold up your heads, oh ye Helots, blood potential flows through your veins. All of us have monarchs and sages for kinsmen; nay, angels and archangels for cousins; since in antediluvian days, the sons of God did verily wed with our mothers, the irresistible daughters of Eve. Thus all generations are blended: and heaven and earth of one kin: the hierarchies of seraphs in the uttermost skies; the thrones and principalities in the zodiac; the shades that roam throughout space; the nations and families, flocks and folds of the earth; one and all, brothers in essence—oh, be we then brothers indeed! All things form but one whole; the universe a Judea, and God Jehovah its head. Then no more let us start with affright. In a theocracy, what is to fear? Let us compose ourselves to death as fagged horsemen sleep in the saddle. Let us welcome even ghosts when they rise. Away with our stares and grimaces. The New Zealander's tattooing is not a prodigy; nor the Chinaman's ways an enigma. No custom is strange; no creed is absurd; no foe, but who will in the end prove a friend. In heaven, at last, our good, old, white-haired father Adam will greet all alike, and sociality forever prevail. Christian shall join hands between Gentile and Jew; grim Dante forget his Infernos, and shake sides with fat Rabelais; and monk Luther, over a flagon of old nectar, talk over old times with Pope Leo. Then, shall we sit by the sages, who of yore gave laws to the Medes and Persians in the sun; by the cavalry captains in Perseus, who cried, "To horse!" when waked by their Last Trump sounding to the charge; by the old hunters, who eternities ago, hunted the moose in Orion; by the minstrels, who sang in the Milky Way when Jesus our Saviour was born. Then shall we list to no shallow gossip of Magellans and Drakes; but give ear to the voyagers who have circumnavigated the Ecliptic; who rounded the Polar Star as Cape Horn. Then shall the Stagirite and Kant be forgotten, and another folio than theirs be turned over for wisdom; even the folio now spread with horoscopes as yet undeciphered, the heaven of heavens on high. (I, 24–25)

Given the theocracy, the universe with God Jehovah at its head, then "the shades that roam throughout space," such as the narrator, Jarl, and Samoa, are of one kin with the seraphs, such as Yillah, a "seraph from the sun." They are indeed what they claim to be after Taji's apotheosis, "all strolling divinities." All of them have monarchs such as Media and sages such as Babbalanja for kinsmen. The nations and families, flocks and folds of the earth, such as the world of Mardi, named for a nation of wandering herdsmen, are brothers in essence to the constellations and worlds in the Milky Way, the thrones and principalities in the Zodiac, such as Arcturus in Boötes, the herdsman. Even the space travel promised in the latter half of the passage becomes a reality; angels and archangels conduct through creation the man who can call, as Babbalanja finally does, "Oh, Alma, Alma! prince divine." When Babbalanja recognizes the theocracy and avows the supreme royalty of Alma, he is immediately rewarded by the vision which the narrator fruitlessly and eternally seeks.

The chapter entitled "Babbalanja Relates to Them a Vision" parallels point by point the astronomical voyage of the narrator. But whereas the narrator voyages as a lost soul, roaming throughout space as a damned comet, Babbalanja voyages as a soul surely guided by an angel. Babbalanja, his eyes "fixed on heaven," first sees the angel as a "shining spot, unlike a star." Then he sees not the vacuity which Taji finds beyond the Mardian Milky Way or the unformed chaos on the edge of the universe, but a mystical world, also imaged forth in terms of a tropical voyage:

"Then, as white flame from yellow, out from that starry cluster it emerged; and brushed the astral Crosses, Crowns, and Cups. And as in violet, tropic seas, ships leave a radiant-white, and fire-fly wake; so, in long extension tapering, behind the vision, gleamed another Milky-Way.
"Strange throbbings seized me; my soul tossed on its own tides."

When the angel asks him what he has learned from the "grace of Alma," Babbalanja presents his passport for mystical space travel: "This have I learned, oh! spirit!—In things mysterious to seek no more; but rest content, with knowing naught but love." They immediately embark:

"We clove the air; passed systems, suns, and moons: what seem from Mardi's isles, the glow-worm stars.
"By distant fleets of worlds we sped, as voyagers pass far sails at sea, and hail them not. Foam played before them as they darted on; wild music was their wake; and many tracks of sound we crossed, where worlds had sailed before.
"Soon, we gained a point, where a new heaven was seen; whence all our firmament seemed one nebula. Its glories burned like thousand steadfast-flaming lights.
"Here hived the worlds in swarms; and gave forth sweets ineffable.
"We lighted on a ring, circling a space, where mornings seemed for ever dawning over worlds unlike.
" 'Here,' I heard, 'thou viewest thy Mardi's Heaven.' "

A greater angel then takes Babbalanja and his guide far above, to a point from which "Your utmost heaven is far below." From this point, Babbalanja "beheld an awful glory": "Sphere in sphere, it burned:—the one Shekinah!"

Mardi culminates in a heavenly reward through Alma and a

hellish punishment for spurning Alma. Of course the conclusion does not merely exalt Alma at Taji's expense. Taji, though a damned soul, is also glorious. Taji's gloriousness considerably weakens the emotional effects of Alma's glories, and one can hardly understand either Melville or *Mardi* without recognizing Taji's glorification. Yet the fact remains that Taji is damned and those who follow Alma are saved. And unlike many of the later works, *Mardi* does not make those who are saved appear contemptible. Melville's failure to order coherently the ambiguities of this ending may explain in part the failure of the entire book. For, after all, *Mardi* provides no reasonable basis for Taji's glorification. He is no demon-hunting Ahab nor even a Bulkington, heroically steering away from the dangerous safety of the shore. On the physical level, "Taji" is only the assumed name of a runaway sailor chasing a girl. And on the allegorical level, which is more important, Taji is a phony demigod chasing a phantom. He refuses to recognize the simple fact that the Alma of Serenia is the only true god in Mardi, that this Alma is truly the Christ, Saviour, Messiah, and Sun.

Once we recognize the fact that there is only one true sun, one divine light, one supreme prince, one Absolute in Mardi, we may return to the myths about other incarnate suns, other divine princes, other absolutes. The true Alma appears in a world swarming with dangerous myths, including the most dangerous myth of all, the myth of Alma.

The mythologists of the Mardian world create myths which support courts and churches, which absolve man from responsibility, which turn strangers into gods, which merely entertain, which explain obscure natural events, which fill gaps in metaphysical theories, which satisfy emotional needs, which order all the parts of the Mardian world. The myth of Alma does all that these myths do. It supports kings and clerics, making its Pontiff Hivohitee the most powerful of princes, "prince, priest, and god, in his own proper person; great lord paramount over many kings in Mardi; his hands full of sceptres and crosiers." Just as Azzageddi, *"in propria persona,"* absolved Babbalanja from responsibility, the myth of Alma, defined by an official

Pontiff as a "god, in his own proper person," transfers man's moral and spiritual responsibility to his priests and church. Alma himself, when he had come as a stranger to the Holy Island, had not, like Taji, found safety in his deification; but the mythic Alma is there enshrined. Alma's myth, officially chronicled, proves as entertaining as any other of Mohi's legends. Defined by both church and state, Alma's myth officially fills all metaphysical gaps, supplies all religious needs, explains all obscure events, and orders the Mardian archipelago.

The official myths defined by Maramma and chronicled by Mohi provide no way of distinguishing between the divine and the mythical. The myth of Alma is like all the other myths of man. But the true Alma is not a "prince divine" because of his legendary past, supernatural character, or prophetic destiny. The basis of his divinity is not that of Peepi, Media, Taji, the deified maker of plantain pudding, or even the Alma of Maramma. The Alma enshrined as a god on the Holy Island of Mar*amma* is no more divine than Yillah, who was "enshrined as a goddess" on the holy island of *Amma*. The avatars of Alma inscribed in the chronicles of Mohi are no more divine than the "Avatar" of "white Taji." The temporal Pontiff of Alma may entertain only equivocal "incorporeal deities from above passing the Capricorn Solstice at Maramma." Alma is divine on Serenia only because Alma on Serenia is Reason.

The psychological qualities which Taji and, for a time, Yoomy adore in Yillah are misplaced, just as are the metaphysical properties which Babbalanja locates in an abstract absolute, the royal divinity located in Mardian royalty, the astronomical attributes falsely defined by all. Only the message of Serenia accurately defines Alma's divinity:

"Right-reason, and Alma, are the same; else Alma, not reason, would we reject. The Master's great command is Love; and here do all things wise, and all things good, unite. Love is all in all. The more we love, the more we know; and so reversed. Oro we love; this isle; and our wide arms embrace all Mardi like its reef. How can we err, thus feeling? We hear loved Alma's pleading, prompting voice, in every breeze, in every leaf; we see his earnest eye in every star and flower." (II, 358–59)

It is essential to note that the Serenians define Alma as the embodiment of intuitive moral and psychological perceptions which they call "right reason." This is not discursive reason, nor is it merely feelings. It is the reason of the heart, which establishes a religion of the heart.

Only the Serenian definition of Alma, as first Babbalanja and then Yoomy, Mohi, and Media discover, can validate the passport to heaven. In their Mardian voyage, the questors met this definition only once, in the mouth of a youthful pilgrim to Maramma. This young disciple of the religion of the heart becomes a sacrifice to the mythological religion of Maramma. When he pleads Oro's message in his heart to excuse himself from abasement before Oro's idol, the priests of Alma seize him: " 'Impious boy,' cried they with the censers, 'we will offer thee up, before the very image thou contemnest. In the name of Alma, seize him.' " When the priests of Alma sacrifice in his name they equate their god with Apo, the god to whom Aleema was to sacrifice Yillah, the god who bears one name of the great Serpent, the Evil Being.[11]

In *Mardi*, mythical truth is irrelevant to religious truth, and may, in fact, destroy it. The youth, although a disciple of the religion of the heart, does not consistently practice it. He makes a pilgrimage to the place of his destruction because he does accept one myth, a myth about Alma's ascension, the very myth about which Mohi and Babbalanja had disputed inconclusively: "But though rejecting a guide, still he clings to that legend of the Peak."

The epistemological dead ends of Mardi turn all history, poetry, and philosophy into myth. By dramatizing the identity of Sir William Jones's four sources of mythology, Melville rejects the mythological basis of religion. In a world in which history, poetry, and philosophy offer mere myths, the only safe basis for religion seems to be intuitive psychological and moral truth.

CHAPTER 3

MOBY-DICK
An Egyptian Myth Incarnate

One way and another, it has begotten events so remarkable in themselves, and so continuously momentous in their sequential issues, that whaling may well be regarded as that Egyptian mother, who bore offspring themselves pregnant from her womb. MOBY-DICK

. . . M. Volney, M. Bailli, and other professed infidels of the age [have insinuated] . . . that the noble system of the national Theology rests upon no more substantial a basis than an Egyptian allegory. . . . I must again assert my perfect coincidence with the opinion of Sir William Jones, whom an intimate acquaintance with the mythology and history of Oriental nations availed not to make a skeptic, that if the Mosaic history be indeed a fable, the whole fabric of the national religion is false, since the main pillar of Christianity rests upon that important original promise, that the Seed of the woman shall bruise the head of the Serpent.

THE REVEREND THOMAS MAURICE, as quoted in his
obituary in the *Gentleman's Magazine*, May 1824

In *Mardi* Melville plays off contemporary mythological theories against contemporary religious orthodoxy in order to exalt a non-mythic religion. The myths which make the god-priests of Maramma supreme in Mardi are as fabulous, as dangerous, and as official as the myths which uphold all the Mardian god-kings. The Alma of Maramma, the last avatar, is at least as monstrous as the other major mythic figures—Media, the euhemerist demigod, a tyrant who learns better; Taji, the astronomical demigod, a fraud who destroys himself;

Yillah, the false goddess and false sun, who leads her followers to destruction and damnation. The religion of Alma is true only because and only to the extent that its Alma equals Reason. This non-mythic truth of Alma is both psychological and moral—psychological in so far as Reason is defined in merely Transcendental terms, moral in so far as Reason retains its Aristotelian-Thomistic values. In *Moby-Dick,* Melville more destructively attacks religious and mythological orthodoxy and more constructively creates a new myth. He violently brings together the cracked and flawed old myths. From the shattered fragments he pieces together the cosmic struggle of Ahab and the White Whale.

Moby-Dick defines historical truth, psychological truth, metaphysical truth, and moral truth with much greater precision and with much greater complexity than does *Mardi*. In one of the many senses in which it is a book of revelation, *Moby-Dick* reveals, layer by layer, the kinds of truth incarnated by the White Whale. As each layer is stripped off and examined in historical, psychological, metaphysical, and moral terms, it is found to be enormous and, in different senses, mythological. No analysis can tell the whole truth of even one of these layers. But by focusing first on the one chapter which most concentrates the whale's various truths, it is possible to see their outlines.

In the chapter "Moby Dick," historical, psychological, metaphysical, and moral truth all meet in the myth of the White Whale, the myth serving, as it serves throughout the book, to mediate these several kinds of myth. The chapter defines more extensively than any other chapter Moby Dick's history, what he represents to the minds of men, and what he symbolizes philosophically and morally. Yet it tells practically nothing of the whale that is not, at least in the most general sense, mythical. The whale's history is as dubious, as equivocal, and as mysterious as his divinity and his malignancy. The entire chapter, while continually defining the myth of Moby Dick, continually insists that the myth is mythical. Almost every detail of his history is questioned as it is presented. Only his physical appearance, his ferocity, and the fact that he encountered Ahab are not to

other in Western thought at least since the fifth century before Christ —the historical and the psychological. (Like most distinctions, those which separate these two schools exist more in theory than in fact. But these theoretic distinctions have their usefulness.) Myth, by definition, cannot be history. Myths may be events of human and natural history as they are distorted, fictionalized, or allegorized by the mind. Or myths may be events of the mind as they are dramatized in narrative form, that is, in terms of natural or historical events. In either case, they are products of the interaction of psychological processes and external reality, combining something of both psychological events and historical or natural events. The distinction which I am going to make between the "historical" and the "psychological" schools is this: the historical school assumes that myth is natural or human history veiled by psychology; it seeks to remove that veil and to discover historical truth. The psychological school assumes that myth is psychology veiled by its narrative formulation; it seeks to remove that veil and to discover psychological truth. The two schools thus agree that myth equals history plus psychology but disagree about the relative importance of the two ingredients. Returning to *Mardi,* we can compare Sir William Jones and Melville in terms of this working distinction. Jones is as good a specimen as one finds of the historical school; Melville, although he admits and dramatizes Jones's theories, overrides these theories with psychological concerns and ultimately enrolls himself in the psychological school. Jones lists four ways in which the human mind, by distorting external reality, produces mythology. The historian perverts history perhaps to curry favor with his king, ignorant awe makes a people personify astronomical objects and events, poets plant nymphs in nature to entertain, and philosophers incarnate their metaphysics in the physical world. Jones seeks to restore what he considers historical and natural truth, the truth of the Judaic-Christian revelation. Melville dramatizes the mythologizing described by Jones, but he turns from the thing distorted—external reality, which remains an enigma—to the distorter, human psychology. Jones finds that myth yields an absolute truth about its ultimate object, God, who fashions and truly reveals history and nature. Melville suggests that the only ultimate truth that myth yields is a truth about its ultimate source, the human mind.

In the chapter "Moby Dick" these two ways of looking at myth are related with great precision and great complexity. The history of Moby Dick is related to the myth of Moby Dick exactly as typical contemporaneous works of comparative mythology of the historical school related history to myth. One of the favorite phenomena of the eighteenth- and nineteenth-century historical school was known as the "Asiatic" or "Oriental" imagination. With one hand, the apologists could explain any differences between the Bible and current archaeology, geology, paleontology, biology, astronomy, or Common Sense by pointing to the "Oriental style" of the transcribers of Scripture; with the other hand, they could wave off other scriptures as mere products of the "Oriental imagination." The skeptics, of course, were using both hands to combine the tricks; the Bible was only one more collection of the fantastic products of the Oriental imagination, which, for both groups, was a compound of ignorance, superstition, and fancy overblown by a hot climate and wild geography. Melville's substitute for the Oriental imagination is the whaleman's imagination—something even wilder than the common seaman's imagination—and he offers it as the explanation of those "wild rumors of all sorts" which did not "fail to exaggerate, and still the more horrify the true histories of these deadly encounters":

For not only do fabulous rumors naturally grow out of the very body of all surprising terrible events . . . but, in maritime life, far more than in that of terra firma, wild rumors abound, wherever there is any adequate reality for them to cling to. And as the sea surpasses the land in this matter, so the whale fishery surpasses every other sort of maritime life, in the wonderfulness and fearfulness of the rumors which sometimes circulate there. For not only are whalemen as a body unexempt from that ignorance and superstitiousness hereditary to all sailors; but of all sailors, they are by all odds the most directly brought into contact with whatever is appallingly astonishing in the sea . . . the whaleman is wrapped by influences all tending to make his fancy pregnant with many a mighty birth.

No wonder, then, that ever gathering volume from the mere transit over the widest watery spaces, the outblown rumors of the White Whale did in the end incorporate with themselves all manner of morbid hints, and half-formed foetal suggestions of supernatural agencies, which eventually invested Moby Dick with new terrors unborrowed from anything that visibly appears.   (Pp. 176–77)

What may have been a direct source for this passage, David Hume's *Natural History of Religion,* defines part of what Melville is here doing:

The absurdity [of anthropomorphism] is not less, while we cast our eyes upwards; and transferring, as is too usual, human passions and infirmities to the deity, represent him as jealous and revengeful, capricious and partial, and, in short, a wicked and foolish man, in every respect but his superior power and authority. No wonder, then, that mankind, being placed in such an absolute ignorance of causes, and being at the same time so anxious concerning their future fortune, should immediately acknowledge a dependence on invisible powers, possessed of sentiment and intelligence. . . .

In proportion as any man's course of life is governed by accident, we always find, that he encreases in superstition; as may particularly be observed of gamesters and sailors, who, though, of all mankind, the least capable of serious reflection, abound most in frivolous and superstitious apprehensions.[2]

Melville, like Hume, is showing how the human imagination projects itself into the inscrutable physical world, transforming inscrutability into mythic religion. Unlike Hume, however, he takes seriously the most superstitious, unsubstantial, nonphysical, and supernatural rumors, hints, and suggestions.

Before presenting these rumors, hints, and suggestions, Melville points out that similar things "in former legendary times" had been thought about the Sperm Whale in general, an object of great superstitious dread. Finally, the suggestions are made, and very important suggestions to *Moby-Dick* they prove to be—the ubiquity in time and space of the White Whale. But these suggestions are offered only as the distortion of historical truth by ignorance, fear, and superstition, represented by the whaleman's imagination:

One of the *wild suggestings* referred to, as at last *to be linked* with the White Whale *in the minds of the superstitiously inclined,* was the *unearthly conceit* that Moby Dick was ubiquitous . . .

Nor, *credulous* as such minds must have been, was this *conceit altogether without some faint show of superstitious* probability. . . .

. . . it cannot be much matter of surprise that *some whalemen* should go still further in their *superstitions*; declaring Moby Dick not only ubiquitous, but immortal . . .   (Pp. 178–79) [Italics mine.]

We may tend to accept Moby Dick's ubiquity in time and space, but we should never forget that this ubiquity is dubious in so far as it is presented as historical truth. Nonetheless it is ultimately of the greatest truth. Although perhaps not historical fact, it is a psychological and hence a metaphysical and moral fact, and a very real, very important fact. Since historical truth cannot be known, other truths prevail.

Here, as in *Mardi,* Melville confronts the epistemological dead end, retraces his steps, and heads in a different direction. The historical truth about the White Whale, like the historical truth about Alma's avatar, is unknowable. But the psychological truth about the White Whale's ubiquity, his intelligent malignity, and his demonism can, like the psychological truth about the revelations of Alma, be known. The most important passage in *Moby-Dick* is the one which presents the psychological truth of the White Whale:

Small reason was there to doubt, then, that ever since that almost fatal encounter, Ahab had cherished a wild vindictiveness against the whale, all the more fell for that in his frantic morbidness he at last came to identify with him, not only all his bodily woes, but all his intellectual and spiritual exasperations. The White Whale swam before him as the monomaniac incarnation of all those malicious agencies which some deep men feel eating in them, till they are left living on with half a heart and half a lung. That intangible malignity which has been from the beginning; to whose dominion even the modern Christians ascribe one-half of the worlds; which the ancient Ophites of the east reverenced in their statue devil;—Ahab did not fall down and worship it like them; but deliriously transferring its idea to the abhorred white whale, he pitted himself, all mutilated, against it. All that most maddens and torments;

all that stirs up the lees of things; all truth with malice in it; all that cracks the sinews and cakes the brain; all the subtle demonisms of life and thought; all evil, to crazy Ahab, were visibly personified, and made practically assailable in Moby Dick. He piled upon the whale's white hump the sum of all the general rage and hate felt by his whole race from Adam down; and then, as if his chest had been a mortar, he burst his hot heart's shell upon it. (P. 181)

Ahab's madness turns the wild fantasies of the whaleman's imagination into psychological, metaphysical, and moral fact. Moby Dick's ubiquity in time and his malignity, so equivocal in the whalemen's legends, are certainty to Ahab; he assumes without question "that intangible malignity which has been from the beginning." And his madness combines with the whaleman's imagination, embodied by the *Pequod*'s crew, to create a myth which determines the fate of both captain and crew.

In a world in which historical truth is attainable, Ahab's insanity would be defined as the difference between the real world and the world of Ahab's mind. But in the external world of *Moby-Dick* the White Whale's historical truth consists merely in visible objects which are but as pasteboard masks. Ahab's mind is free to define Moby Dick. This is not to say that Ahab's psychological truth is the only possible psychological truth. There is indeed a tension between Ahab's psychological truth and, say, Starbuck's. When, however, Starbuck's "soul" is "overmanned" by "a madman," the White Whale is defined not only as Ahab's "intellectual and spiritual exasperations," but as "all evil . . . visibly personified." The crew sees the whale through Ahab's mind: they share his hate, his enemy, and his pursuit; Ishmael abandons his mind to Ahab's, though in Moby Dick he can see "naught but the deadliest ill." Since the *Pequod*'s polyglot crew, that "Anacharsis Clootz deputation," represents all mankind, the fact that Ahab's psychological truth becomes theirs is of utmost significance. When Ahab's mind speaks to theirs, and their minds, as one, echo his, their enemy appears as a monster from the mind:

How it was that they so aboundingly responded to the old man's ire—by what evil magic their souls were possessed, that at times his hate seemed almost theirs; the White Whale as much their insufferable foe as his; how all this came to be—what the White Whale was to them, or how to their unconscious understandings, also, in some dim, unsuspected way, he might have seemed the gliding great demon of the seas of life,—all this to explain, would be to dive deeper than Ishmael can go. (P. 184)

These terms locate the action of *Moby-Dick* within the area of modern psychological theories of mythology, a stream which has been growing steadily from Bayle to Hume to Jung. With no system and no jargon, Melville penetrates deeply enough to reveal the psychological truth of the White Whale. Ahab, by reaching the unconscious understandings of the crew, succeeds in piling "upon the whale's white hump the sum of all the general rage and hate felt by his whole race." He succeeds in evoking a myth, succeeds in completing the formula of one of Melville's mythologically oriented literary contemporaries: "In the mythus a superhuman intelligence uses the unconscious thoughts and dreams of men as its hieroglyphics."[3] Ahab succeeds in fashioning Moby Dick into "the gliding great demon of the seas of life."

This gliding great demon which swims out of the collective unconscious of the race swims also out of many myths consciously known both to the race and to Melville. In *Mardi,* Melville described both the Mardian and extra-Mardian myths only to demolish them with the psychological truth of Alma. *Moby-Dick* first establishes the psychological truth of Ahab's mythic struggle with the White Whale, and then it redefines the various myths of the world by comparing them with its own central myth. It dramatizes some of these myths as ridiculous and others as more or less half-truths. But there is one of the world's myths to which *Moby-Dick* assigns a transcendent importance. This myth is central to Melville's conception, and it maintains a central order in the book. To understand its full significance, we must first examine the myths which are more peripheral.

Despite all the heterodoxy of opinion on *Moby-Dick,* few critics doubt that Moby Dick is a god.[4] There is less agreement, of course, as to which god or what kind of god, for *Moby-Dick* defines the whale's divinity in many ways. A scattering of historical details, the various attributes described second- or third-hand in the *Pequod*'s nine gams, "fabulous rumors," the whaleman's imagination, the madness of Ahab, and the madness of Gabriel all *dramatize* the whale's historical and psychological divinity. In addition, the whale's divinity is defined *discursively* by manifold allusions, references, suggestions, images, hints, and metaphors which relate the whale to other gods. These vary in their degree of specificity, some implying no more than an undefined divine nature, some suggesting a particular divine characteristic, some comparing the whale explicitly to a particular god; and they also vary syntactically and rhetorically in the degree to which they maintain what they imply or assert. Thus we can define even among the least specific suggestions many degrees of assertiveness, from the innocuous adjective ("this high and mighty god-like dignity inherent in the brow") to the apparent similitude (the spirit spout "seemed some plumed and glittering god uprising from the sea") to the belief of a "mad" character (Ahab says that the *Pequod*'s hull when attacked by Moby Dick is "god-bullied") to the narrative statement ("the grand god revealed himself"). The more specific the suggestion, the more complicated it may be. Since we can draw only a vague relationship between the whale and an undefined "god," the less specific suggestions can define the whale's divinity only in vague and general terms. If Moby Dick were small, weak, harmless, mundane, petty, amusing, and restricted in time, space, intelligence, and malice to the usual bounds of an animal, then the terms "god-like" or "the grand god" would ironically indicate his lack of divinity. But because he is enormous, powerful, dangerous, mysterious, grand, fearful, apparently ubiquitous and immortal, and apparently of intelligent malignity, these generalized suggestions only emphasize his divinity. Expressions like "god-like" and "some plumed and glittering god," much as they suggest divinity, tell almost nothing about the nature of that divinity. When, however, syntactical, rhetorical, or dramatic devices link the whale to a particular god, we can make complicated and precise relations between the whale and our knowledge of that god. We can, in short, define the whale's divinity. We are not restricted to vague, general impressions; deity by deity, divine attributes may be added or subtracted, modified or intensified with ease. At the same time, the particular god is redefined in terms of the whale.

The definition of both the whale and the particular god is a product of the syntax, the speaker, the rhetorical figure or figures, the tone, and the context. If, for instance, in a whimsical tone and a fanciful conceit, a particular god considered to be a preserver of man is held up to the whale, the whale's malice may be intensified while the preserving god may be made to seem equivocally frivolous. Or if a treacherous god is compared to Moby Dick in a context describing the whale's treachery, this attribute of the whale and of the other god may be at once intensified and made more significant. Nevertheless—and this is what distinguishes the particular from the general suggestion—knowledge of the particular god is necessary to understand what the suggestion is. This knowledge may override syntactical relations and may redefine the rhetorical context. An apparent similitude, a belief of an insane character, and a direct narrative statement were all offered as examples of the general suggestion and were all found to mean ultimately the same thing: Moby Dick is divine. An apparent similitude, an idea of an insane character, and a direct narrative statement may now serve as examples of the particular suggestion, and they will be found to mean quite different things.

As the *Pequod* follows "the grand Armada" through the Straits of Sunda into "the Oriental seas," a simile likens Moby Dick to an Oriental deity: "And who could tell whether, in that congregated caravan, Moby Dick himself might not temporarily be swimming, like the worshipped white-elephant in the coronation procession of the Siamese!" This simile can hardly have great significance. Perhaps the proximity of the *Pequod* to Siam suggests the way the Siamese worship their idols; perhaps not. At most, this simile does little more than state a comparison between Moby Dick and a specific "plumed and glittering god," perhaps merely as a descriptive touch. We assume that the simile is of no great significance for only one reason: we assume that the Siamese white elephant is of no great significance. If the same syntactical and rhetorical context likened Moby Dick to a major figure in a "major" religion, the suggestion would have major importance. We find quite significant even a suggestion, explicitly insane, that the whale might be worshiped by even a minor sect of a Western religion; we learn a good deal from mad Gabriel, when, "in his gibbering insanity," he pronounces "the White Whale to be no less a being than the Shaker God incarnated."

As a book of revelation, *Moby-Dick* becomes increasingly explicit about the nature of the White Whale. In the last few chapters Moby Dick is physically revealed for the first time, allowing us to measure the accuracy of the whalemen's superstitions and the mythic creation of Ahab's mind. Moby Dick manifests the intelligence, the malice, and the powers ascribed to him, so far as these attributes can be visibly and physically manifested. The first close sight of Moby Dick prepares for one of the great moments of revelation in literature. It is a revelation of horror, the revelation of fearfully potent malice masked by graceful beauty. But the mask itself hints of what lies beneath:

> A gentle joyousness—a mighty mildness of repose in swiftness, invested the gliding whale. Not the white bull Jupiter swimming away with ravished Europa clinging to his graceful horns; his lovely, leering eyes sideways intent upon the maid; with smooth bewitching fleetness, rippling straight for the nuptial bower in Crete; not Jove, not that great majesty Supreme! did surpass the glorified White Whale as he so divinely swam. (P. 539)

The language, the syntax, and the rhetoric form a mask which corresponds to the mask of Moby Dick and Jove. The language of beauty lies on the surface: "graceful," "lovely," "smooth bewitching fleetness," "nuptial bower," "glorified," "divine." But what are "graceful" are "horns"; what are "lovely" are "leering eyes"; the "nuptial bower" is intended for rape; "bewitching" and "divine" mean something quite different from the same words in nineteenth-century romance or twentieth-century advertising. "That great majesty supreme," so "bewitching" and "divine," that leering, ravishing god, is destructive to humankind even in his love. The syntax veils the explicit meaning of the sentence and sets up a startling reversal, the revelation that "not Jupiter," "not Jove," "did surpass the glorified White Whale."

It is in this context that the whale finally displays his divinity and malignity, showing himself to be what the mind of Ahab had conceived him to be. While swimming, the whale hides half his physical nature: "Moby Dick moved on, still withholding from sight the full terrors of his submerged trunk, entirely hiding the wrenched hideousness of his jaw." Soon, however, "the fore part of him slowly rose from the water," and, at this point, not only his natural but also his supernatural character is revealed: "the grand god revealed himself, sounded, and went out of sight." When he reappears, it is to evince, as much as a mute animal can, the intelligent malignity previously ascribed to him by rumors, superstitions, and the mind of Ahab. Ahab tries to avoid the jaws of the whale, "But as if perceiving the strategem, Moby Dick, with that malicious intelligence ascribed to him, sidelingly transplanted himself, as it were, in an instant, shooting his pleated head lengthwise beneath the boat." Soon, after "the whale dallied with the doomed craft in [a] devilish way," his malice and intelligence become unquestionable: "retribution, swift vengeance, eternal malice were in his whole aspect."

To understand any of the many comparisons of Moby Dick with another deity, it is necessary to recognize that the purpose of these comparisons is not to show that Moby Dick is divine. The psychological truth of Moby Dick having been established, he is, as an assumed fact and as a matter of definition, a god. As a god to Ahab and the *Pequod*'s crew, Moby Dick may be a false god, but he must be a god. When the whale is compared to a particular god, it is not to suggest that Moby Dick is a god; it is to limit, not to extend, to define rather than to embellish his godhood. In the narrative itself, these comparisons define Moby Dick always in dramatic or descriptive rather than discursive terms and always in terms that are highly serious. In some of the cetology chapters, these comparisons are made in essentially different terms, terms at once discursive, whimsical, and rather easily misunderstood. The narrative comparisons are largely psychological, and they move toward an identification of Ahab's idea of the whale and the narrative description of the whale; the whimsically discursive comparisons parody contemporaneous comparative mythology, particularly of the historical school, and they move toward an exaltation of the myth of the whale at the expense of the myths of the world.[5] The whimsical and discursive mock-extensions of the myth of the whale are similar in tone and purpose to the myths in *Mardi* which parallel, in ridiculous terms, the myth of Alma. But the central myth in *Moby-Dick* has a validity and an effect entirely foreign to the central myth in *Mardi*.

The comic myths become more comic in relation to the serious central myth, which is intensified by the comic parallels. Just as comic subplot heightens tragedy, what may be called the comic sub-myth heightens the mythic drama. The difference between the comic submyths in *Mardi* and in *Moby-Dick* is simple and highly significant: the comic submyths in *Mardi* are inventions of *Mardi*'s mythologists—historian, poet, philosopher, king, priest, and voyager. The comic subplot heightens tragedy, what may be called the comic sub-world's major religions—Hinduism, Judaism, and Christianity. *Mardi,* concerned with the mythmaking process and its distortion of innate psychological truth, ridicules the various kinds of mythmaking. In *Moby-Dick* there is no innate truth; man's deepest psychological processes produce not the absolute nonmythic truth of Serenia but the relative mythic truth of the demon hunt. The wild mythmaking of the sea attains the highest seriousness, and ridicule is reserved for the particular myths of the world's lands.

Melville uses one of Bayle's formulas to help concoct his wicked mixture of Christian, Hebrew, and pagan stories,[6] but he also uses the formulas of the Christian mythologists responding to the attacks of Bayle, Voltaire, Hume, Dupuis, and Volney. Bayle piled ridiculous and similar detail upon ridiculous and similar detail until all myths collapsed; the apologists segregated similar details into two piles in order to ridicule one and exalt the other. They set "Oriental" myth, garnished with extravagant rhetoric and fanciful details, alongside simply, seriously told Christian story. Similarities faded under the lights of different narrative and rhetorical styles and techniques. Always operating on the assumption that the Truth is obvious, known, and given by divine revelation, they often set Judaic-Christian truth against the false myths of the pagans to show just how ridiculous the fanciful, elaborate, distorted, embellished, in short Oriental, versions were. Melville sets against the truth of Moby Dick, defined in part by the mind of Ahab, fishy myths of the Hindus, the Philistines, the Hebrews, the Greeks, and the Christians, all of which he piles atop one another in a Bayle-like heap. Using all the tricks of both skeptics and apologists, he exalts the myth of the great White Whale by ridiculing the fanciful, elaborate, distorted, and embellished versions of the "Oriental" religions, which are clearly absurd in their absurd similarities.

It is easy to misunderstand Melville's comparative mythology, particularly if one fails to read it in the context of contemporaneous comparative mythology. Not read in this context, Melville's ridicule of other myths has often been mistaken for an identification of the whale with the ridiculed mythic gods. To assume that any mention of another god extends the White Whale into other mythologies is to obscure the precise definition of Moby Dick and the exaltation of *Moby-Dick*'s mythology above all others. One important example should suffice.

In two chapters, Melville comments at length on the "Matse Avatar" of Vishnu. These passages have been offered as proving an identification of Moby Dick with Vishnu. When this identification was developed to its logical conclusion, the critic who made it, confronted with the total incompatibility of the destroying whale and the preserving god, concluded that Moby Dick transcended Hinduism by partaking of it: "The great fish of the Hindus becomes the primal God."[7] But *Moby-Dick* presents the great fish of the Hindus as a fishy myth indeed. Vishnu is first mentioned in the chapter entitled "Monstrous Pictures of Whales," which proposes "to set the world right in this matter, by proving such pictures of the whale all wrong." Beginning at the beginning, Melville examines "the most ancient extant portrait *anyways purporting to be the whale's* [which] is to be found in the famous cavern-pagoda of Elephanta, in India" [italics mine]. Then comes one of the two passages which allegedly establish the identity of Moby Dick and the great fish of the Hindus:

The Hindoo whale referred to, occurs in a separate department of the wall, depicting the incarnation of Vishnu in the form of leviathan, learnedly known as the Matse Avatar. *But though this sculpture is half man and half whale, so as only to give the tail of the latter, yet that small section of him is all wrong.* It looks more like the tapering tail of an anaconda, than the broad palms of the true whale's majestic flukes. [Italics mine.]

After demonstrating that the sculpture of the Matse Avatar does not even have the tail of a whale, Melville turns to "a great Christian painter's portrait of this fish" and discovers that "he succeeds no better than the antediluvian Hindoo." Hindus and Christians are victims of the same joke. The other mention of Vishnu comes toward the end of the chapter entitled "The Honor and Glory of Whaling." This chapter shows Melville's Bayle-like techniques at their best. "Perseus, a son of Jupiter, was the first whaleman," but there are similarities between his story and Jonah's. Furthermore, "akin to the adventure of Perseus and Andromeda—indeed, by some supposed to be indirectly derived from it—is that famous story of St. George and the Dragon." And "this whole story will fare like that fish, flesh, and fowl idol of the Philistines, Dagon by name; who being planted before the ark of Israel, his horse's head and both the palms of his hands fell off from him, and only the stumpy or fishy part of him remained." The next difficulty is "whether to admit Hercules among us or not": "concerning this I long remained dubious . . . But, by the best contradictory authorities, this Grecian story of Hercules and the whale is considered to be derived from the still more ancient Hebrew story of Jonah and the whale; and vice versa; certainly they are very similar. If I claim the demigod then, why not the prophet?" Melville thus heaps pagan and sainted Christian dragon slayers and the fishy myths of the Philistines, Hebrews, and Greeks into one absurdity, and he crowns it all with the second of the two passages allegedly showing Moby Dick's identity with Vishnu:

Nor do heroes, saints, demigods, and prophets alone comprise the whole roll of our order. Our grand master is still to be named; for like royal kings of old times, we find the headwaters of our fraternity in nothing short of the great gods themselves. That wondrous oriental story is now to be rehearsed from the Shaster, which gives us the dread Vishnoo, one of the three persons in the godhead of the Hindoos; gives us this divine Vishnoo himself for our Lord;—Vishnoo, who, by the first of his ten earthly incarnations, has for ever set apart and sanctified the whale. When Brahma, or the God of Gods, saith the Shaster, resolved to recreate the world after one of its periodical dissolutions, he gave birth to Vishnoo, to preside over the work; but the Vedas, or mystical books, whose perusal would seem to have been indispensable to Vishnoo before beginning the creation, and which therefore must have contained something in the shape of practical hints to young architects, these Vedas were lying at the bottom of the waters; so Vishnoo became incarnate in a whale, and sounding down in him to the uttermost depths, rescued the sacred volumes. Was not this Vishnoo a whaleman, then? even as a man who rides a horse is called a horseman?

Perseus, St. George, Hercules, Jonah, and Vishnoo! there's a member-roll for you! What club but the whaleman's can head off like that?

Melville's obvious ridicule of the Vishnu myth should be sufficient to discourage identification of Moby Dick with Vishnu. Indeed, Melville makes it clear that Vishnu is not to be taken as any fish at all.

In the earlier chapter "Monstrous Pictures," Melville refers to "the incarnation of Vishnu in the form of leviathan." In the passage just quoted, he qualifies this incarnation with two short words, "in him": "so Vishnoo became incarnate *in* a whale, and sounding down *in him* to the uttermost depths." This locution no more describes an incarnation of a god *as* a fish than does Father Mapple's statement, "God came down upon him in the whale." And just to make sure that the reader doesn't think that Vishnu was incarnate *as* a whale, Melville asks the specific questions, "Was not this Vishnoo a whaleman, then? even as a man who rides a horse is called a horseman?" Then he reads the roll of his "whalemen," that is, by the definition of the chapter, men or gods who have either killed or been in a whale: "Perseus, St. George, Hercules, Jonah, and Vishnoo! there's a member-roll for you!" Vishnu whimsically regarded sets the stage for the next chapter, "Jonah Historically Regarded." Vishnu is taken no more seriously than Jonah or Saint George, Perseus or Dagon.

Many critics have mentioned many other fish and dragon myths in connection with *Moby-Dick*—Beowulf's battle with Grendel, Chinese dragon myths, Rustam's fight with the White Demon, and the Babylonian Bel-Merodach's struggles with the dragon Tiamat. All these suggestions have some validity, and in a sense it is true that "the White Whale represents the mythological dragons of both Western and Eastern tradition."[8] The most important of these suggestions is the one introduced by Ahab's name, which, as has been often noted, introduces the mass of contemporaneous accounts of the Canaanite Baal and the Babylonian Bel. The Biblical King Ahab "took to wife Jezebel the daughter of Ethbaal king of the Zidonians, and went and served Baal, and worshipped him" (I Kings 16:30–31). But the many various forms and accounts of Baal and Bel, both of which mean "lord," could easily lead into a random confusion. When Bildad urges Queequeg to "remain not for aye a Belial bondsman" but to "spurn the idol Bell, and the hideous dragon," he assumes the identity of the Hebrew word Belial and the Babylonian god Bell. And as Vincent and Mansfield note, "the Biblical scholarship of Melville's day" not only "inclined to equate the Tyrian Baal whom Jezebel induced Ahab to worship and the Babylonian Bel," but also identified "them both as sun gods." Because Baal and Bel occur in the forms of both water dragons and sun gods who hunt the dragon, both destroyers and saviors, they could not coherently order or define the action of *Moby-Dick*. Like the many other myths which contribute to *Moby-Dick*, they are finally subsumed under and redefined by the particular myth which is central to the entire work.

One mythic dragon or monster is mentioned again and again in *Moby-Dick*. This dragon is Leviathan, and Leviathan leads directly to the particular myth which does both order and define the action of *Moby-Dick*.

The Leviathan of Isaiah 27, of Job 3 and 41, of Psalm 74 and Psalm 104 was, according to various scholars, a crocodile, a whale, a serpent, and a megalosaurus. Whatever animal he was, he was what Melville's quotation from Isaiah in the "Extracts" indicates, a dragon:

"In that day, the Lord with his sore, and great, and strong sword, shall punish Leviathan the piercing serpent, even Leviathan that crooked serpent; and he shall slay the dragon that is in the sea." Leviathan was, of course, particularly in later use, a name for Satan. But according to some skeptics, including Melville, Leviathan, like Jehovah, was originally an Egyptian, not a Hebrew, conception.

The eleventh Extract in *Moby-Dick* alludes to Moses as the creator of the Leviathan in Job; Moses' royal Egyptian upbringing was, as we saw in the last chapter, embarrassing to the apologists. Behind Leviathan loomed the Egyptian god Set, or, to use the name given him by the Greek mythographers and generally used by Western mythographers until the late nineteenth century, Typhon. The struggle between Osiris and Typhon forms a basic part of the conception of Ahab's struggle with Moby Dick. The Egyptian myth explains much about Melville's myth, and Melville's myth, when compared with the Egyptian myth, explains much about Melville's mythology.[9]

The third word of *Moby-Dick* suggests the origin of its central myth. For Ishmael's namesake married an Egyptian (Genesis 21:21) and became a patriarch of Egypt. As Dorothée Finkelstein has shown, references to Egyptian history and mythology permeate Melville's work.[10] They are nowhere more pervasive than in *Moby-Dick*. The whale is "physiognomically a Sphinx"; Starbuck is "like a revivified Egyptian"; "the earliest standers of mast-heads were the old Egyptians"; " 'Ahab seemed a pyramid' "; in short, "whaling may well be regarded as that Egyptian mother, who bore offspring themselves pregnant from her womb." This Egyptian mother is Nut, the mother of Isis, who came pregnant from the womb, of Osiris, who impregnated Isis while he lay in the womb with her, and of Typhon, who was to be the eternal archnemesis of the god Osiris and of all men.

Before we see how the Osiris-Typhon myth partly shapes *Moby-Dick*, it would be useful to answer two questions: Why should Melville choose the Egyptian rather than the Hindu mythic struggle between the destroying and the preserving powers? Why should he then ridicule the Hindu myth, whose similarities to the Egyptian myth were a common set-piece for the comparative mythologists? There are several possible answers. (1) In the Hindu myth, the fish incarnates the preserving power. (Moby Dick is the Destroyer,) and Melville's precise ridicule of the Matse Avatar forestalls any mythological mitigation of this fact. (2) The similarities between the Egyptian and Hindu myths were not consistently embodied by parallel deities. The standard notion which equated Osiris with Siva created more problems than it solved.[11] Maurice's explanation of the difficulties is manifestly unsuitable for fictionalization: "When the Egyptians borrowed, as it is probable they did, this doctrine from the Hindoos, it appears to me that they confounded the persons and symbols of the deities they adopted."[12] There are a few hints that Melville at one time had considered using more symbols from the worship of Siva the Destroyer, but the only important remnant of this consideration is Fedallah. (3) Since the cosmic struggle between Vishnu and Siva ultimately resolves into the unity of the Trimurti, this struggle cannot support a tragic conception. (4) Just as Melville apparently construed Hebrew myth as a later misinterpretation of Egyptian myth, there was evidence in the ancient Sanskrit texts that modern Hindu myths had been imposed on a more ancient, differently conceived, mythology. (5) The Hindu myths were first recorded in an Indo-European language, but the Egyptian myths, like the Hebrew, were not. (6) Most important of all, Melville's audience was deeply concerned with the geographical, historical, and mythological proximity of the Egyptians to the Hebrews.

Hunting for all the direct sources of Melville's knowledge of the Osiris myth would be as pointless as hunting for the direct sources of his knowledge of the Apollo myth. Egyptology had been a Western pastime for at least 2,300 years, and thousands of classical and contemporary versions of the Osiris myth were available in English.[13] But the ultimate sources of Melville's knowledge are beyond doubt Herodotus' *History,* Diodorus' *The Library of History,* and, by far the most important, Plutarch's "Isis and Osiris." Melville owned

Herodotus' *History*,[14] and the Extracts at the beginning of *Moby-Dick* include a passage from Plutarch's *Morals,* which contains the essay "Isis and Osiris." Melville uses both books for other purposes in *Moby-Dick* (the notes to the Hendricks House edition cite each work four times). And as Sir James Frazer later pointed out, "The story of Osiris is told in a connected form only by Plutarch, whose narrative has been confirmed and to some extent amplified in modern times by the evidence of the monuments."[15] For contemporaneous versions and explanations Melville could have opened the pages of innumerable magazines, travel books, encyclopedias, and polemical tracts. Maurice's volumes are full of detailed references to the Osiris myth and lengthy apologist explanations of it. For convenience I shall refer primarily to Plutarch and Maurice. These two sources will not materially limit the choice of versions: they define Osiris' slayer, for instance, as a crocodile, a hippopotamus, the Nile, the ocean, his brother and conspirators at a feast, a hot desert wind, small fish, a huge fish, one or several constellations, the winter solstice, the autumnal equinox, a snake, a scorpion, and incarnate hate, destructiveness, or evil.

This version may be found in Plutarch and Maurice: Osiris is a priest-king-god who sails the world in a ship which later becomes the constellation Argo. He hunts Typhon, who is usually represented by some kind of aquatic monster and who symbolizes the ocean and all in nature that is malignant to man. Once a year, Typhon dismembers Osiris. When this happens—the date is variously given as the autumnal equinox, the winter solstice, and the period in between —Osiris disappears for a certain length of time, which is also variously given. During this absence from earth, he rules the infernal regions and a ship sails the world bearing his coffin. During this time, also, his phallus is missing and the land lies infertile. In a vernal phallic ritual, Osiris is healed and the fertility of the land is restored. His dismemberment in the fall or winter symbolizes the seasonal disaster in nature. The seasonal resurrection of the sun causes, symbolizes, or is symbolized by his resurrection.

Ahab is also a priest-king-god who sails the world in a ship which is equated with the constellation Argo. He also hunts an aquatic monster who symbolizes the ocean and all in nature that is malignant to man. Once a year, for three successive years, he is dismembered by the aquatic monster which he hunts. The first two times, he also disappears for a length of time and then is healed with the advance of the sun. Ahab also is described as ruler of the infernal regions. Phallic rituals, fire worship, and infernal orgies are conducted on his ship, which also sails the world bearing a coffin.

Many details of Ahab's story parallel details in the story of Osiris. Some of these seem minor or merely curious, such as, for example, the three main symbols of Osiris—the hawk, the coffin, and the phallus. The hawk, the "most common symbol of Osiris,"[16] is nailed as an emblem to the mast of the sinking *Pequod*; after a coffin is nailed and caulked just as Osiris' coffin was, comes the question, "Were ever such things done before with a coffin?"; the last symbol, as we shall see, performs a most unusual function on the *Pequod*. But much of the Osiris story shapes *Moby-Dick* in ways far more important.

In a passage that appears to be merely fanciful, Ishmael astronomically and mythologically defines the whale hunt:

> Nor when expandingly lifted by your subject, can you fail to trace out great whales in the starry heavens, and boats in pursuit of them. . . . Thus at the North have I chased Leviathan round and round the Pole with the revolutions of the bright points that first defined him to me. And beneath the effulgent Antarctic skies I have boarded the Argo-Navis, and joined the chase against the starry Cetus far beyond the utmost stretch of Hydrus and the Flying Fish. (Pp. 271–72)

Maurice claims that the same mythological story often was symbolized by several constellations in different parts of the zodiac. But probably none was as ubiquitous as the Osiris-Typhon struggle: "the greater part of the Egyptian zodiac apparently alludes to the contests of these two mythological personages for the empire of the skies."[17] From the northern polar dragon down through the equatorial Hydrus and Cetus to the antarctic Argo, Maurice traces the outlines of Typhon's "everlasting wars with the beneficent Osiris."[18] He defines both constellations defined by Ishmael: he asserts that "the celestial Draco, or great Polar dragon of the northern sphere, shedding pernicious influences on man and beast, is no other than the Evil Principle in nature personified, or, in other words, the Lucifer of Sacred writ";[19] he claims that the antarctic "Argo was the sacred ship of Osiris."[20] But, it may be objected, Leviathan and Lucifer are specifically Hebrew figures, Argo and Cetus specifically Greek figures, and none an Egyptian figure. Plutarch answers the Greek question, for he is Maurice's authority for claiming that the Greek Argo was really the ship of Osiris.[21] And on the question "Hebrew or Egyptian?" centered many mythological battles.

The notion that Egypt might have been the birthplace of the gods was central to all Western comparative mythology, both ancient and modern. The three most important classical documents on Egyptology—Book II of Herodotus' *History,* Book I of Diodorus' *Library of History,* and Plutarch's "Isis and Osiris"—all demonstrate that Greek theology, ritual, and myth originated in Egypt, that, in the words of Diodorus, "the gods are fabulously reported to be born in Egypt."[22] It was not until the late eighteenth-century discoveries in Sanskrit that the question became, as we saw it was with Sir William Jones, one of deciding prior antiquities among three religions, the Hindu, the Egyptian, and the Hebrew. Before that, Egyptologists, even the apologists, generally assumed that at least the non-Judaic-Christian gods were first worshiped in Egypt. The highest landmark of post-Renaissance Egyptology, Athanasius Kircher's mountainous *Oedipus Aegyptiacus,* had made Egypt the birthplace not only of all the pagan gods but also of all the sciences, all the arts, and all systematic thought.[23] Kircher and other orthodox Christian Egyptologists of course excluded their own uncreated God from the Egyptian cradle, although they frequently recognized an archetypical trinity in Osiris, Isis, and Horus. Many of the eighteenth-century skeptical mythologists sneered at this exclusion, pointing out that it would have been meaningless to ancient mythographers, who were unable to distinguish between the Jewish and the Egyptian religions: "It is strange that the EGYPTIAN religion, though so absurd, should yet have borne so great a resemblance to the JEWISH that ancient writers, even of the greatest genius were not able to observe any difference between them."[24]

Melville not only saw the striking similarities between the Egyptian and Hebrew religions, but he also ascribed to the skeptical explanation of these similarities—the Jews had taken their theology from the Egyptians. As we saw in the last chapter, he is quite explicit about this in his *Journal,* where he gives the usual skeptical interpretation of Acts 7:22, "Moses learned in all the wisdom of the Egyptians": "I shudder at idea of ancient Egyptians. It was in these pyramids that was conceived the idea of Jehovah. Terrible mixture of the cunning and awful. Moses learned in all the lore of the Egyptians. The idea of Jehovah born here." In *Moby-Dick* he gives to the Egyptians the idea of Leviathan also.

To suggest that Leviathan is Egyptian rather than Hebrew in origin, Melville introduces the zodiac on the planisphere of the temple at Denderah in Egypt. He is here following an established skeptical tradition. In an article entitled "The Zodiac of Denderah," the *North American Review* had ascribed "the love of the marvelous or worse reasons" to the skeptics, who had urged "the extreme antiquity" of the Denderah zodiac and who had even carried it "back to an epoch anterior by far to the Mosiac chronology."[25] Melville prefaces his description of the Denderah zodiac by referring to the "antemosaic" terrors of Leviathan and by syntactically making the "almost fossiliferous" Egyptian tablets which record his existence seem older than the "pre-adamite traces" which he has left in rock:

I am horror-struck at this antemosaic, unsourced existence of the unspeakable terrors of the whale, which, having been before all time, must needs exist after all humane ages are over.

But not alone has this Leviathan left his pre-adamite traces in the stereotype plates of nature, and in limestone and marl bequeathed his ancient bust; but upon Egyptian tablets, whose antiquity seems to claim for them an almost fossiliferous character, we find the unmistakable print of his fin. In an apartment of the great temple of Denderah, some fifty years ago, there was discovered upon the granite ceiling a sculptured and painted planisphere, abounding in centaurs, griffins, and dolphins, similar to the grotesque figures on the celestial globe of the moderns. Gliding among them, old Leviathan swam as of yore; was there swimming in that planisphere, centuries before Solomon was cradled. (P. 454)

Here and elsewhere in *Moby-Dick*, Egypt and Egyptian stand for an unfathomable antiquity and a religious awe never associated with things Hebrew. In the chapter "The Sphinx" the head of the whale itself partakes of the awesome antiquity and inscrutability of Egypt. Later, in commenting again on the silence of that head, Ishmael mentions pyramids and thus thinks of Egypt:

. . . pyramidical silence. And this reminds me that had the great Sperm Whale been known to the young Orient World, he would have been deified by their child-magian thoughts. They deified the crocodile of the Nile, because the crocodile is tongueless; and the Sperm Whale has no tongue, or at least it is so exceedingly small, as to be incapable of protrusion. (P. 345)

The ultimate source of this passage is a statement in Plutarch's "Isis and Osiris," of suggestive significance for *Moby-Dick*:

Neither is the crocodile set so much by among them, without some probable cause: For they say that in some respect he is the very image representing god: as being the onely creature in the world which hath no tongue: for as much as divine speech needeth neither voice nor tongue.[26]

Maurice, drawing on Plutarch, calls "the crocodile the acknowledged symbol of Typhon."[27] And Typhon's symbolic meaning is central to Melville's conception of "the gliding great demon of the seas of life."

When in *Clarel,* I, xxxi, Rolfe suggests that the Christ story may be merely one version of the Osiris story, he also, by using Python for Typhon, suggests that the Apollo story may be another version. Later (III, iii, 25–26), Rolfe defines Python precisely as Maurice had defined "the Lucifer of Sacred writ"—"the great polar dragon of the northern sphere, shedding pernicious influences on man and beast . . . no other than the Evil Principle in nature personified."[28] Plutarch and Maurice define the symbolic meaning of Typhon in the same terms, terms which may also define the White Whale:

Plutarch's "Isis and Osiris" (Holland's translation)

When the Egyptians "would describe hatred, they draw or purtray a fish." (P. 1300)

Typhon is "neither drought alone, nor winde, nor sea ne yet darknesse; but all that is noisome and hurtful whatsoever, and which hath a special part to hurt and destroy, is called *Typhon*." (P. 1305)

The Egyptians attribute "all dangerous wicked beasts . . . unto *Typhon*, as if they were his workes, his parts or motions." (P. 1308)

Maurice's Indian Antiquities

"By Typhon, I have repeatedly observed, must be understood whatever in nature was gloomy and malignant." (III, 243)

The Egyptians "considered Typhon, to whom, among other symbols, was allotted that of the Ocean . . . as *every part of nature which can be considered as noxious and destructive* to mankind. Like time and death, Typhon devoured all things." (III, 255)

Ahab sees in Moby Dick "that intangible malignity which has been from the beginning." In fact, "all evil, to crazy Ahab," becomes "visibly personified and made practically assailable in Moby Dick." Thus Ahab's psychological truth defines the White Whale as Typhon.

Philemon Holland's translation of "Isis and Osiris" pluralizes Typhon to describe all things harmful and destructive in nature. According to Holland's interpretation, any single natural evil may be called a Typhon. In *Moby-Dick,* what is harmful and destructive in nature takes three major forms. The first is the Ocean itself, seething with sharkish ferocity, the home of the great white squid as well as of the great White Whale, persistently slaughtering even its own children. The second is Moby Dick, who, like Typhon, incarnates both the Ocean and "every part of nature which can be considered noxious and destructive to mankind." The third is the Typhoon which strikes the *Pequod,* which singles out Ahab's seat in his whale boat for destruction, which reverses Ahab's compasses and his ship's course, which lights the *Pequod*'s masts and Ahab's harpoon, which is personified, worshiped, and defied by Ahab.

The Typhoon is an alternative manifestation of Ahab's Typhon. As the *Oxford English Dictionary* explains, Typhon was not only "the name of a giant or monster of ancient Greek mythology," but, "in later use partly suggested by TYPHOON," "a whirlwind, cyclone, tornado; a violent storm of wind, a hurricane." The *OED* goes on to show the "interrelationship of the two different oriental words, the first possibly an adoption of Gr. TYPHON" and "also used as a name for the Egyptian evil divinity Set." Melville used the uncapitalized word "typhoon" frequently in his earlier works and several times early in *Moby-Dick*. Late in *Moby-Dick* the word begins to appear capitalized, and shortly thereafter the "Typhoon" strikes the *Pequod*. This Typhoon is not only capitalized by Melville, but is also addressed as a god by Ahab. Melville apparently knew or guessed the inter-relationship of the two Oriental words.

He apparently also knew this etymology from Plutarch's "Isis and Osiris": "And *Typhon,* as we have already said, is named *Seth, Baebon* and *Smy,* which words betoken all, a violent stay and impeachment, a contrariety and a diversion or turning aside another way." As a form of Typhon, the Typhoon violently stays the *Pequod,* turns it aside, and sends it in the direction exactly opposite to Ahab's course.

In the midst of the storm, Starbuck cries out, "let the Typhoon sing, and strike his harp here in our rigging." Starbuck's cry is both an etymological and a mythological joke. The blocks and pins of the *Pequod* had been made from the bones of whales; a harp was fabled to have been made from the bones of Typhon. The jokes about other gods emphasize their dissimilarities to Moby Dick, who surpasses both Jupiter and "Visnu, the Indian Jupiter."[29] This joke depends upon the etymological identity of Typhoon and Typhon, the mythological identity of Typhon and Moby Dick, and the symbolic identity of the storm and the whale.

The whale's identity with the storm is more important than the joke, of course, and it explains the oracular Manxman's prophecy in the chapter "The Doubloon":

"If the White Whale be raised, it must be in a month and a day, when the sun stands in some one of these signs. I've studied signs, and know their marks; they were taught me two score years ago, by the old witch in Copenhagen. Now, in what sign will the sun then be? The horse-shoe sign; for there it is, right opposite the gold. And what's the horse-shoe sign? The lion is the horse-shoe sign—the roaring and devouring lion. Ship, old ship! my old head shakes to think of thee." (P. 431)

The sun is in Leo from July 23 to August 22. The voiceless White Whale is not raised until after Christmas. But the roaring and de-vouring Typhoon strikes the *Pequod* while she sails the Sea of Japan in summer, on the day she turns to meet her Typhon in the Season-on-the-Line.

More important than the contrariety of the storm, Starbuck's un-conscious joke, or the Manxman's unconsciously fulfilled prophecy is Ahab's conscious and defiant worship of the Typhoon as the de-structive force. This defiant worship was not unprecedented in Egyp-tian ritual. A Greco-Egyptian ritual magic text, along with threats to cow the inferior divinities who try to stop the ship of Osiris, gives the formula for invoking Typhon in the storm:

"Pursue me not, thou. . . . I carry the coffin of Osiris . . . I invoke thee, thou who art in the void, wind, or terrible, invisible, all-powerful god of gods, thou who destroyest and renderest desert . . . Thou art surnamed *He who breaks every thing, and is not conquered.* I invoke thee, *O Typhon Seth!*"[30]

The Typhoon is one manifestation of Typhon, and Moby Dick is another. What, then, is Ahab?

In the chapter "Moby Dick," after we learn that Ahab had "piled upon the whale's white hump the sum of all the general rage and hate felt by his whole race from Adam down," and before we learn that Ahab's "gliding great demon of the seas of life" was also that of the crew, "the White Whale as much their insufferable foe as his," we learn the genesis of Ahab's psychological definition of the whale. Ahab's first dismemberment begins his monomaniac incarnation of all evil in the whale, and the mad incarnation of himself as the destroyer of that evil. His monomania probably did not take "its instant rise at the precise time of his bodily dismemberment. . . . Yet, when by this collision forced to turn towards home, and for long months of days and weeks, Ahab and anguish lay stretched

together in one hammock, rounding in mid winter that dreary, howl-
ing Patagonian Cape; then it was that his torn body and gashed soul
bled into one another; and so interfusing, made him mad." The
fact that Osiris' bodily dismemberment symbolizes midwinter and
the fact that "dismemberment" and "torn body" appear frequently
in translations of "Isis and Osiris" and in commentaries on the Osiris
myth hardly prove that Melville is thinking of Osiris' dismemberment while describing Ahab's. But, in the following sentence, Ahab's
chest is called "his Egyptian chest," and, two sentences later we learn
that Ahab revives, like Osiris, when the sun revives. When then we
learn that Ahab is intent on a "supernatural revenge" against the
demon of life, we may ask whether, in this revenge, Ahab somehow
conceives of himself in the role of Osiris, whether somehow, when
"his torn body and gashed soul bled into one another, and so interfusing made him mad," Ahab's madness was assuming the torn body
and gashed soul of the Egyptian god.

In Ahab's struggle, in which he "lay like dead for three days and
nights," Ahab becomes literally an Osiris. The Egyptians identified
every man who died with the god Osiris and gave the name of the
god to the deceased.[31] Just as everything in nature malignant to man
was a Typhon, every man who died was an Osiris. Just as Moby Dick
embodies Typhon, Ahab embodies Osiris.

If Ahab is playing the role of Osiris, he plays it as well as his
"ungodly" nature will permit. Ahab's dismemberment, like Osiris',
is central to his story, and like Osiris' recurs each year. Ahab's dismemberment the next year is represented by the bone of a whale
inexplicably stakewise smiting his groin:

For it had not been very long prior to the Pequod's sailing from Nantucket, that he had been found one night lying prone upon the ground,
and insensible; by some unknown, and seemingly inexplicable, unimagina-
ble casualty, his ivory limb having been so violently displaced, that it
had stake-wise smitten, and all but pierced his groin; nor was it without
extreme difficulty that the agonizing wound was entirely cured. (P. 460)

The nature of this wound makes Ahab's "monomaniac mind" turn
to the idea of the fertility of natural events:

Nor, at the time, had it failed to enter his monomaniac mind, that all the anguish of that then present suffering was but the direct issue of a former woe; and he too plainly seemed to see, that as the most poisonous reptile of the marsh perpetuates his kind as inevitably as the sweetest songster of the grove; so, equally with every felicity, all miserable events do naturally beget their like. Yea, more than equally, thought Ahab; since both the ancestry and posterity of Grief go further than the ancestry and posterity of Joy. (P. 460)

Ahab's groin injury is indeed both the ancestry and posterity of grievous events. His first dismemberment begets its like; walking upon the bone of his foe, he is smitten by that bone. As a result, he relives the solitary suffering which followed his first dismemberment:

With many other particulars concerning Ahab, always had it remained a mystery to some, why it was, that for a certain period, both before and after the sailing of the Pequod, he had hidden himself away with such Grand-Lama-like exclusiveness; and, for that one interval, sought speechless refuge, as it were, among the marble senate of the dead. Captain Peleg's bruited reason for this thing appeared by no means adequate; though, indeed, as touching all Ahab's deeper part, every revelation partook more of significant darkness than of explanatory light. But, in the end, it all came out; this one matter did, at least. That direful mishap was at the bottom of his temporary recluseness. And not only this, but to that ever-contracting, dropping circle ashore, who, for any reason, possessed the privilege of a less banned approach to him; to that timid circle the above hinted casualty—remaining, as it did, moodily unaccounted for by Ahab—invested itself with terrors, not entirely underived from the land of spirits and of wails. (P. 461)

From this solitary agony Ahab revives, as he did from the first dismemberment and as Osiris revives from his periodic dismemberment, when the sun revives. Preceding this last quotation is an awkward apology which leads us back twenty-eight chapters to Ahab's disappearance and emergence at the start of the *Pequod*'s voyage: "Unwittingly here a secret has been divulged, which perhaps might more properly, in set way, have been disclosed before.[32] When the *Pequod* sailed, "Captain Ahab remained invisibly enshrined within his cabin." Then "for several days after leaving Nantucket, nothing above hatches was seen of Captain Ahab." This "supreme lord and dictator" remained "unseen by any eyes not permitted to penetrate into the now sacred retreat of the cabin." As the *Pequod* runs south, Ahab emerges "with a crucifixion in his face." Then, like the sun, he is visible longer and longer each day:

As the sky grew less gloomy; indeed, began to grow a little genial, he became still less and less a recluse; as if, when the ship had sailed from home, nothing but the dead wintry bleakness of the sea had then kept him so secluded. And, by and by, it came to pass, that he was almost continually in the air . . . (P. 122)

Ahab's descent and solitary confinement after each of his first two dismemberments are something like death. "His visits were more to the cabin, than from the cabin to the planks," and, he says, "it feels like going down into one's tomb." When he orders Stubb below decks, he hints, in tragic irony, that his own descent, like the descent of the crew, foreshadows the descent to come after his third and final annual dismemberment: "Below to thy nightly grave; where such as ye sleep between shrouds, to use ye to the filling one at last." But although Ahab's dismemberments and descents are in several ways like those of Osiris, they are, in one way, tragically different. Like Osiris' periodic dismemberments, Ahab's periodic dismemberments are related to natural fertility and astronomical events and are inflicted by his eternal foe, the demon of life. Like Osiris' descents, Ahab's are periodic, are related to natural fertility and astronomical events, and are infernal. Unlike Osiris, however, Ahab is mortal; from one dismemberment he does not recover, from one descent he does not arise. These differences and similarities between Ahab's role and Osiris' role in part define the nature and tragedy of Ahab's cosmic struggle. They also in part define Ahab as something like, and something unlike, four kinds of god—the sun-god, the infernal god, the fertility god, and the savior god.

THE SUN-GOD

The Season-on-the-Line forms the chronological and geographical center of *Moby-Dick*. At that time and place the whale for the first and last times dismembers Ahab. One Season-on-the-Line passes between these two; precisely at this time, Christmas Day, the twice-maimed Ahab begins his fiery hunt. Although Ahab's second injury comes shortly before the Season-on-the-Line, all three injuries coincide with the various dates given for the dismemberment of Osiris, sometime between the autumnal equinox and the winter solstice. Although *Moby-Dick* defines its dates with no more precision than do the accounts of the Osiris myth, this much is explicitly clear: not only is each of Ahab's three injuries related to the position of the sun in the zodiac, but also the annual catastrophe and revival of Ahab, like those of Osiris, suggest and are suggested by the annual catastrophe and revival of the sun.

Ahab's revivals form one part of an astronomical drama. We have seen another part, the relation of Ahab's ship, his hunt, and his prey through the constellations Argo, Draco, and Cetus to astronomical events. The seasonal, geographical, and whaling occurrence known as the Season-on-the-Line brings together all the astronomical symbolism:

For there and then, for several consecutive years, Moby Dick had been periodically descried, lingering in those waters for awhile, as the sun, in its annual round, loiters for a predicted interval in any one sign of the Zodiac. There it was, too, that most of the deadly encounters with the white whale had taken place; there the waves were storied with his deeds; there also was that tragic spot where the monomaniac old man had found the awful motive to his vengeance. (P. 198)

Why Ahab sails the world to meet his foe in this "set time and place" is in part made clear by the "Doubloon" chapter, which explains the significance of the zodiac in the structure of *Moby-Dick*. On the doubloon itself "arching over all was a segment of the partitioned zodiac and signs all marked with their usual cabalistics, and the keystone sun entering the equinoctial point at Libra." So "this equatorial coin" made in Ecuador, "a country planted in the middle of the world, and beneath the great equator, and named after it; and . . . cast midway up the Andes, in the unwaning clime that knows no Autumn," embodies nevertheless the autumnal equinox. The coin, which, "like a magician's glass, to each and every man in turn but mirrors back his own mysterious self," represents Truth; since it

means everything, it means nothing absolutely; since it means everything, it means anything its interpreters see in it. (Or as Pip puts it,
"I look, you look, he looks; we look, ye look, they look"; "when
aught's nailed to the mast it's a sign that things grow desperate.")
Although the text is rendered variously, it is "still one text," and the
renderings all reflect it. The text indeed, as Stubb says, is that "your
zodiac here is the life of man in one round chapter." For Flask, that
life may be "nine hundred and sixty" cigars "at two cents the cigar";
for Queequeg, the primitive, that life may be represented by what he
finds "in the vicinity of his thigh—I guess it's Sagittarius, or the
Archer";* for Starbuck that life may be the alternation of darkness
with the heavenly light of faith; for Stubb that life may be a jollity
that "wheels through toil and trouble." All of course are relatively
right and absolutely wrong. The difference between the relative
truths created by their minds and the unperceived absolute truth
created by their cosmic predicament forms Ahab's cosmic tragedy.
To Stubb, the sun's adventures are only a jolly sermon for the adventures of man: "the sun goes through it every year, and yet comes out
of it all alive and hearty. Jollily he, aloft there, wheels through toil
and trouble; and so, alow here, does jolly Stubb." But for Ahab,
although he knows that man, rather than come out of it all alive and
hearty, must be "born in throes," "live in pain and die in pangs," the
life of man must be an attempt to be the sun, to be a god.

Maurice scattered through all his volumes interminable readings
of the Trinity into and out of medals and coins.[33] Starbuck, like
Maurice, calls the coin's three peaks "three mighty heaven-abiding
peaks, that almost seem the Trinity." Ahab sees this Trinity as himself:

"There's something ever egotistical in mountain-tops and towers, and all
other grand and lofty things; look here,—three peaks as proud as Lucifer.
The firm tower, that is Ahab; the volcano, that is Ahab; the courageous,
the undaunted, and victorious fowl, that, too, is Ahab; all are Ahab . . ."

(P. 428)

---

* Melville makes a similar phallic joke in *Mardi*. The great "Archer" of
Mardi is "the god Upi" (I, 249).

Though Ahab's soul may be as proud as Lucifer, he understands what it is to be the sun: " 'Methinks now this coined sun wears a ruddy face; but see! aye, he enters the sign of storms, the equinox! and but six months before he wheeled out of a former equinox at Aries! From storm to storm! So be it, then.' " Ahab, that "hot old man" with a "fiery hot" body, whose soul is symbolized by a fire-laden ship, sails on his "fiery hunt" from equinox to equinox, from storm to storm, until he fancies that he brings the sun to the world in his ship. The Egyptians not only believed that Osiris was the sun, but "they affirme also, that the Sunne and Moone are not mounted upon chariots, but within bardges or boates continually do moove and saile as it were round about the world."[34] Shortly after Ahab cries out "I am immortal then, on land and sea . . . Immortal on land and sea!" he speaks with the voice of the sun-god. On the day after the Typhoon, the sea is as golden as the doubloon: "The sea was as a crucible of molten gold, that bubblingly leaps with light and heat." Ahab sees the sea and the sun and shouts: " 'Ha, ha, my ship! thou mightest well be taken now for the sea-chariot of the sun. Ho, ho! all ye nations before my prow, I bring the sun to ye! Yoke on the further billows; hallo! a tandem, I drive the sea!' " But Ahab is going the wrong way.

When the narrator of *Mardi* passed himself off as a demigod from the sun, he had at least been traveling for a long time the same way as the sun. Ahab has been going in the opposite direction ever since he set sail—south while the sun was moving north, north while the sun was moving south, and always east while the sun moves west. Only when deluded by the Typhoon into heading away from his quest does he sail with the sun. When Ahab reasserts his lordship over the level loadstone, reverses the compasses, and again sails east, "In his fiery eyes of scorn and triumph, you then saw Ahab in all his fatal pride."

Neither Ahab nor the whale, which loiters like the sun in the zodiac, is the sun. The sun is their creator, and though perhaps only "another lonely castaway," is "the loftiest and the brightest." As the high source of all life, it can see both man and the demon which glides around man; it can also look beyond, into the unknown. Ahab gazes at the "solar fire" and says:

"Thou sea-mark! thou high and mighty Pilot! thou tellest me truly where I *am*—but canst thou cast the least hint where I *shall* be? Or canst thou tell me where some other thing besides me is this moment living? Where is Moby Dick? This instant thou must be eyeing him. These eyes of mine look into the very eye that is even now beholding him; aye, and into the eye that is even now equally beholding the objects on the unknown, thither side of thee, thou sun!" (Pp. 493–94)

As the creator of all, the sun is the god of both man and whale. Like Ahab, the dying whale "worships fire; most faithful, broad, baronial vassal of the sun."

Ahab, like the sun, seems to feed on himself: "For a long time now, the circus-running sun has raced within his fiery ring, and needs no sustenance but what's in himself. So Ahab." The monomaniac purpose which infused itself into Ahab's being after his first dismemberment feeds on him both as a god and as a fire:

But as the mind does not exist unless leagued with the soul, therefore it must have been that, in Ahab's case, yielding up all his thoughts and fancies to his one supreme purpose; that purpose, by its own sheer inveteracy of will, forced itself against gods and devils into a kind of self-assumed, independent being of its own. Nay, could grimly live and burn, while the common vitality to which it was conjoined, fled horror-stricken from the unbidden and unfathered birth. Therefore, the tormented spirit that glared out of bodily eyes, when what seemed Ahab rushed from his room, was for the time but a vacated thing, a formless somnambulistic being, a ray of living light, to be sure, but without an object to color, and therefore a blankness in itself. God help thee, old man, thy thoughts have created a creature in thee; and he whose intense thinking thus makes him a Prometheus; a vulture feeds upon that heart for ever; that vulture the very creature he creates. (P. 200)

Both as fire and as god, this purpose destroys Ahab, burning out his soul and overlording his reason. Throughout the "fiery hunt," Ahab, consuming himself continually with his own fire, is called hot and fiery, burning and smoking, from the time when "he would burst from his state room as though emerging from a bed of fire" until he stands untottering, "his eyes glowing like coals, that still glow in the ashes of ruin." Starbuck is a close witness of Ahab's fire: "I have sat before the dense coal fire and watched it all aglow, full of its tormented flaming life; and I have seen it wane at last, down, down, to dumbest dust. Old man of oceans! of all this fiery life of thine, what will at length remain but one little heap of ashes!" Ahab's internal fire and Ahab's worship of fire consummatingly meet when the corposants leap from the *Pequod*'s masts in the Typhoon. After Ahab seizes the last link of the lightning chain and grounds the current by placing his foot upon the Parsee, "he stood erect before the lofty tri-pointed trinity of flames." Then, in defiant prayer, he explains both his internal fire and his worship of fire, though fire itself be but a "lonely castaway":

"Oh! thou clear spirit of clear fire, whom on these seas I as Persian once did worship, till in the sacramental act so burned by thee, that to this hour I bear the scar; I now know thee, thou clear spirit, and I now know that thy right worship is defiance. . . . Oh, thou clear spirit, of thy fire thou madest me, and like a true child of fire, I breathe it back to thee."

[*Sudden, repeated flashes of lightning: the nine flames leap lengthwise to thrice their previous height. . . .*]

"I own thy speechless, placeless power; said I not so? Nor was it wrung from me; nor do I now drop these links. Thou canst blind; but I can then grope. Thou canst consume; but I can then be ashes. Take the homage of these poor eyes, and shutter-hands. I would not take it. The lightning flashes through my skull; mine eye-balls ache and ache; my whole beaten brain seems as beheaded, and rolling on some stunning ground. Oh, oh! Yet blindfold, yet will I talk to thee. Light though thou be, thou leapest out of darkness; but I am darkness leaping out of light, leaping out of thee! The javelins cease; open eyes; see, or not? There burn the flames! Oh, thou magnanimous! now do I glory in my genealogy. But thou art but my fiery father; my sweet mother, I know not. Oh, cruel! what hast thou done with her? There lies my puzzle; but thine is greater. Thou knowest not how came ye, hence callest thyself unbegotten; certainly knowest not thy beginning, hence callest thyself unbegun. I know that of me, which thou knowest not of thyself, oh, thou omnipotent. There is some unsuffusing thing beyond thee, thou clear spirit, to whom all thy eternity is but time, all thy creativeness mechanical. Through thee, thy flaming self, my scorched eyes do dimly see it. Oh, thou foundling fire, thou hermit immemorial, thou too hast thy incommunicable riddle, thy unparticipated grief. Here again with haughty agony, I read my sire. Leap! leap up, and lick the sky! I leap with thee; I burn with thee; would fain be welded with thee; defyingly I worship thee!"

(Pp. 500–501)

THE INFERNAL GOD

To explain why Osiris the sun-god rules the infernal regions, comparative mythologists turned to the annual adventures of the sun and to the various mythological and ritual representations of these adventures. When the sun sinks below the equator at the autumnal equinox, it is, as Ahab observes when looking at the doubloon, a death. Between the autumnal equinox and the winter solstice the sun, for those in the Northern Hemisphere, may be construed mythologically as descending to rule the infernal regions, from which it slowly emerges as the vernal equinox approaches.

When Ishmael gazes into the fire of the *Pequod*'s tryworks, he, like Ahab, is blinded, inverted, and deadened. He recovers to warn: "Give not thyself up, then, to fire, lest it invert thee, deaden thee; as for the time it did me." What he had seen, what had fixed his attention on the fire, was the vision of Ahab's soul, represented by the hell and "the Tartarean shapes" which Ahab ruled:

. . . as to and fro . . . the harpooneers wildly gesticulated with their huge pronged forks and dippers; as the wind howled on, and the sea leaped, and the ship groaned and dived, and yet steadfastly shot her red hell further and further into the blackness of the sea and the night, and scornfully champed the white bone in her mouth, and viciously spat round her on all sides; then the rushing Pequod, freighted with savages, and laden with fire, and burning a corpse, and plunging into that blackness of darkness, seemed the material counterpart of her monomaniac commander's soul. (P. 421)

Ahab, "more a demon than a man," evokes and rules over "the infernal orgies, which are part of the ritual initiation of the crew, making them sharers in Ahab's vengeance against the great demon of the seas of life. These infernal orgies immediately precede the

chapter which defines the psychological and mythological truth of
the whale; they immediately follow the first ceremonies at which
Ahab is the high priest. Ahab calls upon his mates and harpooneers
to "'commend the murderous chalices'": "'Oh, my sweet cardinals!
your own condescension, *that* shall bend ye to it. I do not order ye; ye
will it.'" He consummates his high infernal priesthood with the
diabolical baptism of his harpoon: "Ego non baptizo te in nomine
patris, sed in nomine diaboli!"

THE FERTILITY GOD

After Osiris' dismemberment and while he rules the infernal
regions, the land lies infertile because, of all the members of Osiris
scattered by Typhon, only the phallus was not found. Therefore a
large replica of Osiris' phallus became the center of Egyptian fertility
rites.

When Ahab recovers from his groin injury and emerges from his
tomb-like cabin, he readies himself for the hunt by presiding as high
priest over infernal rituals. Then, whenever a whale is slain in Ahab's
hunt, the enemy is burned with other infernal rituals by the Tartarean harpooneers in the hellish tryworks. But to prepare the marine
harvest for the tryworks, another type of priestly ritual must first be
performed. "The Cassock," the chapter immediately preceding "The
Try-Works," describes this ritual.

Ahab's priest in this ceremony is clad in the pelt of the whale's
phallus, as "jet-black as Yojo, the ebony idol of Queequeg."

And an idol, indeed, it is; or, rather, in old times, its likeness was. Such
an idol as that found in the secret groves of Queen Maachah in Judea;
and for worshipping which, king Asa, her son, did depose her, and destroyed the idol, and burnt it for an abomination at the brook Kedron,
as darkly set forth in the 15th chapter of the first book of Kings. (P. 417)

Throughout the eighteenth and nineteenth centuries, comparative
religion and mythology examined each detail of ancient and modern
priestly ritual and dress, searching for correspondences which might
indicate origins and influences. Of all the priestly dress, the Christian
cassock proved perhaps the most fertile for skeptical deductions.[35] Of

all the priestly ceremonies, phallic rituals proved perhaps the most attractive not only to the skeptics but even to such orthodox comparative religionists as the Reverend Thomas Maurice. Melville constructs his own comparative religion from contemporaneous theories about both priestly vestments and phallic rituals. He relates the phallic rites on the *Pequod* to contemporaneous Western rituals and implies that the modern Western priests have their phallic progenitors:

> The mincer now stands before you invested in the full canonicals of his calling. Immemorial to all his order, this investiture alone will adequately protect him, while employed in the peculiar functions of his office.
>
> That office consists in mincing the horse-pieces of blubber for the pots; an operation which is conducted at a curious wooden horse, planted endwise against the bulwarks, and with a capacious tube beneath it, into which the minced pieces drop, fast as the sheets from a rapt orator's desk. Arrayed in decent black; occupying a conspicuous pulpit; intent on bible leaves; what a candidate for an archbishoprick, what a lad for a Pope were this mincer!*
>
> * Bible leaves! Bible leaves! This is the invariable cry from the mates to the mincer.

(P. 418)

Melville's punning joke is much more than a joke. It brings the study of comparative mythology in *Moby-Dick* almost full circle, almost to the final and most important resemblance between Ahab and Osiris.

Earlier, in the chapter entitled "The Whiteness of the Whale," Melville refers to the meaning of white in some of the world's religions. From nearly every reference later rises an important structural component of the comparative mythology in *Moby-Dick*. After referring, among many other things, to the great white elephant of Siam, Melville brings his two-page sentence to the point, the archetypical significance of whiteness:

> . . . though even in the higher mysteries of the most august religions it has been made the symbol of the divine spotlessness and power; by the Persian fire worshippers, the white forked flame being held the holiest on the altar; and in the Greek mythologies, Great Jove himself made incarnate in a snow-white bull; and though to the noble Iroquois, the midwinter sacrifice of the sacred White Dog was by far the holiest festival of

their theology, that spotless, faithful creature being held the purest envoy they could send to the Great Spirit with the annual tidings of their own fidelity; and though directly from the Latin word for white, all Christian priests derive the name of one part of their sacred vesture, the alb or tunic, worn beneath the cassock; and though among the holy pomps of the Romish faith, white is specially employed in the celebration of the Passion of our Lord; though in the Vision of St. John, white robes are given to the redeemed, and the four-and-twenty elders stand clothed in white before the great white throne, and the Holy One that sitteth there white like wool; yet for all these accumulated associations, with whatever is sweet, and honorable, and sublime, there yet lurks an elusive something in the innermost idea of this hue, which strikes more of panic to the soul than that redness which affrights in blood. (P. 186)

We have now seen how "sweet," how "honorable," and how "sublime" are all but one of these "higher mysteries of the most august religions." "The white flame" of the Persian fire worshipers "but lights the way to the White Whale"; "Great Jove . . . incarnate in a snow-white bull" is a leering, lustful, menacing incarnation of treachery; "the midwinter sacrifice of the sacred White Dog" is paralleled by the midwinter sacrifice of Ahab to the White Whale; the "sacred vesture . . . worn beneath the cassock" of Christian priests is, in wicked metaphorical fact, worn beneath the modern counterpart of the pelt worn by primitive phallic priests. The one mystery which has not been revealed is primitive Christianity, which in *Mardi* Melville sharply distinguished from institutionalized Christianity. When Melville asserts in a Bayle-like footnote to the next paragraph that the "heightened hideousness" of the polar bear "only arises from the circumstance, that the irresponsible ferociousness of the creature stands invested in the fleece of celestial innocence and love," one may wonder if *Moby-Dick* is to distinguish quite so sharply between the ferocious ecclesiastical monstrosity of Alma's priests and the blissful celestial innocence of Alma's teachings.

THE SAVIOR GOD

In Mohi's chronicles the treatment of Christ, Brahma, and Manco Capac as avatars of the same god reflects a discovery that was being made with increasing frequency in the late eighteenth and first half of the nineteenth centuries, the discovery that a savior of mankind was central to many of the world's religions; and Mohi's account of Alma, Brami, and Manko is a conventional description of the savior gods. It lacks only one important element which the mythographers found common to most of the savior myths—the assault or temptation by the power of evil. The conflict with the evil principle was of course central to the myth of Osiris, the Egyptian savior god. In the following description—taken from a standard mid-nineteenth-century work on ancient Egypt—we may see a bridge between the mythology of *Mardi* and the mythology of *Moby-Dick*:

In the fabulous history of Osiris, we may trace a notion, common to all nations, of a God, who in the early ages of their history lived on earth, and was their King, their instructor, and even the father of their race; who taught them the secrets of husbandry, the arts of civilisation, and the advantages of social intercourse; and who, extending his dominion over the whole world, permitted all mankind to partake of his beneficent influence. They represent him to have been assailed by the malignant attacks of some monster, or enemy of man, either as an evil principle, or the type of a destructive power. He is sometimes exposed to the waters of the sea.[36]

This description is strikingly similar to Mohi's description of the Mardian savior gods, but the "malignant attacks of some monster, or enemy of man, either as an evil principle, or the type of a destructive power," measure part of the distance between Alma and Ahab.

That Ahab plays a role like that of Osiris we cannot doubt. Nor can we doubt that Melville saw similarities between Osiris and Christ. *Clarel* I, xxxi, demonstrates that at one other time Melville entertained the possibility that the Christ myth was only a later version of the Osiris myth. If the Egyptians conceived Leviathan and Jehovah, perhaps they also conceived Jehovah's Son and His conflict with Leviathan.

According to much of the skeptical literature available to Melville, when the sun reached the winter solstice, all Asia Minor and the entire Mediterranean world celebrated the birth of a savior. This savior was born on the date the *Pequod* sails, December 25. (The precession of the equinoxes explains why the present date of the solstice is four days earlier.) The following long quotation from Godfrey Higgins's *Anacalypsis, an Attempt to Draw Aside the Veil of the Saitic Isis; or, An Inquiry into the Origin of Languages, Nations, and Religions** shows what significances even a self-professed Christian could find in December 25:

Osiris, Bacchus, Adonis, were all incarnate Gods: taught by the priests; despised by the philosophers; believed by the rabble. They were probably all derived from the story of Cristna born in the eighth month, which answers to our December, on a Wednesday at midnight . . .

Thus the *verbum caro factum est* is not peculiar to the Christians, but was in fact acknowledged in almost every nation of the world. This was the Logos of the Persians and the Greeks, whose birth was originally fixed to the moment of the winter solstice. This Logos, we have seen, was the second person of the Trinity—the Iao of the Gentiles.

Tertullian, Jerom, and other fathers of the church, inform us, that the Gentiles celebrated, on the 25th of December or on the 8th day before the calends of January, the birth of the God Sol, under the name of Adonis, in a cave, like that of Mithra, (in Persia *Mithra*; in Egypt, Phoenicia, and Biblis, *Adonis,*) and that the cave wherein they celebrated his mysteries was that in which Christ was born in the city of Bethlehem, or, according to the strict meaning of the word Bethlehem, *in the city of the house of the sun.* This God Adonis is really and literally the Hebrew word אדן, *Adn,* yet retained in the Welsh Celtic *Adon,* which is translated into Latin *Dominus,* into Greek Κυριος, and into English *Lord,* the peculiar name of honour given to Jesus Christ.

. . .

The same God was believed, by the inhabitants of Persia, Asia Minor, and Armenia, under the name of Mithra, to have been born in a cave on the 25th of December, to have been put to death, and to have risen again on the 25th of March. In their mysteries the body of a young man, apparently dead, was exhibited, which was feigned to be restored to life. By his sufferings he was believed to have worked their salvation, and on this account he was called *their Saviour.* His priests watched his tomb to the midnight of the vigil of the 25th of March, with loud cries, and in darkness; when all at once the light burst forth from all parts, and the priest

* *Anacalypsis* is one of the curiosities of the age. Its two hefty folios are at once a skeptical attack on orthodox apologists (Jones and Maurice in particular) and a mystical collection of strange lore. It was widely used as a literary source book.

cried, Rejoice, oh sacred *initiated,* your God is risen. *His death, his pains, and sufferings have worked your salvation.*

. . .

At the first moment after midnight of the 24th of December, all the nations of the earth, by common consent, celebrated the accouchement of the Queen of Heaven, of the Celestial Virgin of the sphere, and the birth of the God Sol, the infant Orus or Aur, the God of Day, called by the Gentiles *the hope and promise of all nations, the Saviour of mankind* from the empire of Ahriman and darkness.

The Egyptians celebrated the birth of the son of Isis on the 25th of December, or the 8th day before the calends of January. This Eratosthenes says was the God of Day, and that Isis or Ceres was symbolical of the year. The son of *the Holy Virgin,* as they called Ceres, was Osiris: he was born on the 25th of December. At his birth, Plutarch says, that a voice was heard, saying, "On this day is born the *supreme Lord of the universe,* the beneficent king Osiris." On this day, at the same moment, the Romans began to celebrate the feast of the Brumalia in honour of the birth of the God of Day—of the Sol invincible.[37]

Ahab, who begins his hunt on Christmas, who bears a "crucifixion" on his face, who metaphorically wears the crown made of the nails used in the Crucifixion,[38] and who arises after he "lay like dead for three days and nights," may perhaps be playing the roles of both the Egyptian savior and the later Hebrew Saviour. And the narrative compares him explicitly to at least four other mythological saviors—Perseus, Prometheus, Noah, and Zoroaster.

The first paragraph that describes Ahab compares him to "Cellini's cast Perseus," and "the gallant Perseus, a son of Jupiter," plays the role of "the first whaleman" in two of the chapters that directly parody contemporaneous comparative mythology (56 and 82). Ahab's similarities to and differences from Prometheus are central to an entire book on Melville's work.[39]

Noah is at least as important as these two saviors. If the whaleship were told that another flood had come, the crew would only say, "Well, boys, here's the ark"; Ahab says about the sea that it is "The same!—the same!—the same to Noah as to me"; while lifting casks from the *Pequod*'s hull, "you almost looked for some mouldy cornerstone cask containing coins of Captain Noah, with copies of the posted placards, vainly warning the infatuated old world from the flood." Ahab's almost cabalistic lordship over the loadstone may possibly be another reflection of Melville's reading in Maurice, who suggested that the magnetic compass was God's revelation to Noah in the ark "to direct its devious course, amidst the boundless darkness that reigned around, and the united fury of the conflicting elements."[40] And Ishmael's boarding of Osiris' ship, the Argo-Navis, would in no way be inconsistent with his boarding Noah's ark, for, as Maurice says, "Argo was the sacred ship of Osiris, and no other than the ark."[41] Maurice speaks in a well-established tradition. In the historical-diffusionist school of comparative mythology, an entire orthodox department taught that Noah was the archetypical Helio-Arkite god, the father in fancy as well as in flesh of all but one of the savior gods. The skeptics merely reversed the orthodox chronology, making Noah the fanciful descendant of Osiris.

Millicent Bell has shown how Bayle's account of Zoroastrianism became raw material for the Manichean universe of *Moby-Dick* and how Melville invests Ahab with "symbols taken chiefly from Bayle's important essay on Zoroaster."[42] Zoroaster, who, according to Maurice, purged the Persian mythology of its "impurities," substituting instead "the simple adoration of the solar orb and fire as the purest symbol of the Deity,"[43] was thought by many skeptics to be merely another manifestation of the archetypical savior myth, perhaps the one who introduced the cassock now worn by Christian priests.[44] When Ahab cryptically shouts, "Oh! thou clear spirit of clear fire, whom on these seas I as Persian once did worship," he says a great deal about his nature. He shows that he himself consciously conceives of his own acts in terms of other religions, and he shows that his rituals previously have taken other forms. His words suggest that we see him only in his most recent avatar, that he has in fact appeared before as other forms of the savior.

We realize that particular pagan gods were important to Melville, and that some of them helped form, in detail, the cosmic and mythic tragedy of *Moby-Dick*. But perhaps ultimately it makes little difference to us that Ahab may be playing the role of a *particular* non-

Judaic-Christian god. The battles of faith have long since left the fields of the literalness, the exclusiveness, and the originality of the Judaic-Christian revelation; the psychological facts of religion no longer engage directly with the historical facts; Osiris is neither an opponent nor an avatar of Christ. If Ahab has appeared before as other forms of the savior and if he is symbolically associated with Persian, Hebrew, and Greek saviors, what is the special significance of the Egyptian savior?

The answer is simple. Melville saw Egyptian mythology as the direct source of the Hebrew mythology and therefore of the myth of the Christ.

Confronted with the solecisms of the Old Testament's prophecies of the Saviour and the New Testament's biography of the Saviour, he turned to what he considered their Egyptian source. There he found a picture of the savior which seemed to describe more accurately what he could see. He drew from this source his own version of the savior myth—*Moby-Dick,* which he submits to us as a kind of truth not found in Christian, Hebrew, or Egyptian mythology.

Moby-Dick concerns both Moby Dick the god and Ahab the man. Comparisons between Moby Dick and similar deities in the world's mythologies exalt the whale and ridicule the religions based on the other mythologies. Comparisons between Ahab and various gods of the world equivocate the other gods because Ahab is mortal, and, for the same reason, exalt Ahab while making his mortality the basic fact of his tragedy.

The narrator of *Mardi* plays the role of Taji, a minor sun-god, and therefore plunges deeper into destruction and damnation. Ahab plays the role of Osiris, not only as sun-god but also as fertility god, infernal god, and the savior of man, the dragon slayer, hunter of the gliding great demon of the seas of life. He, like Taji, plunges to destruction and damnation. Perhaps Taji might be considered a sacrifice who, though he himself races back into chaos, brings his followers to Serenia. But Ahab takes with him Man, embodied by the polyglot crew of the *Pequod.* Only one escapes to tell the tale. Whether Moby Dick is in historical fact the gliding great demon is unknowable; but because Ahab succeeds in defining him psychologically, metaphysically, and morally as the Dragon, the Leviathan, the Typhon, the whale becomes in mythic fact that great demon. When Ahab's monomania makes him re-enact the role of the dragon slayer, makes him play Osiris to Moby Dick as Typhon, perhaps therefore Christ to Moby Dick as Leviathan, he dramatizes the full implication of being a "grand ungodly godlike man." Playing the role of a god is the most complete ungodliness.

Ahab, in seeking to become the savior god, turns away from the teachings of the savior gods. He, like Taji, spurns the Reason of Alma and himself plays the role of avatar to the hell at the end of the hunt. After rejecting the brotherly bonds of the *Rachel,* after rejecting the lessons of mortality presented by the *Delight*—turning his taffrail to "the resurrection and the life," and after rejecting the Right Reason for which Starbuck pleads, Ahab meets the demon he seeks. But to say that Ahab's destruction is caused by following the mythological actions rather than the moral and metaphysical teachings of the savior gods is not to say that the moral and metaphysical teachings of the savior gods lead to salvation. Within a year Melville published a book whose tragic hero ignores the mythological actions of the savior gods and tries only to embody their moral and metaphysical teachings. Pierre learns that being a rock of faith can be as disastrous as the most self-assertive god-playing, can lead in fact to playing a most stony and defiant mythological role.

CHAPTER 4

PIERRE; OR, THE AMBIGUITIES
The Petrifaction of Myth

And every one that hath forsaken houses, or brethren, or sisters, or father, or mother, or wife, or children, or lands, for my name's sake, shall receive an hundredfold, and shall inherit everlasting life.
CHRIST'S ANSWER TO PETER, MATTHEW 19:29

And I say also unto thee, That thou art Peter, and upon this rock I will build my church; and the gates of hell shall not prevail against it.
MATTHEW 16:18

And did all drink the same spiritual drink: for they drank of that spiritual Rock that followed them: and that Rock was Christ.
I CORINTHIANS 10:4

The story of Pierre, the hero of *The Ambiguities,* is the story of a Christian youth, who, by trying to become symbolically and ethically a new Christ, becomes symbolically and ethically a pagan god; who, in trying to be a savior, becomes the destroyer of all that he tries to save.

The story opens by showing Pierre in a pastoral paradise (his hereditary country estate, Saddle Meadows) and in an idyllic romance (with Lucy). With the arrival of Isabel, probably Pierre's illegitimate half-sister, all idylls end. Pierre faces his central ethical problem: should he publicly avow his sister and give her the love which his father's sins have denied her? If he does, he knows that he will thereby disgrace his father and destroy his mother. He believes that the only answer to his problem is to avow Isabel but not as a sister.

This, he realizes, will destroy Lucy, but he sees the "all-including query" as "Lucy or God?" He decides to save everybody except Lucy by pretending to marry Isabel and then taking her to the city. Pierre thus leaves his conventional and conventionally pious mother in order to uphold the name of his dead, unconventional, sinning father (whom he had previously regarded as a kind of god); thus he rejects the fair, virtuous, and innocent Lucy, who seems to represent Heaven, in order to accept completely the mysterious dark lady, Isabel, who seems to represent Nature; he abandons his country paradise and enters the hellish city; he renounces society, law, and custom to follow what seems to him the transcendent ethic of Christ. The central irony develops when Pierre, by embracing what seems Christ's message coming from his heart, finds himself incestuously embracing his sister.

In *Moby-Dick* the evils of the world are largely physical, and the ravening sea and the monsters it contains immediately suggest large symbolic values. Because evil in *Pierre* is largely social and ethical, large symbolic values do not grow so naturally out of its action. Yet the symbolism of *Pierre* is ponderous. In fact, because the symbolic action is often too heavy for the physical action, the book often breaks down and its language flies out of control. But the symbolic action itself remains intact.

Pierre; or, The Ambiguities is symbolically the other side of the *Moby-Dick* coin. Ahab begins his hunt by creating the myth of the White Whale; Pierre begins by seeing his only myth destroyed. Ahab succeeds in making all evil "practically assailable" in the White Whale; for Pierre, though "he had bitter cause for quarrel," "there was none to strike."[1] Ahab could at least dart harpoons into a demon monster of the sea; Pierre can only shoot down his own cousin on a pavement in the stony city. Ahab rules a world as a mythic figure, and he leads this world through his myth into destruction; Pierre is impotently cast out, thrown down, imprisoned, and destroyed by the world. *Moby-Dick,* the sea story, moves toward the symbolic demon who glides through the seas of life; *Pierre,* the land story, grinds incessantly among symbolic rocks. On the sea, Ahab shouts at his God in the roaring Typhoon; on the land, Pierre finds that "Silence is the only voice of our God," that those who think they have heard from this God are as absurd "as though they should say they had got water out of stone; for how can a man get a voice out of silence?"

Because *Pierre* is a land story, taking place in a world in which God is a stony silence, it uses rocks and stones for its chief symbols, for its title, and for its title character. Pierre, the stone of the title, begins as a follower of Peter, and then becomes gradually more and more identified with a real stone. First he submits himself to the "Memnon" or "Terror Stone," a huge balancing rock which serves the function of a *logan,* a huge Druidic balancing rock. This commits him to Isabel and his renunciation of the Saddle Meadows paradise. Following all but two of the major events in the novel, Pierre sees himself in a dream vision metamorphosed into a huge rock, Enceladus, the heaven-defying Titan. And finally, entombed in a stone prison, he becomes in all respects a rock.

The language, imagery, and symbolism of rocks, stones, bricks, and marble are explicit in more than a fifth of the pages of the book.[2] *Pierre's* world is peopled by stones, vaulted by "seven-fold stony skies" supported by a sinister-veined "marble pillar that stands beneath the all-comprising vault"; it is created by a stony Silence which sends down its Son as a "meteoric stone" and rains down "vindictive peltings of hail-stones." Even the past of this world wears a "marble face." When the creatures of this world build, they imitate their Creator, creating a "granite hell" in the heart of a Tartarus of paving stones, "stony walls," "stone lions," "stony roofs," and "mortar and brick"; they even cement each other into their own designs.

The institutions of this world are conceived of in stony terms, and they seek to embody themselves in terms of stone. After "hereditary beliefs, and circumstantial persuasions" crumble, "the fair structure of the world must . . . be entirely rebuilt again, from the lowermost corner stone up"; this process is symbolized in the city's stony hell by the Apostle's Tower, which was originally designed as a "supplemental edifice" to the abandoned church, like the church itself "to be promiscuously rented to the legal crowd": "But this new building very much exceeded the body of the church in height. It was some seven stories; a fearful pile of Titanic bricks, lifting its tiled roof almost to a level with the top of the sacred tower." This tower is also a symbol of the central structural principle of *Pierre,* the metamorphosis of Pierre himself from a holy temple to a fearful mass of Titanic stone.

Pierre begins as an innocent child in the little ordered paradise of his family's estate; he ends as an impotent Titan, borne down into hell, but struggling to assault heaven. In his dream vision at the end he sees himself as Enceladus, an uncarved mass of stone, half-buried in rocky earth, threatening with his armless trunk to batter the heaven which has cast him down. His metamorphosis is externally paralleled by his trip from Reverend Falsgrave's "beautiful little marble church" in the country to Plotinus Plinlimmon's pile of Titanic bricks in the churchyard in the stony city. Three internal images embody his metamorphosis—petrifaction, the fallen statue in the ruined temple, and birth.

The petrifaction image is central, uniting the other two. Yet the cause of this petrifaction remains part of the ambiguities. Pierre's heart is "turned to stone" by Lucy's tears; he vows to the "Black Knight" to "see thy face, be it Gorgon!"; the "heavenly waters" of his childhood "marbleized" his father's memory in his heart as "some rare waters in Derbyshire will preserve birds'-nests"; he discovers that by his own beauty he has been made "stone-blind"; *Hamlet* and the *Inferno* make "his petrifying heart" drop like a "pebble."

Only Isabel is explicitly exonerated from Pierre's petrifaction. First the narrator says that the terrors of Isabel's face are "not those of Gorgon." Later, when Isabel asks "is my face Gorgon's?" Pierre answers, "Nay, sweet Isabel; but it hath a more sovereign power; that turned to stone; thine might turn white marble into mother's milk." Isabel, to whom the solid physical world seems unreal and who makes it seem unreal to Pierre also, in one sense causes Pierre himself to dissolve. Pierre's final cry to her shows in what sense she might turn white marble into mother's milk: "Girl! wife or sister, saint or fiend! in thy breasts, life for infants lodgeth not, but death-milk for thee and me!—The drug!" Isabel's milk dissolves Pierre's identity, leaving only his stony body in his stony hell.

Placed against the country-raised Isabel, who dissolves reality, whose symbols are water and vegetative nature, is Lucy, who was born "among brick and mortar in a sea-port," who comes to represent the purity, the pure sterility, and the solidity of marble. When Pierre tells Lucy of his "marriage," she is described as a "snowy, marble statue"; later, she is called "so marble-white," a "marble girl"; she has become the replacement of what previously stood in the marble shrine of Pierre's heart, "the perfect marble form of his departed father; without blemish, unclouded, snow-white, and serene; Pierre's fond personification of perfect human goodness and virtue":

And as if her body indeed were the temple of God, and marble indeed were the only fit material for so holy a shrine, a brilliant, supernatural whiteness now gleamed in her cheek. Her head sat on her shoulders as a chiseled statue's head; and the soft, firm light in her eye seemed as much a prodigy, as though a chiseled statue should give token of vision and intelligence. (P. 385)

But whether this marble girl petrifies Pierre or whether Pierre is petrified by his father or by the "Black Knight," through his head or through his heart, remains ambiguous.

The second image which embodies Pierre's metamorphosis internally is the fallen statue in the ruined temple. This image first appears in what seems a conventional lesson on pride and fate drawn from a conventional set of ruins:

For in the ruddiness, and flushfulness, and vain-gloriousness of his youthful soul, he fondly hoped to have a monopoly of glory in capping the fame-column, whose tall shaft had been erected by his noble sires.

In all this, how unadmonished was our Pierre by that foreboding and prophetic lesson taught, not less by Palmyra's quarries, than by Palmyra's ruins. Among those ruins is a crumbling, uncompleted shaft, and some leagues off, ages ago left in the quarry, is the crumbling corresponding capital, also incomplete. These Time seized and spoiled; these Time crushed in the egg; and the proud stone that should have stood among the clouds, Time left abased beneath the soil.   (Pp. 6–7)

But this lesson becomes an unconventionally physical part of the structure of *Pierre*. "Now Pierre stands on this noble pedestal," but soon he is buried under the ruins of the temple in which he had worshiped both his earthly and heavenly creator. Even in its glory, this temple hints of its flaws:

> There had long stood a shrine in the fresh-foliaged heart of Pierre, up to which he ascended by many tableted steps of remembrance; and around which annually he had hung fresh wreaths of a sweet and holy affection. Made one green bower of at last, by such successive votive offerings of his being; this shrine seemed, and was indeed, a place for the celebration of a chastened joy, rather than for any melancholy rites. *But* though thus mantled, and tangled with garlands, this shrine was of marble—a niched pillar, *deemed* solid and eternal, and from whose top radiated all those innumerable sculptured scrolls and branches, which supported the *entire one-pillared* temple of his moral life; as in some beautiful *Gothic* oratories, *one central pillar, trunk-like, upholds the roof.* In this shrine, in this niche of this pillar, stood the perfect marble form of his departed father; without blemish, unclouded, snow-white, and serene; Pierre's *fond* personification of perfect human goodness and virtue. Before this shrine, Pierre poured out the fullness of all young life's most reverential thoughts and beliefs. *Not to God had Pierre ever gone in his heart, unless* by ascending the steps of that shrine, and so making it the vestibule of his *abstractest* religion. (P. 79) [Italics mine.]

The equivocal syntax which describes Pierre's worship indicates the shakiness of this shrine.

Only "deemed" solid and eternal, the shrine collapses. When Pierre's father dies, writhing in the knowledge of his sin, "the fire in the hearth lay in a broken temple." The sins of his father are only one of the fatal flaws in Pierre's temple, his idol, and his worship. After Pierre finds "the perfect marble form" of his earthly father grossly imperfect, there are dark hints that his heavenly father may be equally imperfect.

Pierre's shrine is totally destroyed by the knowledge of his father's sin, which "rolled down on his soul like melted lava, and left so deep a deposit of desolation, that all his subsequent endeavors never restored the original temples to the soil." "The mild statue of the saint" is buried "beneath the soul's temple itself." The deep deposit of desolation left by the tide of lava buries Pierre, who comes to embody both the incomplete abandoned capital in the Palmyra quarry and the statue that has fallen from his ancestral column.

The third internal image of Pierre's metamorphosis—birth and growth—pushes up through this deposit. The thing born in Pierre as a "heaven-begotten Christ" matures ineluctably into the monstrous stone Enceladus, cast down from heaven and imprisoned by earth. This metamorphosis measures the distance between the heaven-begotten Jesus and the Titanic son of earth and grandson of heaven.

The image of birth and growth presents special problems, for it connects Pierre's spiritual to his sexual urges. The ambiguities of both these urges make a simple understanding of them impossible. To argue that Pierre's literally enthusiastic plunge into his relation with Isabel is either simply foolish, simply lustful, or simply divine is grossly to oversimplify *Pierre*. Pierre's enthusiasm, which metamorphoses the unfettered boy into the buried giant, is at once ambiguously foolish, lustful, and divine. This is Pierre's cross and the crux of *Pierre*.

One passage focuses on the problem, and this passage offers the best evidence to those who maintain that Pierre's enthusiasm is more lustful than divine. In this passage Melville points to Isabel's actual beauty and raises the spectre of her hypothetical ugliness. When he asks whether Pierre's divine urges would have been so strong without sexual reinforcements, he shows, finally, one thing: the religion of the heart is profoundly dangerous. For the heart cannot be trusted; it is imperfect; through it, Eros, as well as Alma, may speak. But because Pierre trusts his possibly corrupt heart, Melville does not therefore brand him a fool or a lecher. The passage begins by asserting that Pierre was "charged with the fire of all divineness." When this divineness proves itself imperfect, Divinity becomes just as ambiguously imperfect as Pierre:

But Pierre, though charged with the fire of all divineness, his containing thing was made of clay. Ah, muskets the gods have made to carry infinite combustions, and yet made them of clay!

Save me from being bound to Truth, liege lord, as I am now. How shall I steal yet further into Pierre, and show how this heavenly fire was helped to be contained in him, by mere contingent things, and things that he knew not. But I shall follow the endless, winding way,—the flowing river in the cave of man; careless whither I be led, reckless where I land.

Was not the face—though mutely mournful—beautiful, bewitchingly? How unfathomable those most wondrous eyes of supernatural light! In those charmed depths, Grief and Beauty plunged and dived together. So beautiful, so mystical, so bewilderingly alluring; speaking of a mournfulness infinitely sweeter and more attractive than all mirthfulness; that face of glorious suffering; that face of touching loveliness; that face was Pierre's own sister's; that face was Isabel's; that face Pierre had visibly seen; into those same supernatural eyes our Pierre had looked. Thus, already, and ere the proposed encounter, he was assured that, in a transcendent degree, womanly beauty, and not womanly ugliness, invited him to champion the right. Be naught concealed in this book of sacred truth. How, if accosted in some squalid lane, a humped, and crippled, hideous girl should have snatched his garment's hem, with—"Save me, Pierre—love me, own me, brother; I am thy sister!"—Ah, if man were wholly made in heaven, why catch we hell-glimpses? Why in the noblest marble pillar that stands beneath the all-comprising vault, ever should we descry the sinister vein? *We lie in nature very close to God*; and though, further on, the stream may be corrupted by the banks it flows through; yet at the fountain's rim, where mankind stand, *there the stream infallibly bespeaks the fountain*.

So let no censorious word be here hinted of mortal Pierre.

(Pp. 126–27) [Italics mine.]

Part of the case against Pierre's enthusiasm is based on Pierre's own questionings of it late in the book. Pierre comes to believe that his "mystic and transcendental persuasions" that Isabel was indeed his sister were "originally born, as he now seemed to feel, purely of an intense procreative enthusiasm." Some critics read "procreative" here as "lustful," making Pierre's acknowledgment of Isabel purely a product of lust masked by foolish rationalization. There are several things wrong with this reading: procreative neither means lustful nor very precisely describes Pierre's sexual attraction to Isabel; there is no reason to assume, despite the ambiguous basis of Pierre's knowledge, that his "mystical and transcendental persuasions" were erroneous; the word "procreative" in this passage refers, quite explicitly and precisely, to the birth of Pierre's enthusiasm; that birth makes the irony of this word refer only secondarily to his incestuous predicament. The earlier passage which describes that birth shows what his "intense procreative enthusiasm" begets—a Christ:

> Not that at present all these things did thus present themselves to Pierre; but these things were foetally forming in him. Impregnations from high enthusiasms he had received; and the now incipient offspring which so stirred, with such painful, vague vibrations in his soul; this, in its mature development, when it should at last come forth in living deeds, would scorn all personal relationship with Pierre, and hold his heart's dearest interests for naught.
>
> Thus, in the Enthusiast to Duty, the heaven-begotten Christ is born; and will not own a mortal parent, and spurns and rends all mortal bonds.
>
> (P. 125)

This Christ, which is Pierre and yet has no personal relationship with Pierre, is most similar to the Prometheus-vulture which feeds on Ahab's heart, "a vulture the very creature he creates"—most similar in all but two respects: Ahab's divinity is infused into his being by hate, but Pierre's divinity is conceived in him by love; Pierre, unlike Ahab, only gradually metamorphoses into the very creature he creates. This metamorphosis is most insistently defined and visually bodied forth.

The divine conception in Pierre becomes an infant soul, described literally as a "little soul-toddler" born of the union of "its mother the world, and its father the Deity" and turned loose by both mother and father:

> When at Saddle Meadows, Pierre had wavered and trembled in those first wretched hours ensuing upon the receipt of Isabel's letter; then humanity had let go the hand of Pierre, and therefore his cry; but when at last inured to this, Pierre was seated at his book, willing that humanity should desert him, so long as he thought he felt a far higher support; then, ere long, he began to feel the utter loss of that other support, too; ay, even the paternal gods themselves did now desert Pierre; the toddler was toddling entirely alone, and not without shrieks. (P. 349)

The image of birth and growth then connects with the stone imagery. As Pierre's toddler-soul arises slowly from the "deposit of desolation" which covers "the prostrated ruins of the soul's temple," its size, divinity, and significance become manifest:

Now he sees, that with every accession of the personal divine to him, some great land-slide of the general surrounding divineness slips from him, and falls crashing away. Said I not that the gods, as well as mankind, had unhanded themselves from this Pierre? So now in him you behold the baby toddler I spoke of; forced now to stand and toddle alone. (P. 359)

The toddler image disappears when Pierre's metamorphosis reaches its Titanic consummation. At the same time "the general surrounding divineness" is defined as an imprisoning divine sterility, the earthly mother and heavenly father are defined in terms of Greek rather than Christian mythology, and Pierre's vision of himself serves as the measure of the distance between Christ and Enceladus. In order to understand not only *Pierre* but all Melville's later works at least through *The Confidence-Man,* one question must be answered with as much precision as possible: how great a distance does Melville place between Christ and the impotent, heaven-begotten, earthly-born giant who demonstrates by storming the gates of heaven that he "came from thither"?

The Mount of Titans itself offers a complicated metamorphosis which corresponds to Pierre's metamorphosis. Just as Pierre's soul was first described in Christian and now in pagan terms, the Mount of Titans is a pagan name which has replaced and extinguished its Christian "former title—The Delectable Mountain—one long ago bestowed by an old Baptist farmer, an hereditary admirer of Bunyan." Just as for Pierre the "interregnum of all hereditary beliefs" had signalized the overturn of "his whole previous moral being," for the mountain the change of name seems to signalize a complete physical overturn:

For as if indeed the immemorial mount would fain adapt itself to its so recent name, some people said that it had insensibly changed its pervading aspect within a score or two of winters. Nor was this strange conceit entirely without foundation, seeing that the annual displacements of huge rocks and gigantic trees were continually modifying its whole front and general contour. (Pp. 402–3)

Just as the temple of Pierre's soul lies beneath the "melted lava" which rolled down upon it, the Titanic rocks "thrown off from the rocky steep" are "igneous" and Enceladus himself raises his "turbaned head of igneous rock . . . from out the soil." "The imprisoning earth" from which Enceladus half emerges manifests physically the deep "deposit of desolation" on Pierre's soul. Enceladus' earthly burden puts "forth a thousand flowers, whose fragile smiles disguised his ponderous load"; but these flowers are the "celestial" and sterile amaranthine which represents "the ever-encroaching appetite for God." Pierre's final burial strips the disguise of smiling flowers from earth's load:

> That sundown, Pierre stood solitary in a low dungeon of the city prison. The cumbersome stone ceiling almost rested on his brow; so that the long tiers of massive cell-galleries above seemed partly piled on him. His immortal, immovable, bleached cheek was dry; but the stone cheeks of the walls were trickling. (P. 424)

These trickling stones are also the "dark-dripping rocks" of the Mount of Titans, "the four blank walls" of Pierre's room in the Apostle's Tower, that "Titanic pile of bricks," which his vision transforms into the Mount of Titans, and the marble temples, both external and internal, of Saddle Meadows, which Pierre's enthusiasm transmutes into the Mount of Titans.

Pierre's "impregnations from high enthusiasms" are born as the "heaven-begotten Christ"; they mature as the toddler-soul deprived of "its mother the world, and its father the Deity"; they reach their destined growth when Pierre sees that upon the phantom Enceladus "his own duplicate face and features magnifiedly gleamed upon him with prophetic discomfiture and woe":

> Old Titan's self was the son of incestuous Coelus and Terra, the son of incestuous Heaven and Earth. And Titan married his mother Terra, another and accumulatively incestuous match. And thereof Enceladus was one issue. So Enceladus was both the son and grandson of an incest; and even thus, there had been born from the organic blended heavenliness and earthliness of Pierre, another mixed, uncertain, heaven-aspiring, but still not wholly earth-emancipated mood; which again, by its terrestrial taint

held down to its terrestrial mother, generated there the present doubly incestuous Enceladus within him; so that the present mood of Pierre— that reckless sky-assaulting mood of his, was nevertheless on one side the grandson of the sky. (P. 408)

There is no doubt that the transformation of the heaven-begotten Christ into Enceladus, the doubly incestuous grandson of heaven, embodies Pierre's metamorphosis. The most important question is this: is Enceladus a debased Christ, an unmasked Christ, or merely a matured Christ, transformed only by growth. Pierre himself and his earthly and spiritual relations provide the answer.

Just as Enceladus is the grandson of heaven, Pierre has a heavenly grandfather, a "sweet-hearted, charitable Christian" who had "annihilated two Indian savages by making reciprocal bludgeons of their heads"—"in fine, a pure, cheerful, childlike, blue-eyed, divine old man; in whose meek, majestic soul, the lion and the lamb embrace— fit image of his God." The portrait of this divine personage directly influences Pierre's high enthusiasms and metaphorically represents their ultimate source:

The majestic sweetness of this portrait was truly wonderful in its effects upon any sensitive and generous-minded young observer. For such, that portrait possessed the heavenly persuasiveness of angelic speech; a glorious gospel framed and hung upon the wall, and declaring to all people, as from the Mount, that man is a noble, god-like being, full of choicest juices; made up of strength and beauty. (Pp. 33–34)

It is precisely because Pierre believes "that man is a noble, god-like being" that he is destroyed. By deifying first his grandfather, father, and mother, then Lucy, then Isabel, and finally himself, he kills one of his idols and drags the remaining living ones to death in the granite hell. If Christ is the ultimate source for Pierre's destructive belief in man's godliness, then Christ in *Pierre* is the deceiver which he appears to be in *The Confidence-Man* and the "torturer" which he is called in *Clarel* (I, xiii, 99). And at least in *Pierre,* Christ's message is precisely the message of Pierre's heavenly grandfather.

The introduction to Plinlimmon's pamphlet "Chronometricals and Horologicals" explicitly equates the two messages. The "Sermon on the Mount"—"that greatest real miracle of all religions"—aggravates the solecism of Christly renunciation and Christian Mammonism, of heavenly and worldly time, by doing what the heavenly portrait does, impregnating the youthful soul with high enthusiasms:

From that divine mount, to all earnest-loving youths, flows an inexhaustible soul-melting stream of tenderness and loving-kindness; and they leap exulting to their feet, to think that the founder of their holy religion gave utterance to sentences so infinitely sweet and soothing as these; sentences which embody all the love of the Past, and all the love which can be imagined in any conceivable Future. Such emotions as that Sermon raises in the enthusiastic heart; such emotions *all youthful hearts refuse to ascribe to humanity as their origin. This is of God! cries the heart, and in that cry ceases all inquisition.* Now, with this fresh-read Sermon in his soul, the youth again gazes abroad upon the world. Instantly, in aggravation of the former solecism, an overpowering sense of the world's downright positive falsity comes over him; *the world seems to lie saturated and soaking with lies.* (P. 243) [Italics mine.]

This dissolving doctrine together with the rest of the Bible contradicts all those "good and wise people" who "sincerely say" that "there is much truth in this world." But the soul-melting stream which flows from the mount has been defined previously as the peach-juice inscription of the words of God: "Love is both Creator's and Saviour's gospel to mankind; a volume bound in rose-leaves, clasped with violets, and by the beaks of humming-birds printed with peach-juice on the leaves of lilies."

After posing this conflict between the apparent world and the world as it is apparently defined by the apparent Word of God, Melville makes as explicit a statement of his own view of the conflict as can be found in the entire corpus of his works. This statement must be read in the context of all the action and imagery, and read furthermore as an introduction to the anti-Christian "Chronometricals and Horologicals," which is central to Melville's work from this date on. So read, it lays bare the role of Christ in this work:

Hereupon then in the soul of the enthusiast youth two armies come to the shock; and unless he prove recreant, or unless he prove gullible, or unless he can find the talismanic secret, to reconcile this world with his own soul, then there is no peace for him, no slightest truce for him in this life. Now without doubt this Talismanic Secret has never yet been found; and in the nature of human things it seems as though it never can be. Certain philosophers have time and again pretended to have found it; but if they do not in the end discover their own delusion, other people soon discover it for themselves, and so those philosophers and their vain philosophy are let glide away into practical oblivion. Plato, and Spinoza, and Goethe, and many more belong to this guild of self-impostors, with a preposterous rabble of Muggletonian Scots and Yankees, whose vile brogue still the more bestreaks the stripedness of their Greek or German Neoplatonical originals. That profound Silence, that only Voice of our God, which I before spoke of; from that divine thing without a name, those impostor philosophers pretend somehow to have got an answer; which is as absurd, as though they should say they had got water out of stone; for how can a man get a Voice out of Silence? (P. 244)

Since Christ's message is the subject of this passage, the preceding passage, and the pamphlet which they introduce; since the fact that Christ's teachings have been "let glide away into practical oblivion" is the cause and the aggravation of the very problem being considered; since Christ's Sermon on the Mount claimed to reveal the Talismanic Secret which "without doubt . . . has never yet been found"; since "from that divine mount . . . flows an inexhaustible soul-melting stream" which makes the world seem "to lie saturated and soaking with lies"; since Christ, like "those impostor philosophers," pretended to have gotten "a Voice out of Silence"; since Christ in fact purported to be the Logos of God; since God is elsewhere in *Pierre* described in stony terms; since Greece, as *Clarel* (III, vi) indicates, was a source of Christ's stream; and since Pierre is both petrified and dissolved as he proves "gullible" to this stream; it does not seem entirely unreasonable to think not only that Christ is being included among the "many more" who "belong to this guild of self-impostors," but that the Messiah himself in fact is the veiled subject of the entire passage.

"Chronometricals and Horologicals" states the case against Christ's teachings. Whether Melville agrees with or is mocking the pamphlet is an idle question. Melville's narrative masks display his only possible judgment of the pamphlet, "the excellently illustrated re-state-

ment of a problem," perhaps no solution but perhaps the only possible human solution, both "exceedingly trivial" and "so profound,
that scarce Juggularius himself could be the author." Undoubtedly
the pamphlet is subjected to ironies, perhaps most significantly in that
it assumes an oracular tone and indeed takes its title ("*El*") from
the oracle at Delphi, while attacking the Christian oracle. In a sense,
it offers a discredited pagan revelation as a substitute for the Christian
revelation which it seeks to discredit. But despite any and all ironies
to which the pamphlet may be subjected, it does describe with great
precision what the imitation of Christ leads to, at least in the world
of *Pierre*:

Though Christ encountered woe in both the precept and the practice of
his chronometricals, yet did he remain throughout entirely without folly
or sin. Whereas, almost invariably, with inferior beings, the absolute effort
to live in this world according to the strict letter of the chronometricals is,
somehow, apt to involve those inferior beings eventually in strange, *unique*
follies and sins, unimagined before. (Pp. 249–50)

The narrator of *Mardi* thinks Yillah is divine, spurns the divine
Reason of Alma, and assumes the role of a god. As a result, he
plunges to destruction and damnation. Ahab assumes the role of a
god and spurns the Right Reason of Christian Starbuck. As a result,
he is dragged to destruction and hell. Pierre, while embracing the
gospels of Christianity, thinks that his father, mother, and earthly
lover are divine Christian saints. When he sees his earthly divinities
crumble and his heavenly Deity become obscure, he tries to play the
role of the moral Christ. In so doing he is taking to his heart, not
spurning, the ultimate message of Christ: "Follow me." But this
role leads him into a granite hell and self-destruction. It also destroys
all those whom he believed divine.

The iteration of Lucy's divinity is too persistent to need verifying
quotation. Both narrator and characters continually call her an angel,
a saint, and a goddess. (To say that this is merely a convention of
mid-nineteenth-century romance is to miss the significance of the convention; it is also to miss the effect which these titles have on the other
characters and on the action.) But Lucy may not be the most divine

saint, angel, or deity in Pierre's paradise. His earthly father, as we have seen, is deified in the same breath and worshiped in the same temple as his heavenly Father. His mother, whom he significantly calls Sister Mary, "had ever seemed to Pierre . . . a beautiful saint, before whom to offer up his daily orisons." When Pierre's heart's temple is desolated, his "sacred father" becomes "no more a saint," Lucy becomes not the representative of but the grand alternative to God (one question remained—"Lucy or God"), and his mother becomes a monster of haughtiness fashioned by the "Infinite Haughtiness." Isabel at first seems a substitute "half unearthly" "saint enshrined," but she ultimately becomes as ambiguous as Pierre's original saints: " 'Girl! . . . saint or fiend!' "

As Frank Manuel has demonstrated, one of the great achievements of the eighteenth-century comparative mythologists was the creation of the systematic idea of a primitive mind. To understand fully the function of Isabel in *Pierre* it is necessary to understand the nature and function of the primitive mind in the mythology of the eighteenth and early nineteenth centuries. The nature of Isabel's mind is consistently dramatized: she cannot understand abstract language; she conceives only of physical objects; she thinks many inanimate objects are alive and talks to them; she has difficulty distinguishing between cats, stones, trees, and people; she is childlike; she was once thought to be mad and has spent part of her life in a madhouse.

The idea that the primitive ancestors of contemporary Europeans had a psychological make-up, a human nature, that was essentially different from Hume, de Brosses, and Vico, and that it was similar in general character to contemporary aborigines, to children, to benighted common people—in a word, that there was a distinctive primitive mentality—had been gaining ever greater force in European thought since the seventeenth century. There are even hints, though only hints, that madness too could be assimilated to this state of being. The momentous analogy was fed by volumes of empirical observation. Europeans had been watching and writing about savages for over two hundred years [notice how conventional are the accounts of the savage mind in *Typee* and *Omoo*]; a growing interest in child behavior is attested in works on education; and madmen, particularly demoniacs, had been the subject of medical analysis during the seventeenth-century outbursts of witchcraft. At the turn of the century Fontenelle had still regarded the difference between the primitive mind and the contemporary principally as one of degree; in later eighteenth-century writers the mentality of the primitive became more distinct, individualized to the point where a different human nature was recognized. Turgot even suggested that this early stage involved a different mode of perception from later metaphysical and scientific thinking—his famous anticipation of the Comtian law of three states.

The identification of the early mind with the concrete, the visual, as contrasted with the abstract capacity of the civilized man can of course already be found in Fontenelle and Vico, and even earlier in the father of them all—John Locke.[3]

Perhaps the most characteristic and least disputed concept of the primitive mind may be discovered when the nature of the primitive mind is used as a known given quantity. Vico assumes this knowledge while trying to establish the primitive characteristics of *il mondo fanciullo*:

Vico had also seen the "vulgar" who, when aroused by strange phenomena, "make of all nature a vast animate body which feels passions and effects"; he had heard them say that a "magnet loves iron"; he had watched children "take inanimate things in their hands and play with them and talk with them as if they were living persons." [Note particularly Isabel's behavior with the guitar.] Primitives were endowed with the same "corporeal imagination," a capacity to "feign" the living existence of natural bodies, and then to believe what they had just feigned.[4]

Once the existence of a distinctive primitive mentality became a widely accepted basic assumption, a vital question arose to confront all the mythologists—orthodox, heretical, and skeptical: what god or gods does the primitive mind worship? The apologists had long maintained that primitive man had worshiped one god, that monotheism always preceded polytheism, that the many pagan gods and idols were perversions of an originally pure, simple, primitive religion. One of Hume's most revolutionary heterodoxies was making polytheism precede monotheism, a pointed inversion of the orthodox sequence.[5] When the apologists responded to Hume, they found it necessary to fight on his ground, to recognize some sort of psychological basis for religious belief. Thus we found Sir William Jones, an orthodox apologist of the historical school, promulgating four different psychological bases for mythological inventions (inventions which he of course defined as human perversion or embellishment of sensory and divine revelation).

Isabel is exactly the sort of primitive mentality with which the comparative mythologists were most concerned, a primitive created by isolation from all culture rather than immersion in a primitive culture. As we might expect, Isabel's religious beliefs cast a new light on the religious beliefs of the society which she enters as a full-grown, sane, intelligent primitive. When Isabel comes to use the language of the Anglo-American religion, she uses it Transcendentally, equating its "God" with her "impulse." More important, her religion is exactly balanced against "the hereditary beliefs and circumstantial persuasions" of the religion which "the first Glendinning had brought over sea, from beneath the shadow of an English minister," the faith which Pierre finds to be misplaced:

". . . I thanked—not God, for I had been taught no God—I thanked the bright human summer, and the joyful human sun in the sky; I thanked the human summer and the sun, that they had given me the woman; and I would sometimes steal away into the beautiful grass, and worship the kind summer and the sun; and often say over to myself the soft words, summer and the sun." (P. 145)

Isabel's religion is not tangential to the action; it moves the action from within. After she avows her primitive worship of "the human summer and the sun," Pierre, "bewitched" and "enchanted" by her, can neither sleep nor any longer maintain his relations in the civilized world. He, too, steals away, leaves this world behind, and enters the primeval world of nature. There he encounters the Memnon or Terror Stone, the first of his two symbolic pagan stones:

Pierre plunged deep into the woods, and paused not for several miles; paused not till he came to a remarkable stone, or rather, smoothed mass of rock, huge as a barn, which, wholly isolated horizontally, was yet sweepingly overarched by beechtrees and chestnuts. (P. 154)

Melville describes in detail this rock, which is about to become not only an important dramatic device and an important symbol, but also an important piece of raw archaeological evidence:

It was shaped something like a lengthened egg, but flattened more; and, at the ends, pointed more; and yet not pointed, but irregularly wedge-shaped. Somewhere near the middle of its under side, there was a lateral ridge; and an obscure point of this ridge rested on a second lengthwise-sharpened rock, slightly protruding from the ground. Beside that one obscure and minute point of contact, the whole enormous and most ponderous mass touched not another object in the wide terraqueous world. It was a breathless thing to see. One broad haunched end hovered within an inch of the soil, all along to the point of teetering contact; but yet touched not the soil. Many feet from that—beneath one part of the opposite end, which was all seamed and half-riven—the vacancy was considerably larger, so as to make it not only possible, but convenient to admit a crawling man; yet no mortal being had ever been known to have the intrepid heart to crawl there. (Pp. 154–55)

In one direction, the Memnon Stone explicitly extends Pierre's tragedy back into Egyptian mythology:

For, not to speak of the other and subtler meanings which lie crouching behind the colossal haunches of this stone, regarded as the menacingly impending Terror Stone—hidden to all the simple cottagers, but revealed to Pierre—consider its aspects as the Memnon Stone. For Memnon was that dewy, royal boy, son of Aurora, and born King of Egypt, who, with enthusiastic rashness flinging himself on another's account into a rightful quarrel, fought hand to hand with his overmatch, and met his boyish and most dolorous death beneath the walls of Troy. His wailing subjects built a monument in Egypt to commemorate his untimely fate. Touched by the breath of the bereaved Aurora, every sunrise that statue gave forth a mournful broken sound, as of a harp-string suddenly sundered, being too harshly wound. (P. 159)

Throughout the ages many thought that it was the Egyptian priests who caused the sound to come from the statue of Memnon. If this was true, these were not the only priests who pretended to get the voice of a god from a stone. The Druids, according to Maurice and many others, got from stones the most important pronouncements of their gods.

The Terror Stone, with its "other and subtler meanings," extends the religious symbolism of *Pierre* back into Druidic ritual. The year before *Pierre* appeared, a major archaeological study compared rocks found near Pierre's Terror Stone both to Druidic and Polynesian rocks.[6] Two things seemed to bring the Druidic past to Melville's mind: modern English priests (as in *Clarel,* which makes the "Druid priest Melchizedek" parallel the modern Anglican priest whose name means Druid, and in *Billy Budd,* which, as we shall see, focuses at once on ancient and modern British ritual), and primeval rock and stone worship—as in the Stonehenge-like rocks of the Typee valley. A few shadowy hints relate the modern priests of the imported English religion in *Pierre* with the Welsh Druidic past—both Lucy (the true Christian) and the anti-Christian Plotinus Plinlimmon (priest of the Apostles trying to recapture the "pure archetypical faith") had Welsh origins. As several critics have noticed, Pierre's movement into the primeval religious past and present world of nature clearly recalls the movement into the primeval Typee valley.[7] The stones which form the Typee Stonehenge stand under "a wilderness of vines, in whose sinewy embrace many of the stones lie half hidden" (*Typee,* p. 658). As Pierre slowly metamorphoses into a rock, he moves toward his extinction in the stone prison and Isabel's last embrace, described by the words which end the book: "she fell upon Pierre's heart, and her long hair ran over him, and arbored him in ebon vines." One of the first stages of the metamorphosis takes place under the Terror Stone, where Pierre, just plunged from the civilized to the primitive world, relives a primitive Druidic ritual.

Maurice describes this ritual in his discussion of Druidic human sacrifices and stone worship in consecrated groves:

These grotesque and ponderous masses of unhewn stone, which, among a barbarous people were reverenced as the symbols of deity, were not always pyramidal nor placed in an erect posture. Sometimes they were recumbent, and poised on their own base, as in the case of the immense ovals, which, in Cornwall, are called LOGAN, rocking or bowing stones. These prodigious stones the Druids had the art to persuade their infatuated disciples were inspired with the spirit of the indwelling deity, and to this awful test they brought the supposed criminal, over whose head the

sword of justice was suspended, and the descent of which was alone de-
layed, till the animated mass, as he approached to touch it, by its tremu-
lous motion declared him guilty.[8]

Pierre under the spell of the primitive Isabel sees an anthropomorphic
natural world, ironically endows a stone with divinity, and submits
himself to the test imposed by Druid priests on "their infatuated disciples" among "a barbarous people":

But never had he been fearless enough—or rather fool-hardy enough, it
may be, to crawl on the ground beneath the vacancy of the higher end;
that spot first menaced by the Terror Stone should it ever really topple.

Yet now advancing steadily, and as if by some interior predetermina-
tion, and eyeing the mass unfalteringly; he then threw himself prone upon
the wood's last year's leaves, and slid himself straight into the horrible
interspace, and lay there as dead. He spoke not, for speechless thoughts
were in him. These gave place at last to things less and less unspeakable;
till at last, from beneath the very brow of the beetlings and the menacings
of the Terror Stone came the audible words of Pierre:—
    "If the miseries of the undisclosable things in me, shall ever unhorse
me from my manhood's seat; if to vow all Virtue's and all Truth's, be but
to make a trembling, distrusted slave of me; if Life is to prove a burden
I can not bear without ignominious cringings; if indeed our actions are
all fore-ordained, and we are Russian serfs to Fate; if invisible devils do
titter at us when we most nobly strive; if Life be a cheating dream, and
virtue as unmeaning and unsequeled with any blessing as the midnight
mirth of wine; if by sacrificing myself for Duty's sake, my own mother
re-sacrifices me; if Duty's self be but a bugbear, and all things are allow-
able and unpunishable to man;—then do thou, Mute Massiveness, fall on
me! Ages thou hast waited; and if these things be thus, then wait no
more; for whom better canst thou crush than him who now lies here
invoking thee?"   (Pp. 157–58)

Pierre's attempt to restore a pure moral religion first pushes him into
a primitive ritual under a pagan stone. This action is later comically
paralleled by the Apostles' efforts to achieve "a spiritually-minded and
pure archetypical faith," efforts which daily begin with the grotesque
rituals of the flesh-brush. But Pierre's new religion is ultimately more
transcendental than the Apostles'. Isabel's mysterious influence leads

Pierre into a primitive worship, the tragic sacrifice of himself, and his own ironic deification in that sacrifice.

Pierre's mother, Pierre himself, the narrator, Lucy, and Isabel all continually refer to Pierre as some kind of divine being. Pierre's mother sees in him an embodiment of both Orpheus and Pluto. Pierre at various times conceives of himself as a Titan and a demigod, and he calls himself a "god." The narrator calls Pierre "god-like," a "demi-god," and a "fair god," and he also sets up this curious definition of Pierre's divinity:

So the country was a glorious benediction to young Pierre; we shall see if that blessing pass from him as did the divine blessing from the Hebrews; we shall yet see again, I say, whether Fate hath not just a little bit of a word or two to say in this world; we shall see whether this wee little bit scrap of latinity be very far out of the way—*Nemo contra Deum nisi Deus ipse.* (P. 14)

Pierre's cumulative self-destruction fully realizes the hinted prophecy: "Himself was too much for himself." Lucy's view of Pierre's divinity, the view of the marble girl who embodies a Christian albeit ambiguous saint, is at least glorifying. Isabel's view, the view of a primitive, establishes the fact of his divinity.

As mentioned in the first chapter, the eighteenth-century notion of a distinctly primitive mind and the eighteenth-century faith in Common Sense as the true divine revelation met in Romanticism. The child, the peasant, the savage, and the madman, being primitives and thus having more of common than of uncommon sense, became the true repositories of Truth, and their words in Romantic literature are very often oracular. Pip, the true oracle of *Moby-Dick,* is the perfect example—at once a child, a Negro, and a lunatic. In *Pierre,* this Romantic convention is widespread, but often ambiguous. The most simple-minded characters speak the truest words, but they are often unaware of what they are talking about: the half-deaf old book-stall man mistakes Pierre's inquiry about the "Chronometrics" for one about the "chronic-rheumatics" and answers, "Never catch 'em!— now's the time, while you're young!—never catch 'em!" Charlie Millthorpe, "gayly laughing" as he disposes of a porter, chuckles "the whole world's a trick"; the turnkey, admitting two visitors at once to the cell in which Pierre, Lucy, and Isabel are dying, pronounces the oracular judgment: "Kill 'em both with one stone, then."

But these characters are only comic foils for Isabel, who thoroughly comprehends what she primitively perceives. And this is why the last speech of the book is perhaps Isabel's and perhaps a stone wall's, why Isabel is at this point identified with the wall, with time, and with Nature, and why this last speech is oracular:

"All's o'er, and ye know him not!" came gasping from the wall; and from the fingers of Isabel dropped an empty vial—as it had been a run-out sand-glass—and shivered upon the floor; and her whole form sloped side-ways, and she fell upon Pierre's heart, and her long hair ran over him, and arbored him in ebon vines.

This ambiguity is perhaps the strangest of all. Earlier, the narrator said that it was "as absurd" to say that a man had got "a Voice out of Silence" as to say that one could get "water out of a stone." The stone wall which now may be speaking also has "stone cheeks" which are "trickling."

The gasp from the wall suggests that the stone-like, time-like, vine-like Isabel has received an exclusive revelation of Pierre. Isabel receives, in fact, two kinds of special revelation: her primitive under-standing reveals unseen realities; Pierre reveals himself to her in secret acts. Only Isabel, therefore, knows Pierre. Earlier, after calling Pierre's love "heavenly" and wondering at his divineness, Isabel defines Pierre: "Thou art a visible token, Pierre, of the invisible angel-hoods. . . . The gospel of thy acts goes very far, my brother. Were all men like to thee, then were there no men at all,—mankind extinct in seraphim!" When she tells him "thou art already sainted," Pierre becomes not only an "enthusiast"—literally, one possessed by a god—who is possessed by a "heaven-begotten Christ," but even a kind of Christ. He symbolizes this by making a sacrament of the bread and wine offered by Isabel: "I do dare to call this the real sacrament of the supper.—Eat with me."

What has been called Pierre's "habit of identifying his father with his God"[9] assumes, after the sacrament, almost explicit significance:

Such, oh, *thou son of man*! are the perils and the miseries thou callest down on thee, when, even in a virtuous cause, thou steppest aside from those arbitrary lines of conduct, by which the common world, however base and dastardly, surrounds thee for thy worldly good. (P. 207) [Italics mine.]

As the "son of man," Pierre sees himself as the sacrificial victim to his "father's fair fame":

Unrecallably dead and gone from out the living world, again returned to utter helplessness, so far as this world went; his perished father seemed to appeal to the dutifulness and mercifulness of Pierre, in terms far more moving than though the accents proceeded from his mortal mouth. And what though not through the sin of Pierre, but through his father's sin, that father's fair fame now lay at the mercy of the son, and could only be kept inviolate by the son's free sacrifice of all earthly felicity;—what if this were so? (P. 208)

If we take Pierre's "father" in this passage to be merely his earthly father, Pierre's predicament is merely foolishness and the rhetoric used to describe it is absurd. But if Melville believed that Christ was in the same predicament as Pierre and that Christ formed the same resolve as Pierre, then the absurdity of the passage becomes almost entirely a matter of opinion. For it is possible to consider the history of Christ what Pierre considers his future—a "pious imposture" which keeps from the world a knowledge of his "father's" imperfections.

Pierre can find no way "to hold his father's fair fame inviolate" "without a most singular act of pious imposture, which he thought all heaven would justify in him, since he himself was to be the grand self-renouncing victim." The incidental agonies which he must inflict "then seemed to him part of the unavoidable vast price of his enthusiastic virtue; and, thus minded, rather would he privately pain his living mother with a wound that might be curable, than cast world-wide and irremediable dishonor—so it seemed to him—upon his departed father." If Pierre is not thinking of his father as God, then this is nonsense. For in what sense could the dishonor of Pierre's earthly father be "world-wide"? Pierre comes to the realization that his family is destined to offer up "one grand victim at the least," and he chooses to be the sacrifice. Immediately upon making this resolution, he is compared to the Greek gods:

We think we are not human; we become as immortal bachelors and gods; but again, like the Greek gods themselves, prone we descend to earth; glad to be uxorious once more; glad to hide these god-like heads within the bosoms made of too-seducing clay. (P. 212)

Pierre was now this vulnerable god . . . Though in some things he had unjuggled himself . . . he was at bottom still a juggler. (P. 213)

Pierre's vulnerability, his temptation to juggle, the tempting bosom made of too-seducing clay is not, as some critics would have us think, Isabel. It is Lucy. Although she is most consistently defined in ethereal and heavenly terms, she is more earthly now than Pierre, the vulnerable god who proposes a pious imposture as a means of sacrificing himself to keep the name of his father inviolate to the world. Thus there is only one question left for Pierre: "Then, for the time, all minor things were whelmed in him; his mother, Isabel, the whole wide world; and one only thing remained to him;—this all-including query—Lucy or God?" These two alternatives exclude all such "minor things" as his mother, the world, and Isabel. Pierre at least thinks he chooses one of the alternatives. He at least thinks he chooses God.

Pierre comes to his resolution just subsequent to Isabel's revelation of himself to himself and their sacramental supper. When he next returns to Isabel he reveals his resolution to her, and only to her. He has chosen to be Christ, and Isabel's final special knowledge is, at least in part, a knowledge of this choice.

"Thou hintest of deceiving one for one's good. Now supposing, sweet Isabel, that in no case would I affirmatively deceive thee;—in no case whatever;—wouldst thou then be willing for thee and me to piously deceive others, for both their and our united good?" (P. 222)

"Thou hast not yet answered a question I put to thee but just now. Bethink thee, Isabel. The deceiving of others by thee and me, in a thing wholly pertaining to ourselves, for their and our united good. Wouldst thou?" (P. 223)

Only one other character in *Pierre* thinks of the grand godly sacrifice, and he recommends the role to Pierre: "Pierre, hark in your ears;—it's my opinion the world is all wrong. Hist, I say—an entire mistake. Society demands an Avatar,—a Curtius, my boy! to leap into the fiery gulf, and by perishing himself, save the whole empire of men!" The ironies of Millthorpe's silliness are manifold. Not the least of these is that the divine avatar, here as in *Mardi,* is not what saves men. Indeed, in the world of *Pierre,* Pierre's metamorphosis into a divine avatar leads all who are related to him into destruction and damnation. In *Mardi,* when Christ was considered only as the last avatar, he could not be meaningfully distinguished from any other avatar, and his church could not be meaningfully distinguished from any other institutionalized monstrosity. Only those who followed the divine reason of Christ could dwell in the land of serenity. Theirs was the only true church of Christ, the church of his Reason. In *Pierre* this church is found to be a chronometric impossibility which leads to unique sins and follies, which petrifies the follower of its leader.

Pierre's name, considered in this context, is of the utmost significance. For Pierre's namesake received directly Christ's equivocal definition of the meaning of his name: "thou art Peter, and upon this rock I will build my church; and the gates of hell shall not prevail against it" (Matt. 16 : 18). Pierre does not choose the meaning of this equivoque upon which the priests of *Mardi* built the monstrous establishment of Maramma:

The imperishable monument of his Holy Catholic Church; the imperishable record of his Holy Bible; the imperishable intuition of the innate truth of Christianity;—these were the indestructible anchors which still held the priest to his firm Faith's rock, when the sudden storm raised by the Evil One assailed him. But Pierre—where could *he* find the Church, the monument, the Bible, which unequivocally said to him—"Go on; thou art in the Right; I endorse thee all over; go on." (P. 240)

Pierre chooses instead the meaning chosen by the dwellers on Serenia. But nevertheless he comes to share the fate of Taji, who spurned Serenia. Indeed, Pierre's words contain loud echoes of Taji's words: " 'Lo! I leave corpses wherever I go!' groaned Pierre to himself . . .

'Corpses behind me, and the last sin before, how then can my conduct be right?'" And, as we have seen, the gates of hell do quite literally prevail against Pierre. The "illustrative light" which his "sun-like glories of god-like truth and virtue" shall cast "upon the sapphire throne of God" proves ambiguous indeed.

Pierre's life does not closely parallel the mythical parts of the savior gods' lives. Angels do not announce his birth; he performs no miracles in childhood; he does not heal the sick or raise the dead; he does not bruise the head of the serpent or dragon; he does not rise from the dead. But his life does closely parallel those parts of the saviors' lives which are usually not disputed. He first becomes dissatisfied with his "hereditary persuasions"; he next shows the ethical absurdities of the old religion by disputing with its priesthood; he finally tries to "gospelize the world anew, and show them deeper secrets than the Apocalypse." Yet Pierre's nonmythic role becomes in the end doubly mythical.

Pierre finds that the stone Enceladus, which is physically not even a statue but only a rock randomly cast up and cast down, which is in identity only the fabulous creation of a people distant in time and place, becomes his central fact. In trying to follow, to imitate, and to become Christ, he succeeds only in becoming Enceladus, a stone borne down by the earth into a granite hell. In *Pierre,* Christ's call to follow him becomes ambiguously ironic, the efforts of a man to obey the call become tragic, and a rock is ambiguously offered as the symbol of the divine absolutist.

CHAPTER 5

WORLDLY SAFETY
AND OTHER-WORLDLY SAVIORS

BARTLEBY: THE ASCETIC'S ADVENT

There are essentially three ethics available to man—action in and of the world, action in the world for other-worldly reasons, and non-action, that is, withdrawal from the world. We might call the extreme of the first the ethic of Wall Street, the extreme of the second the ethic of Christ, and the extreme of the third the ethic of the Eastern monk. Wall Street's ethic seeks the world as an end; Christ's ethic prescribes certain behavior in this world to get to a better world; the Eastern monk's ethic seeks to escape all worlds. *Bartleby* is a world in which these three ethics directly confront one another.

To read *Bartleby* well, we must first realize that we can never know who or what Bartleby is, but that we are continually asked to guess who or what he might be. We must see that he may be anything from a mere bit of human flotsam to a conscious and forceful rejecter of the world to an incarnation of God. When we see the first possibility we realize the full pathos of the story; when we see the last possibility we realize that the story is a grotesque joke and a parabolic tragedy.

But of course the possibility that Bartleby may be the very least of men does not necessarily contradict the possibility that Bartleby may be an embodiment of God. For as Christ explains in Matthew 25, the least of men (particularly when he appears as a stranger) is the physical representative and representation of Christ. Upon this identification depend the Christian ethic, the next world to which Christ sends every man, and the central meanings of *Bartleby*:

34 Then shall the King say unto them on his right hand, Come, ye blessed of my Father, inherit the kingdom prepared for you from the foundation of the world:

35 For I was ahungered, and ye gave me meat: I was thirsty, and ye gave me drink: I was a stranger, and ye took me in:

36 Naked, and ye clothed me: I was sick, and ye visited me: I was in prison, and ye came unto me.

37 Then shall the righteous answer him, saying, Lord, when saw we thee ahungered, and fed thee? or thirsty, and gave thee drink?

38 When saw we thee a stranger, and took thee in? or naked, and clothed thee?

39 Or when saw we thee sick, or in prison, and came unto thee?

40 And the King shall answer and say unto them, Verily I say unto you, Inasmuch as ye have done it unto one of the least of these my brethren, ye have done it unto me.

41 Then shall he say also unto them on the left hand, Depart from me, ye cursed, into everlasting fire, prepared for the devil and his angels:

42 For I was ahungered, and ye gave me no meat: I was thirsty, and ye gave me no drink:

43 I was a stranger, and ye took me not in: naked, and ye clothed me not: sick, and in prison, and ye visited me not.

44 Then shall they also answer him, saying, Lord, when saw we thee ahungered, or athirst, or a stranger, or naked, or sick, or in prison, and did not minister unto thee?

45 Then shall he answer them, saying, Verily I say unto you, Inasmuch as ye did it not to one of the least of these, ye did it not to me.

Christ is here saying that the individual comes to God and attains his salvation when he shows complete charity to a stranger, and he rejects God and calls for his damnation whenever he refuses complete charity to *one* stranger, even "the least of these." As the story of Bartleby unfolds, it becomes increasingly apparent that it is in part a testing of this message of Christ. The narrator's soul depends from his actions toward Bartleby, a mysterious, poor, lonely, sick stranger who ends his life in prison. Can the narrator, the man of our world, act in terms of Christ's ethics? The answer is yes and no. The narrator fulfills the letter of Christ's injunction point by point: he offers money to the stranger so that he may eat and drink; he takes him in, finally offering him not only his office but also his home; when he sees that he is sick, he attempts to minister to him; he, alone of all mankind, visits and befriends the stranger in prison. But he hardly fulfills the spirit of Christ's message: his money is carefully doled out; he tries to evict the stranger, offers his home only after betraying him, and then immediately flees from him in the time of his greatest need; it is his demands on the stranger which have made him sick; he visits the stranger in prison only once while he is alive, thus leaving him alone for several days before and after his visit, thus leaving him to die entirely alone. At the heart of both the tragedy and the comedy lies the narrator's view of the drama, a view which sees all but all in the wrong terms: "To befriend Bartleby; to humor him in his strange wilfulness, will cost me little or nothing, while I lay up in my soul what will eventually prove a sweet morsel for my conscience."[1]

According to Christ's words in Matthew 25, it would make no difference to the narrator's salvation whether Bartleby is the Saviour incarnate or merely the least of his brethren. And certainly reading *Bartleby* with Matthew 25 in mind defines the central issues, no matter who Bartleby is. But the story repeatedly suggests that Bartleby may not be merely the least of Christ's brethren but may in fact be the Saviour himself. Again I wish to emphasize that we are certainly not justified in simply taking Bartleby to be an incarnation or reincarnation of Christ (except in the terms of Matthew 25). But if we do not entertain the possibility that Bartleby is Christ, although we still see most of the tragedy, we miss a great deal of the comedy. Bartleby's story is the story of the advent, the betrayal, and torment of a mysterious and innocent being; this is a tragic story no matter who the being is. These events carefully and pointedly re-enact the story of Christ, and there is nothing funny about this. Nor is there anything inherently funny about the fact that for all we know Bartleby may be God incarnate. The central joke of the story is that although the narrator comes close to seeing this possibility without ever seeing what he sees, his language continually recognizes and defines the possibility that Bartleby may be Christ. The narrator's own words define his own tragedy as cosmic and comic.

The narrator tells us that he is an "eminently *safe* man," an "unambitious" lawyer who, "in the cool tranquillity of a snug retreat," does "a snug business among rich men's bonds and mortgages and title-deeds." He tells of receiving the "good old office" of "Master in Chancery," which greatly enlarges his business. This is the time which he significantly labels "the period just preceding the advent of Bartleby." After mentioning this office only once, he digresses for several pages. When he next mentions it, he calls it simply—and significantly—"the master's office." This joke introduces the pointedly ambiguous description of the advent of Bartleby:

> Now my original business . . . was considerably increased by receiving the master's office. There was now great work for scriveners. Not only must I push the clerks already with me, but I must have additional help.
> In answer to my advertisement, a motionless young man one morning stood upon my office threshold, the door being open, for it was summer. I can see that figure now—pallidly neat, pitiably respectable, incurably forlorn! It was Bartleby. (P. 23)

So Bartleby is a being who answers the narrator's call for "additional help" at a time of "great work for scriveners." The narrator responds by placing "this quiet man within easy call, in case any trifling thing was to be done."

Bartleby at first does an "extraordinary" amount of work, but, "on the third day," begins to answer "I would prefer not to" to the narrator's petty orders. Who is this being? The narrator can only tell us that "Bartleby was one of those beings of whom nothing is ascertainable, except from the original sources, and, in his case, those are very small."

As Bartleby, by merely standing, sitting, and lying still, step by step withdraws from the world, the narrator follows him, leaving behind, bit by bit, his worldly values. Slowly the narrator's compassion for Bartleby and his sense of brotherhood with him emerge, and as they emerge we see more and more clearly that the drama involves the salvation of both Bartleby—the poor, lonely stranger—and the narrator—the "safe" man who in many ways represents our world. As this drama becomes clear, the narrator's language becomes more and more grotesquely ironic.

At the beginning of his withdrawal, Bartleby is only saved from being "violently dismissed" because the narrator cannot find "anything ordinarily human about him." In the next stage of his withdrawal, Bartleby stands at the entrance of his "hermitage" and "mildly" asks "What is wanted?" when the narrator "hurriedly" demands that he proofread the copies, Bartleby answers that he "would prefer not to," and the narrator tells us that "for a few moments I was turned into a pillar of salt."

The narrator, as boss of the office, plays god.[2] What he does not realize, but what his language makes clear, is that he may be playing this role with God himself. The narrator tells us that he "again advanced towards Bartleby" because "I felt additional incentives tempting me to my fate." "Sometimes, to be sure, I could not, for the very soul of me," he ironically admits, "avoid falling into sudden spasmodic passions with him."

The narrator even discovers "something superstitious knocking at my heart, and forbidding me to carry out my purpose . . . if I dared to breathe one bitter word against this forlornest of mankind." At this point we need hardly remember Matthew 25 or that Melville referred to Christ as the Man of Sorrows to see why the narrator should look to his salvation instead of his safety. But when the narrator surmises that Bartleby has "nothing else earthly to do," he blandly asks him to carry some letters to the post office.

The narrator then realizes that Bartleby is "absolutely alone in the universe," but his response to this cosmic loneliness is to tell Bartleby that "in six days' time he must unconditionally leave the office." On the appointed day, the narrator tries to dismiss Bartleby with words that become grotesquely ludicrous if they are seen as an inversion of the true roles of these two beings: "If, hereafter, in your new place of abode, I can be of any service to you, do not fail to advise me by letter." Perhaps the narrator has already received in very clear letters all the advice he needs, a description of what service Bartleby might be to him in his new place of abode, and what his own place of abode will be if he rejects the advice and denies the man. (But perhaps, as the last few paragraphs of the story hint, Matthew 25 and its entire context is now the Dead Letter Office.)

Shortly after saying these words, the narrator discovers that this very day is "an election day." Still, "a sudden passion"—the very thing which the narrator's words had recognized as endangering his "very soul"—makes him demand that Bartleby leave him. The scrivener gently replies, "I would prefer *not* to quit you." The narrator reminds Bartleby ironically that he has no "earthly right" to stay; Bartleby "answered nothing" and "silently retired into his hermitage."

This infuriates the narrator; as he says, the "old Adam of resentment rose in me and tempted me concerning Bartleby." But on this election day the narrator saves himself for the time being "simply by recalling the divine injunction: 'A new commandment give I unto you, that ye love one another.'" "Yes," he says, "this it was that saved me." But the narrator fails to grasp what he has seen; he defines this love "as a vastly wise and prudent principle"; "mere self-interest" becomes his most clearly perceived motive to "charity."

After some days pass in which he has had a chance to consult "Edwards on the Will" and "Priestley on Necessity," the narrator has his most complete revelation of his own drama:

Gradually I slid into the persuasion that these troubles of mine, touching the scrivener, had been all predestinated from eternity, and Bartleby was billeted upon me for some mysterious purpose of an all-wise Providence, which it was not for a mere mortal like me to fathom. Yes, Bartleby, stay there behind your screen, thought I; I shall persecute you no more; you are harmless and noiseless as any of these old chairs; in short, I never feel so private as when I know you are here. At last I see it, I feel it; I penetrate to the predestinated purpose of my life. I am content. Others may have loftier parts to enact; but my mission in this world, Bartleby, is to furnish you with office-room for such period as you may see fit to remain.

(P. 44)

According to Christ's own words in Matthew 25, the narrator is absolutely right; he has finally seen his mission in the world.

But the narrator's resolution of his dilemma is short-lived. It withers quickly under the "uncharitable remarks obtruded upon" him by his "professional friends." He confesses that the whispers of his professional acquaintance "worried me very much." When he then thinks of the possibility of Bartleby's "denying my authority," outliving him, and claiming "possession of my office by right of his perpetual occupancy," the narrator resolves to "forever rid me of this intolerable incubus." Even then, after he informs Bartleby that he must leave, and after Bartleby takes "three days to meditate upon it," he learns that Bartleby "still preferred to abide with" him, that "he prefers to cling to" him. This sets the stage for the narrator's denial of Bartleby, for he decides that "since he will not quit me, I must quit him."

To hear the full significance of his three denials of Bartleby, we must hear the loud echoes of Peter's three denials of Christ. Matthew 26:

> 70 But he denied before them all, saying, I know not what thou sayest.
> 72 And again he denied with an oath, I do not know the man.
> 74 Then began he to curse and to swear, saying, I know not the man.

Even closer are Peter's words in Mark 14:71: "I know not this man of whom ye speak."

The first denial:

> "Then, sir," said the stranger, who proved a lawyer, "you are responsible for the man you left there." . . .
> "I am very sorry, sir," said I, with assumed tranquillity, but an inward tremor, "but, really, the man you allude to is nothing to me." (P. 47)

The second denial:

> "In mercy's name, who is he?"
> "I certainly cannot inform you. I know nothing about him." (P. 47)

The third denial:

> In vain I persisted that Bartleby was nothing to me—no more than to any one else. (P. 48)

After the narrator's three denials of Bartleby, he belatedly makes his most charitable gesture toward him, offering, "in the kindest tone I could assume under such exciting circumstances," to permit him to come to his home. But Bartleby answers, "No: at present I would prefer not to make any change at all." The narrator leaves; the new landlord has the police remove Bartleby to the Tombs. The narrator then learns of Bartleby's procession to his Golgotha:

As I afterwards learned, the poor scrivener, when told that he must be conducted to the Tombs, offered not the slightest obstacle, but, in his pale, unmoving way, silently acquiesced.

Some of the compassionate and curious bystanders joined the party; and headed by one of the constables arm in arm with Bartleby, the silent procession filed its way through all the noise, and heat, and joy of the roaring thoroughfares at noon.   (Pp. 50–51)

"Quite serene and harmless in all his ways," Bartleby is, like Christ, "numbered with the transgressors" (Mark 15:28). The world places him in prison where, amidst "murderers and thieves," he completes his withdrawal from the world.

When the narrator more or less meets the last condition laid down in Matthew 25—visiting the stranger in prison—all his charity is shown to be too little and too late. Before Bartleby leaves the world he says to the narrator, "I know you," and adds, without looking at him, "and I want nothing to say to you." At this point we can hear new ironies in the narrator's attempt to dismiss Bartleby: "If, hereafter, in your new place of abode, I can be of any service to you, do not fail to advise me by letter." Thus, when the narrator retells the rumor of Bartleby's having worked in the Dead Letter Office, he describes in part himself, in part Bartleby, and in part the scriptural letters which spell the hope of salvation. "The master's office" has become the Dead Letter Office.

Dead letters! does it not sound like dead men? . . . pardon for those who died despairing; hope for those who died unhoping; good tidings for those who died stifled by unrelieved calamities. On errands of life, these letters speed to death.

Ah, Bartleby! Ah, humanity!   (P. 54)

But all this is only half the story. For if the narrator is weighed and found wanting, what then of Bartleby himself? At least the narrator at times can show compassion, sympathy, and charity. Indeed, he at times much more than transcends the worldly ethics with which he starts and to which he tends to backslide. (One must bear in mind while evaluating the narrator's behavior that he is continually defending himself from two possible accusations—that he is too hard-hearted and that he is too soft-hearted.) Although he begins by strictly following horological time, he conforms more and more closely to chronometrical time. And he is after all certainly the most charitable character in the story. What time does Bartleby follow, and, finally, how charitable is he? Or is it possible to account for the actions of a being who is almost by definition enigmatic?

Because "Bartleby was one of those beings of whom nothing is ascertainable, except from the original sources, and, in his case, those are very small," he is almost as difficult to judge as to identify. But whether he is finally a god incarnate as a man or only a man playing the role of a crucified god, his behavior fits a pattern which implies an ethic.

If, as the Plotinus Plinlimmon pamphlet asserts in *Pierre,* chronometrical time is an impossibility for man, if man is left with the choice in the world between following chronometrical time and being destroyed or following horological time and being contemptible, if, then, no action in the world can be at the same time safe and worthy of salvation, what is there left for man to do? One answer is that man can try to live out of the world, can withdraw from the world altogether. This is the answer which forms the counterpoint with worldly ethics in both *Bartleby* and *Benito Cereno,* each of which dramatizes a particular and different kind of monasticism.

Bartleby's monkish withdrawal from the world has been described by Saburo Yamaya and Walter Sutton as essentially Buddhistic in nature. Yamaya shows the connections between Buddhist Quietism and the stone imagery of both *Pierre* and *Bartleby,* citing as one of Melville's sources this passage from Bayle's *Dictionary*:

The great lords and the most illustrious persons suffered themselves to be so infatuated with the [Buddhist] Quietism, that they believed insensibility to be the way to perfection and beatitude and that the nearer a man came to the nature of a block or *a stone,* the greater progress he made, the more he was like the first principle, into which he was to return.[3]

Sutton quite accurately perceives (apparently without reference to Yamaya) that Bartleby, in achieving "the complete withdrawal of the hunger artist," has attained what "in Buddhist terms . . . is Nir-

vana, extinction, or nothingness,"[4] and he suggests that at this point
in his life Melville was unconsciously approaching Buddhism. But
Melville was probably quite aware that Bartleby's behavior conforms
very closely to a kind of Oriental asceticism which Thomas Maurice
had spent about fifty pages describing.

The Oriental ascetic who most closely resembles Bartleby is the
Saniassi, a Hindu rather than a Buddhist. It seems probable that once
again Maurice's *Indian Antiquities* served as a direct source for Melville's fiction. Maurice describes in detail the systematic withdrawal
from the world practiced by the Saniassi, and many details have a
surprising—and grotesquely humorous—correspondence to the systematic withdrawal from the world practiced by Bartleby. For instance, in the fifth stage the Saniassi "eats only one particular kind of
food during the day and night, but as often as he pleases."[5] Bartleby
"lives, then, on ginger-nuts . . . never eats a dinner, properly speaking; he must be a vegetarian, then, but no; he never eats even vege-
tables, he eats nothing but ginger-nuts." "During the last three days,"
the Saniassi "neither eats nor drinks."[6] During Bartleby's last few
days, he prefers not to eat.

The fact that external details of Bartleby's withdrawal closely
parallel some of the external details of the Saniassi's withdrawal is
not nearly so significant as this fact: Bartleby's behavior seems to be
the very essence of Maurice's description of the Saniassi's behavior.
In fact, Maurice's general description and judgment of the Saniassi
often seems to be a precise description and judgment of Bartleby.

Most striking are the very things which Maurice claims are peculiar to the Saniassi. He observes that one of the principal ways in
which the Saniassi is distinguished from the Yogi is "by the calm,
the silent, dignity with which he suffers the series of complicated evils
through which he is ordained to toil."[7] The Saniassi "can only be fed
by the charity of others"; "he must himself make no exertion, nor feel
any solicitude for existence upon this contaminated orb."[8] The
Saniassis' design "is to detach their thoughts from all concern about
sublunary objects; to be indifferent to hunger and thirst; to be insensible to shame and reproach."[9]

Perhaps most important to the judgment of Bartleby is the Sani-assis' "incessant efforts . . . to stifle every ebullition of human passion, and live upon earth as if they were already, and in reality, disembodied."[10] This may at once help account for Bartleby's appearing as a "ghost" or as "cadaverous" to the narrator and explain what ethical time he follows, for "it is the boast of the Saniassi to sacrifice every human feeling and passion at the shrine of devotion."[11] Like Bartleby, the Saniassi "is no more to be soothed by the suggestions of *adulation* in its most pleasing form, than he is to be terrified by the loudest clamours of *reproach* . . . By long habits of indifference, he becomes inanimate as a piece of wood or stone; and, though he mechanically respires the vital air, he is to all the purposes of active life *defunct*."[12]

Bartleby is, then, in part the story of a man of the world who receives "the master's office"; who advertises for help; who is thereupon visited by a strange being who in an "extraordinary" way at first does all that is asked of him; who treats this strange being with contempt; who nevertheless receives from this being what seems to be his purpose in life; who betrays this being; and who watches and describes the systematic withdrawal of this being. It is also in part the story of this strange being, who replays much of the role of Christ while behaving like an Hindu ascetic, and who ends by extinguishing himself and making dead letters of the scripture which describes his prototype. As we shall see in *The Confidence-Man,* this role and this extinguishment are a foreshadowing of the apocalypse.

BENITO CERENO: THE ASCETIC'S AGONY

Bartleby ends in a Hindu-like monastic extinction; Benito Cereno's end is extinction in a Catholic monastery. This end is the one change which Melville made in the basic plot of his source, Amasa Delano's *Narrative of Voyages and Travels.* Shortly after introducing Cereno, Melville obscurely and obliquely hints that his end will be monastic retirement, soon followed by death: "His manner upon such occasions was, in its degree, not unlike that which might be supposed to have been his imperial countryman's, Charles V., just previous to the anchoritish retirement of that monarch from the throne." This hint is doubly significant, for it leads to a source in many ways more important than Delano's *Voyages*—William Stirling's *The Cloister Life of the Emperor Charles the Fifth*.

Benito Cereno appeared first in *Putnam's Monthly Magazine* in late 1855. In January of the same year, the *Edinburgh Review* had apologized for quoting from Stirling's *Cloister Life of the Emperor Charles the Fifth*: "We are not sure whether we ought to quote from a book so well known as that of Mr. Stirling."[13] There was some reason to apologize. Stirling's work had first appeared as two articles, entitled "The Cloister Life of the Emperor Charles V," in *Fraser's Magazine* of April and May, 1851. The following year the articles were expanded into a book, which by 1853 had gone into its third edition. The articles themselves were several times reprinted in other magazines, and numerous popular and recondite periodicals continually noticed, reviewed, summarized, and quoted from the book throughout 1853 and 1854.

At the same time many of the same periodicals were noticing, reviewing, summarizing, and quoting from Melville's work. Melville, busily reading his critics, must have read again of Charles V, to whom he had made five detailed references in *Mardi* and *White-Jacket*. In "I and My Chimney," also submitted to *Putnam's* in 1855, the narrator tries to avoid what he likens to the Emperor's abdication and monastic retirement. *Benito Cereno* seems to assume that the readers of *Putnam's* in 1855 were familiar with Stirling's *Cloister Life of Charles*.

Many of the phrases Melville uses to describe Cereno are almost identical to phrases Stirling uses to describe Charles V; many details of Cereno's physical and social environment have precise correspondents in the environment of Charles; almost every trait of Cereno is a trait of Charles. Benito Cereno is, in more than one sense, the ghost of Charles V—he is both his supernatural ghost and his symbolic ghost. Re-enacting Charles's abdication of the Holy Roman Empire and surrender of worldly power, he finally becomes, like Charles himself, the symbolic ghost of all power. The meanings of this strange relationship will become clearer as we examine the evidence that defines it.

What Melville calls "the anchoritish retirement" of Charles V was passed in the mountains of Spain; Benito Cereno's ship seems to be a monastery in the mountains of Spain:

> Upon gaining a less remote view, the ship . . . appeared like a white-washed monastery after a thunder-storm, seen perched upon some dun cliff among the Pyrenees. But it was no purely fanciful resemblance which now, for a moment, almost led Captain Delano to think that nothing less than a ship-load of monks was before him. Peering over the bulwarks were what really seemed, in the hazy distance, throngs of dark cowls; while, fitfully revealed through the open port-holes, other dark moving figures were dimly descried, as of Black Friars pacing the cloisters. (P. 57)

The Black Friars were the Dominicans, who, unbridled by Charles V, became the principal sponsors of the Inquisition. Melville's Black Friars run a ship which he has rechristened the *San Dominick,* patron saint of the Dominican order. (In Delano's narrative the ship's name is *Tryal*.) The captain of this monastic ship resembles "some hypochondriac abbot" and he lives in monastic quarters. The description of his cuddy relates almost every object in it to either monasticism or the Inquisition: the table holds a "thumbed missal"; the bulkhead bears a "meagre crucifix"; cutlasses, a harpoon, and old rigging lie "like a heap of poor friars' girdles"; the settees are as "uncomfortable to look at as inquisitors' racks"; the washstand looks like a "font."[14] Not only does Cereno's monastic cuddy closely resemble Charles V's monastic chambers (even the "large, misshapen arm chair" has an exact counterpart in a large, misshapen arm chair of much interest to all the Emperor's chroniclers), but the exteriors of their quarters are even more curiously similar.

Melville reproduces the physical surroundings of Charles's chambers with an incredible exactitude and a strange effect. The Emperor lived in the second story of a building attached to the church. On the right side (direction defined as usual by the church) were Charles's bedroom and state cabinet, which opened onto a "gallery" that was cut off from below.[15] As Captain Delano stands on "the starboard quarter-gallery" of the *San Dominick,* a retreat "cut off from the deck," onto which formerly opened "the state-cabin door," he is aware of the presence of royal ghosts:

As his foot pressed the half-damp, half-dry sea mosses matting the place, and a chance *phantom* cats-paw—an islet of breeze, *unheralded, unfollowed* [italics mine]—as this ghostly cats-paw came fanning his cheek; as his glance fell upon the row of small, round dead-lights—all closed like coppered eyes of the coffined—and the state-cabin door, once connecting with the gallery, even as the dead-lights had once looked out upon it, but now calked fast like a sarcophagus lid; and to a purple-black tarred-over panel, threshold, and post; and he bethought him of the time, when that state-cabin and this state-balcony had heard the voices of the Spanish king's officers . . . (P. 88)

The imperial monastic gallery overlooked a grand garden composed of "parterres" on "terraces" and a formal "alley of cypress."[16] Delano fancies that he sees just such a garden: "He leaned against the carved balustrade, again looking off toward his boat; but found his eye falling upon the ribbon grass, trailing along the ship's water-line, straight as a border of green box; and parterres of sea-weed, broad ovals and crescents, floating nigh and far, with what seemed long formal alleys between, crossing the terraces of swells, and sweeping round as if leading to the grottoes below." Beyond Charles's garden was a forest, from which the local poachers descended.[17] Delano sees from the balcony a Spanish sailor beckoning from "groves of rigging"; the sailor "as if alarmed by some advancing step along the deck within, vanished into the recesses of the hempen forest, like a poacher." Delano seems to feel the desolation, loneliness, and sense of imprisonment described in the *Cloister Life of Charles*:[18] "Trying to break one charm, he was but becharmed anew. Though upon the wide sea, he seemed in some far inland country; prisoner in some deserted chateau, left to stare at empty grounds, and peer out at vague roads, where never wagon or wayfarer passed."

In the Emperor's garden was a "summer-house,"[19] which, like the other buildings, was later burned. Stirling's book ends with a description of the ruins of the imperial quarters, garden, and church: "The principal cloister was choked with the rubbish of the fallen upper story. . . . Two sides of the smaller and older cloister were still standing, with blackened walls and rotting floors and ceiling."[20] Delano seems to be among these ruins: "And overhanging all was the balustrade by his arm, which, partly stained with pitch and partly embossed with moss, seemed the charred ruin of some summer-house in a grand garden long running to waste." And later, "As with some eagerness he bent forward . . . the balustrade gave way before him like charcoal," causing the fall "of the rotten fragments."

The similarities between Stirling's Charles V and Melville's Captain Cereno are even closer than the similarities between their environments. Charles is "broken in health and spirits";[21] Cereno is "broken in body and mind." Charles, "in the absence of the chief of his household, . . . seems to have fallen in some degree into the hands of the friars";[22] Cereno, in "the absence of those subordinate deck-officers," has fallen into the hands of the "Black Friars." Charles "almost fell into the arms of his attendants";[23] Cereno "fell into the ready arms of his attendant." Stirling describes the abdication ceremony with Charles approaching, "supporting himself on the right with a staff, and leaning with his left hand on the shoulder" of his escort.[24] Captain Cereno approaches his abdication from the ship in the same posture: "the better to support him, the servant, placing his master's hand [left hand, as indicated by the context] on his naked shoulder, and gently holding it there, formed himself into a sort of crutch." Charles and Cereno are each described as exceptionally "punctilious"; they are each shaved at a designated hour of the day. Delano sees in Babo's shaving of Cereno a "play of the barber" and wonders at "the theatrical aspect of Don Benito in his harlequin ensign"; Charles is shaved by "his barber, a malapert of the old comedies."[25] Cereno's barber has supervised the ghastly preparations of Aranda's body and has threatened all the Spaniards' bodies with the same fate; Charles's barber tells the Emperor, "we will take care to bury you with all honours."[26] Charles's body was so tender that when some of the friars shook his hand, "the pain compelled him to withdraw his hand, and say, 'Pray don't, father; it hurts me' ";[27] Delano

wonders about Cereno, "where may one touch him without causing a
shrink." They each relay "commands" to a stream of messengers.
When Charles landed on the Spanish coast on his passage to the monastery, "being worn with suffering and fatigue, he was carried up from
the boat in a chair."[28] As he continued toward the monastery, he was
alternately borne in a litter and carried in the arms of his attendants.
Benito Cereno is "so reduced as to be carried ashore in arms." He
later attends the deposition "in his litter." Charles was "seized with
violent vomitings; and . . . lay motionless, with closed eyes";[29]
Cereno's "cough returned and with increased violence; this subsiding,
with reddened lips and closed eyes." This description of Charles may
have suggested the creation of his supernatural ghost: "He wrapped
his emaciated body in hair-cloth, and flogged it with scourges, which
were afterwards found in his cell, stained with his blood. Restless
and sleepless, he would roam, ghostlike, through the corridors of the
convent."[30] Cereno is called "cadaverous" several times; he is "almost
worn to a skeleton"; "he is like one flayed alive"; he is likened to a
"somnambulist." And he is nothing if not "ghostlike." Delano "began to feel a ghostly dread of Don Benito"; he thinks of "the dark
Spaniard himself, the central hobgoblin of all"; he remarks on "his
usual ghastliness."

The ghostly Benito Cereno captains a ship which is continually
called unreal and enchanted. The *San Dominick* is in fact a ghost
ship, the floating coffin and tomb of the ghost of Charles V. What
Melville calls "a strange craft; a strange history, too, and strange folks
on board" float directly from a funeral procession for Charles:

Its principal feature was a huge galley, large enough for marine service,
placed on a cunningly devised sea, which answered the double purpose
of supporting some isles, emblematic of the Indies, and of concealing the
power which rolled the huge structure along. Faith, Hope, and Charity
were the crew of this enchanted bark.[31]

The sea upon which the *San Dominick* floats also seems devised:
"The sea, though undulated into long roods of swells, seemed fixed,
and was sleeked at the surface like waved lead that has cooled and set

in the smelter's mold"; "the leaden ocean seemed laid out and leaded up." When Delano first boards the ship, he seems to be boarding a ghost ship, an enchanted bark: "The ship seems unreal; these strange costumes, gestures, and faces, but a shadowy tableau just emerged from the deep, which directly must receive back what it gave." The *San Dominick,* that "strange craft" with "enchanted sails" whose bell has a "dreary graveyard toll," is linked at several points to the strange history of Charles's wandering body and coffins.

In a notorious incident, the Emperor performed his own funeral rites before his death, followed his coffin, and perhaps even lay down in it.[32] After his death, his body was guarded by four monks.[33] The *San Dominick* is guarded by the four black oakum-pickers, whose "low, monotonous chant" is likened to a "funeral march." These four are "calkers" who may have some connection with "the state-cabin door . . . now calked fast like a sarcophagus lid." Several years after Charles's death, his body was transferred by Philip II from the monastery to a new coffin in the Escorial. "The repose of the emperor was again broken," when, in 1654, Philip IV removed the body to a new sepulchral chamber.[34] At this time the coffin was opened, and Philip saw the mysteriously preserved body of the Emperor. (The coffin was opened again some months after the publication of *Benito Cereno,* and the body was found to be still in a well-preserved state.[35])

Just before Philip saw death in the person of his forebear, a long sermon was preached on Ezekiel and the valley of dry bones. Just before the first association between death and the *jefe* of *"Seguid vuestro jefe,"* we learn that the *San Dominick*'s "keel seemed laid, her ribs put together, and she launched, from Ezekiel's Valley of Dry Bones":

Rudely painted or chalked, as in a sailor freak, along the forward side of a sort of pedestal below the canvas, was the sentence, *"Seguid vuestro jefe,"* (follow your leader); while upon the tarnished head-boards, near by, appeared, in stately capitals, once gilt, the ship's name, "SAN DOMI-NICK," each letter streakingly corroded with tricklings of copper-spike rust; while, like mourning weeds, dark festoons of sea-grass slimily swept to and fro over the name, with every hearse-like roll of the hull. (P. 58)

Philip IV's rites for Charles are climaxed when he confronts his dead forebear: "It became necessary to remove the previous coverings," and Philip came "face to face with his great ancestor."[36] The climax of *Benito Cereno* is also a confrontation, when his previous coverings are removed, with a dead leader: "But by this time the cable of the San Dominick had been cut; and the fag-end, in lashing out, whipped away the canvas shroud about the beak, suddenly revealing, as the bleached hull swung round towards the open ocean, death for the figure-head, in a human skeleton; chalky comment on the chalked words below, '*Follow your leader.*'"

Stirling's final mention of Charles's first coffin occurs in his concluding description of the monastic ruins: "In a vault beneath, approached by a door of which the key could not be found, I was told that the coffin of chestnut wood, in which the emperor's body had lain for sixteen years, was still kept as a relic."[37] On the *San Dominick*, Captain Delano fancies himself in a "subterranean vault"; later comes that pregnant statement: "If the Deposition have served as the key to fit into the lock of the complications which precede it, then, as a vault whose door has been flung back, the San Dominick's hull lies open today."

The question now is whether we have found a key or a lock, clarification or obscuration of the central meanings of *Benito Cereno*. This question can be answered by turning first to one theme obvious even without the ghost of the Emperor—the fading of his empire to a ghost authority:

Upon a still nigher approach, this appearance was modified, and the true character of the vessel was plain—a Spanish merchantman of the first class, carrying negro slaves, amongst other valuable freight, from one colonial port to another. A very large, and, in its time, a very fine vessel, such as in those days were at intervals encountered along that main; sometimes superseded Acapulco treasure-ships, or retired frigates of the Spanish king's navy, which, like superannuated Italian palaces, still, under a decline of masters, preserved signs of former state. (P. 57)

The Emperor's presence vastly extends this comment on empire.

Charles, who in name held absolute rule over more of the earth's surface than any other man in history, ended by exercising in fact almost as little absolute rule as Cereno. When Melville describes the sea captain as a being like a land monarch, his simile serves to define not only Cereno's role in the story but also the role of his counterpart in history. Since in Cereno "was lodged a dictatorship beyond which, while at sea, there was no earthly appeal," he serves as a well-chosen counterpart for the Holy Roman Emperor, who likewise functions as a well-chosen symbol of all authority on this earth. Thus, when Delano sees in Cereno the embodiment of supreme earthly power, his imperfect awareness applies just as well to Charles: "Lax as Don Benito's general authority might be, still, whenever he chose to exert it, no man so savage or colossal but must, more or less, bow." When this authority is found to be a sham, "and that silver-mounted sword, apparent symbol of despotic command, was not, indeed, a sword, but the ghost of one," the new awareness applies as well to Charles as it does to Cereno.

But Charles, like the "shield-like stern-piece," is, in this regard, only the "principal relic of faded grandeur." Each historical allusion in the story refers to the overthrow or fading of some particular worldly power. Melville compares Cereno to James I: "No sword drawn before James the First of England, no assassination in that timid king's presence, could have produced a more terrified aspect than was now presented by Don Benito." Just as Charles's abdication had marked the passing of the Holy Roman Empire, the accession of James (according to a famous account in Melville's possession), "trembling at a drawn sword,"[38] had marked the passing of a British Empire: "On the day of the accession of James the First our country descended from the rank which she hitherto held, and began to be regarded as a power hardly of the second order."[39] Wounds inflicted on the Negroes are likened to "those shaven ones of the English at Preston Pans, made by the poled scythes of the Highlanders." In the battle of Preston Pans (fought, curiously, on September 21, the anniversary of Charles's death) the royalist forces were defeated by those of the Pretender. Delano compares Cereno's "Christian" steward to George III, loser both of the American colonies and of his own sanity.

A most significant parallel to the successful bloody rebellion of the slaves of the *San Dominick* is the successful bloody rebellion of the slaves on the island of Santo Domingo, a topic of great ante-bellum interest. Babo rises to power on the *San Dominick* in the year in which Toussaint L'Ouverture began extending his rule over all of Santo Domingo. Babo substitutes a skeleton for the *San Dominick's* "proper figure-head—the image of Christopher Colon, the discoverer of the New World." Santo Domingo, not long after its discovery by Columbus, became the seat of Spanish imperial power in the New World. After the Spaniards had exterminated most of the natives, Charles V made Santo Domingo the site of the first large-scale importation of Negro slaves into the Western Hemisphere. Charles's funeral procession, with its "enchanted bark" and "isles emblematic of the Indies," ironically symbolizes the final disintegration of the Spanish New World empire. Not without reason does Captain Delano think that "past, present, and future seemed one."

Melville's central concern is the cause of the overthrow of worldly power, seen in the disintegration of the Spanish empire, its emperor, and its symbolic descendant—Benito Cereno. Stirling shares this concern and defines the cause: "Religion was the enchanted ground whereon his strong will was paralyzed, and his keen intellect fell grovelling in the dust."[40] He charges the Church with responsibility for "the vast fields of intellect which her dark shadow has blighted."[41] The "shadows present, foreshadowing deeper shadows to come" at the beginning of *Benito Cereno* are clearly defined at the end:

> "You are saved," cried Captain Delano, more and more astonished and pained; "you are saved: what has cast such a shadow upon you?"
> "The negro."   (Pp. 139–40)

The Negroes of the *San Dominick* represent not only a malignant destructive force; they also represent the Church.[42] These "friars," "inmates," and "brethren" are strangely similar to Stirling's churchmen. After Cereno's monastic retirement, the monk Infelez assumes the apparent functions of Babo, the "begging friar of St. Francis." Infelez and Babo are described in similar terms, terms very much like those which Stirling used to describe the Bishop of Arras and the famous Jesuit, St. Francis Borja. Babo is not only Cereno's "constant attendant and companion, but in all things his confidant"; Infelez is "his one special guardian and consoler." In Stirling, Borja is Charles V's "old companion and counsellor," whom "alone he had chosen to make the confidant,"[43] and the Bishop of Arras is "his sole counsellor and confidant."[44] Cereno is "attended by the monk Infelez"; Charles is "attended by his confessor."[45] "The emperor lived with the friars on terms of friendly familiarity";[46] Cereno seems to deal with Babo "on no stiffly superior terms but . . . with familiar trust." The Negroes are called "unruly," "stupid," and "ignorant brethren." The friars are called "unruly,"[47] "ignorant and stupid."[48] Delano's reactions to Cereno's command are well described by Stirling: "surprised by his familiarity with the stupid friars . . . marveled at his forebearance with careless servants."[49]

Since Cereno's slaves or friars are really his masters, *Benito Cereno* suggests that Charles's friars were really his masters. It also suggests that the Holy Roman Emperor was not only the slave but also the creation of the Church. When Babo applies the last touches in his shaving and grooming of Cereno, he seemed a "sculptor finishing off a white statue-head." Finally, "the servant for a moment surveyed his master, as, in toilet at least, the creature of his own tasteful hands." Babo himself creates more than this "statue-head"; he also orders the creation of the *San Dominick*'s new "figure-head," the skeleton of Don Alexandro Aranda, the "leader" followed by all.

If the Negroes are an allegorical incarnation of the Church, the skeleton figurehead which they create for all to follow has an obvious significance. As we might expect, Aranda's body disappears "for three days" after his death and reappears "at sunrise." Appropriately it then replaces *Christ*opher Colon. Babo points to his creation and demands that the Spaniards "keep faith with the blacks," threatening that otherwise "you shall in spirit, as now in body, follow your leader."

Thus the Spaniards have several interdependent spiritual and physical leaders: Christ and the Church; Charles and the State; the skeleton figurehead on the *San Dominick*'s prow and the "cadaverous" statue-head created in the *San Dominick*'s monastic cuddy; and the Negroes, who physically create some of these leaders and allegorically create the others. As the ghost of the Catholic monastic Emperor Charles V, Benito Cereno dramatizes the significance of all these leaders.

The common association of royalty with divinity was applied to Charles more literally than to most monarchs. Prior to Charles's abdication, it was not at all clear whether the Pope or the Holy Roman Emperor held the higher Church office. (In fact, Charles not only imprisoned the Pope, but ordered prayers said for him throughout the Church during his captivity.) Even after Charles's abdication, that most devout and orthodox Jesuit, St. Francis Borja, knelt to the Emperor and addressed him as an embodiment of divinity: " 'I humbly beg your majesty . . . to suffer me to continue kneeling; for I feel . . . as if, in the presence of your majesty, I were in the presence of God himself.' "[50] There are many hints that Cereno's "royalty" is also associated with divinity, and that his role is much more significant to the Church than that of a mere "hypochondriac abbot" who retires to the "Hospital de Sacerdotes."

Not only does Cereno appear to have an absolute dictatorship, "but the Spaniard, perhaps, thought that it was with captains as with gods." Delano asks Cereno, "have you appointed them [the oakum-pickers] shepherds to your flock of black sheep?" Cereno replies, "What posts they fill, I appointed them." Cereno says of Atufal, "He must take his stand and abide my coming." Delano conceives "the idea of Don Benito's darkly preordaining Captain Delano's fate," and thinks "that lax as Don Benito's general authority might be, still, whenever he chose to exert it, no man so savage or colossal but must, more or less, bow."

Who or what is this man who in appearance holds supreme power over men and their fates? When Cereno describes to Captain Delano the evidences of his identity, his phrasing is almost precisely that of the famous passage about the Resurrection in Paley's *Evidences of*

Christianity: "They not only saw him, but touched him, conversed with him, ate with him, examined his person to satisfy their doubts."[51] "Said Don Benito, sadly: 'you were with me all day; stood with me, sat with me, looked at me, talked with me, ate with me, drank with me; and yet, your last act was to clutch for a monster, not only an innocent man, but the most pitiable of all men.'" Paley argues at length that Christ, if not the true Messiah, had to be "either an enthusiast or an impostor," suppositions which he attempts to disprove.[52] Delano thinks Cereno's behavior "unaccountable, except on one of two suppositions—innocent lunacy, or wicked imposture," suppositions which he immediately discards. Later, "across the long-benighted mind of Captain Delano, a flash of revelation swept," and, just as with Saul, the "scales dropped from his eyes." Still later, some of Cereno's testimony is "held dubious for both learned and natural reasons," but finally "the revelations of their captain" are accepted. At the last, Delano calls Cereno his savior: "you have saved my life, Don Benito, more than I yours; saved it, too, against my knowledge and will." If Delano's statement is true, then Cereno's denial, "courteous even to the point of religion," is most significantly ambiguous: "Nay, my friend . . . you had the Prince of Heaven's safe-conduct through all ambuscades."

There are several shadowy hints that the relationship between Cereno and Babo is like that between Christ and Judas. Delano, who sometimes obtusely attributes to Cereno characteristics which really belong to Babo, compares Cereno to Judas: "was the Spaniard less hardened than the Jew, who refrained not from supping at the board of him whom the same night he meant to betray?" Christ limits the identity of his betrayer with these words: "But, behold, the hand of him that betrayeth me is with me on the table" (Luke 22:21). At Cereno's last meal on the *San Dominick*, Babo's hand on the table is given an ominous importance: "For nothing was to be seen but the hand of his servant pushing the Canary over towards him." One of Christ's addresses to Judas and the other apostles (John 15:14–15) forms an interesting counterpoint with a passage from *Benito Cereno* (p. 68):

"Ah, master," sighed the black, bowing his face, "don't speak of me; Babo is nothing; what Babo has done was but duty."

Ye are my friends, if ye do whatsoever I command you.

"Faithful fellow!" cried Captain Delano. "Don Benito, I envy you such a friend; slave I cannot call him."

Henceforth I call you not servants; for the servant knoweth not what his lord doeth: but I have called you friends.

John 15:15 goes on to explain: "for all things that I have heard of my Father I have made known unto you." Babo is "in all things his confidant."

The Biblical allusions in *Benito Cereno* are as carefully selected as the historical allusions, and they bear just as heavily on the central meaning. Each alludes to a context which modifies and is modified by the story. To understand this technique, it is only necessary to check the following allusions against their source: the Spanish sailor's "soiled undergarment . . . edged, about the neck, with a narrow blue ribbon" comes from Numbers 15:38; "padlock and key—significant symbols truly" may be explicated by the usual explications of Isaiah 12:22 and Revelations 3:7; Daniel 5 explains the significance of the ship's last bottle of Canary, which is pushed over by "the hand of his servant, mute as that on the wall."

The cumulative effect of all the corresponding historical details and Biblical contexts is twofold. Obviously, they widen the implications of Cereno's destruction. What is not so obvious is the way in which they narrow the definition of that destruction and its cause.

Worldly power, as represented by Benito Cereno, is blighted by "the negro" that "has cast such a shadow" upon him. Worldly power, as represented by Charles V, is "blighted" by the "dark shadow" of the Church. *Benito Cereno* equates the "negro" and the Church by metaphors and by references to *The Cloister Life of Charles the Fifth* and to the Bible. Not only does the shadow of the "negro" represent the shadow of the Church, but it is the heeding of Church teaching, the confidence of Christianity, which destroys Cereno. He had confidence: he followed his leader and trusted the slaves. "None wore fetters, because the owner, his friend Aranda, told him that they were all tractable." As a result, "on Mount Agonia . . . Benito Cereno, borne on the bier, did, indeed, follow his leader." Christ's ultimate message, *"Sequere me,"* has become the text for *Benito Cereno*: *"Seguid Vuestro Jefe."*

When Delano finds Cereno's behavior "unaccountable, except on one of two suppositions,—innocent lunacy, or wicked imposture," he overlooks several other possibilities. Among these is the true explanation of Cereno's behavior—innocent imposture. By consistently maintaining his pose as the real commander of the *San Dominick,* Cereno *saves* Delano. Pierre's imitation of Christ had led to a "pious imposture" in which he had become a kind of Christ. Benito Cereno's innocent imposture dramatizes another part not only of the imitation of Christ, but even of the role of the Saviour.

The question about Cereno is not, as it was with Bartleby, whether he "is" Christ. He obviously is not Christ, but a Spanish sea captain. But as the ghost of Charles V, Cereno re-enacts the Emperor's abdication of the world and servitude to the Church. When he follows the leader of the Church, he, too, is betrayed by the men in whom he has confidence.

THE ASCETICS' ALLEGORICAL MASQUERADE

Bartleby and *Benito Cereno* represent an extremely complicated, extremely well-controlled, and extremely meaningful development of allegory. In both stories the physical action is certainly what one would call realistic (although not commonplace). In fact, *Bartleby* has very little action at all and almost all the action of *Benito Cereno* is copied from a travel book and a history book. This in itself distinguishes these stories from most allegory, which is filled with the most extraordinary kind of adventures. Furthermore, as in the most characteristic "realistic" fiction, great attention is paid to physical details. Of course the ones who pay the greatest attention to minute details are the narrators—the myopic narrator of *Bartleby* and the narrator of *Benito Cereno,* who for the most part is recording the impressions of the myopic Captain Delano. In one sense, this can be taken as a joke on the ethical myopia of the man of the world, but it is also a very serious element in both stories. For in both stories physical details mask allegorical meanings, and meanings and masks redefine each other in a complicated pattern.

The physical action of *Bartleby* is simple. When it is viewed in the light of the message in Matthew 25, however, it assumes an ethical complexity. That is, the enigmatic stranger becomes a representative of Christ and a means of testing the narrator's ability to follow Christ's ethics. Matthew 25 suggests another possibility, which the story insistently reinforces: Bartleby may not merely represent Christ; he may be the Saviour incarnate. Finally, the literal level, the Christian ethical level, and the suggested allegorical level are all redefined by the fact that Bartleby's behavior closely conforms to that of a particular kind of Hindu monk.

Thus we have the following levels of action, each of which requires of us a complicated logical-emotional-ethical response: (1) The physical action of the story. (2) The physical action redefined by Christ's ethics. (3) A suggested religious allegory. (4) A suggested religious allegory redefined by the business-world physical action. (5) The physical action of the story redefined by its consonance with a kind of Hindu monasticism. (6) A suggested religious allegory redefined by its consonance with a kind of Hindu monasticism. As if this were all not complicated enough, we must remember that all these levels come to us through the words of a comically obtuse narrator.

Benito Cereno is even more complicated. In the first place, the physical action in *Benito Cereno* is considerably more involved than the physical action in *Bartleby*. Beyond that, the ethical problems presented by this physical action are also more complex. All parties follow their leaders in brutality. The Spaniards enslave the Negroes; the Negroes brutalize and kill the Spaniards; the Americans shoot and mangle many of the Negroes and shoot a few Spaniards more or less accidentally. Nevertheless, each party follows, in its own peculiar way, some form of Christ.

We have to reckon next with the fact that most of the physical action is derived from Amasa Delano's *Narrative of Voyages and Travels* and William Stirling's *Cloister Life of the Emperor Charles the Fifth*. The story is in a sense a new version of both its sources and therefore a commentary on each. At the same time that the physical action and the ethical action are redefining and being redefined by a book of travels and a history, all the action and one of the sources are suggesting a religious allegory. In this allegory the Catholic Church is embodied by the savage slaves, the slaves create a skeleton figurehead for the leader of their world, and the apparent leader of their world—who is like the apparent leader of the Holy Roman Empire— engages in a Christ-like pious imposture. And all the meanings of worldly and other-worldly power come to us either in the absurd observations of an ethically myopic sea captain or the ridiculous language of official documents which Melville has in large part appropriated from the real-life sea captain's book.

Perhaps the most extraordinary thing about these two extraordinary stories is that they are both highly intense explorations of the meanings of man's gods. Each story presents a mysterious stranger who is more or less like and unlike the mysterious savior central to so many of the world's mythologies. The two stories together ask us to set up a long series of comparisons involving many fictional, historical, and mythical figures.

Bartleby and *Benito Cereno,* great achievements in their own right, also prepare for the next step in Melville's mythology. *The Confidence-Man*: *His Masquerade,* a full-fledged allegory, brings fictional, historical, and mythical figures into a direct confrontation on a Mississippi steamboat known as the *Fidèle.* As men meet their gods, an elaborate pun on confidence displays what the gods mean to man.

CHAPTER 6

THE CONFIDENCE-MAN
The Destroyer's Eastern Masquerade

> *. . . the irresponsible ferociousness of the creature stands invested in the fleece of celestial innocence and love.*
>
> MOBY-DICK

> *In the eyes of Buddhists this personage is sometimes a man, and sometimes a god, or rather he is both one and the other. He is a divine incarnation, a man-god, who came into the world to enlighten men, to redeem them, and point out to them the way of salvation. . . . If we addressed to a Mongol or a Thibetan this question, "Who is Buddha?" he replied instantly, "The Saviour of Men."*
>
> ABBÉ EVARISTE RÉGIS HUC, *A Journey Through the Chinese Empire*

> *Sir Wm. Jones thinks, that the reason christianity is not more readily received among them—is, that they confound their own religion with it, and consider the advent of Christ, as nothing more than one of the incarnations of Vishnu.*
>
> HANNAH ADAMS, *A Dictionary of all Religions*

> *Poor worshippers of Vishnu, how miserably you are striving to hide the realities of the world from your eyes—to strew garlands over the grave! You have never yet dared to pronounce the real name: it is Siva the Destroyer.*
>
> FREDERICK DENISON MAURICE, *The Religions of the World*

The Confidence-Man: His Masquerade is Melville's most nearly perfect work. In no other work—possibly excepting *Bartleby*—is his language under such careful control. Not a word is wasted or misplaced. I say to anybody who thinks he finds a wasted or misplaced word, "Read the book again." In a sense it is a grand *reductio ad absurdum* of the novel form itself. A novel or a prose romance asks us to pay attention to the details of a particular story. These details are words and the physical objects and actions which the words present, describe, and evaluate. *The Confidence-Man* asks us to make this attention extraordinary. We must look at every word, every object, every action as though it represented an ultimate meaning. But every word, every object, and every action in the book is almost endlessly meaningful.

The Confidence-Man is perhaps Melville's most ambitious work. It tries to define every important ethical problem known to man; it tries to dramatize man's epistemological problems; it tries to provide a voice for each way of looking at these problems. On board the *Fidèle* are heard the voices of ancient and modern philosophers, poets, and gods. An incarnation of Plato's Socrates argues with an incarnation of Diogenes; a comic embodiment of Emerson refuses to buy a poem offered by a comic embodiment of Poe; shapes of Manco Capac, Christ, Satan, Vishnu, and Buddha direct the action.[1] *The Confidence-Man* traces Western thought from its origins in the East to its ancient gods and philosophers and to their modern disciples and followers.

The Confidence-Man is Melville's most comic work and his most appalling work. It focuses steadily, although obliquely, on awarenesses in many ways far more terrifying than a knowledge of the great white squid or the great White Whale. It turns universal chaos into a comic cosmos.

But *The Confidence-Man: His Masquerade* is also Melville's most puzzling work. All kinds of verbal and physical tricks and disguises mask the Confidence Man and his world. The reader of *The Confidence-Man* is asked to play a game which is at once amusing and deadly serious. For the game consists of unmasking man's gods and myths.

PRELIMINARY PROBLEMS

Before investigating the mythological structure and meanings of *The Confidence-Man,* I should like to explain what seem to me the three most basic problems in understanding the book. They are: How are we to take the "lamb-like" figure? What are we to do with Black Guinea's list? How can we unmask a confidence man?

a) *The First Avatar?*

The book opens by describing the "advent" of a mysterious figure known as "the man in cream-colors" or the "lamb-like figure." There are few serious students of Melville who doubt that the lamb-like man at least represents Christ and may be an incarnation of Christ. And there are few who doubt that the various avatars of the Confidence Man are all avatars of Satan. Until recently, critics have generally agreed that the lamb-like man is the first avatar of the Confidence Man, that is, either that he is a false Christ or that *The Confidence-Man* presents Christ as an alternative manifestation of the Devil. But most of the criticism of *The Confidence-Man* published in the last few years asserts that the lamb-like man is intended to be a white contrast to Black Guinea, the first avatar of the Confidence Man, that he is a benign Christ who opposes the malign Devil.[2] According to this interpretation, *The Confidence-Man* is a Christian book, at least in so far as it exalts a "true Christianity" by denigrating false Christians and pseudo-Christianity. Another recent interpretation, one that fits the evidence more closely, claims that "the basic structural principle is one that leaves the reader alone with an enigma."[3] Perhaps so. But although the reader is finally left with an enigma, he is also given probable explanations of the enigma. Indeed, with this part of the puzzle, as with all parts (and perhaps with everything), probabilities are all evidence.

The Confidence-Man presents the lamb-like man, who at least represents Christ, as most probably the first avatar of the Confidence Man; the savior is most probably the destroyer. Later we shall see how the book's mythology makes this probable. But we do not need the mythology to perceive eight pieces of circumstantial evidence which indicate that the lamb-like man is probably the first avatar of the Confidence Man:

1. The lamb-like man is introduced with great fanfare and mystery in the opening sentence, and he forms the center of interest in the first two chapters. This pointed introduction certainly encourages the reader to think that the lamb-like man may be the title character of *The Confidence-Man: His Masquerade.*

2. The lamb-like man is in some senses quite literally a confidence man. He introduces the first statements of confidence to the passengers on the *Fidèle*: "Charity thinketh no evil. Charity suffereth long, and is kind. Charity endureth all things. Charity believeth all things. Charity never faileth." What higher or more encompassing confidence can there be?

3. The lamb-like man's mute scriptural message of confidence seems to be the text for the oral polemics of the later avatars. Since the surest way to identify the Confidence Man is to examine the moral and metaphysical contents of his message, the similarity between his mute scripture and their insinuating words constitutes the nearest thing to certainty which is possible in the world of *The Confidence-Man*.

4. After the lamb-like man falls asleep in a retired spot on the forecastle, we never hear another word of him. But in this very place then appears Black Guinea, the first undisputed avatar of the Confidence Man.

5. Immediately after the lamb-like man with his white fleece cap vanishes, we learn of the "black fleece" and "bushy wool" of Black Guinea. Later the word "fleece" becomes one of the puns associated with the Confidence Man.

6. If the lamb-like man is not the Confidence Man of the title, then the Confidence Man's advent is never described. But we know that the lamb-like man boards the *Fidèle* like a god on April Fools' Day.

7. The first of the typically complicated sentences in *The Confidence-Man* begins by describing the lamb-like man and ends by pointedly not repeating the "careful description" which a reward poster gives of "a mysterious imposter, supposed to have recently arrived from the East." Then we learn that the lamb-like man looks as if he had been "traveling night and day from some far country beyond the prairies."

8. The last character to be introduced in *The Confidence-Man* embodies the unity of the lamb-like man and Black Guinea. He is a mysterious boy, thought by his dupe to be a "public benefactor." The boy is the only character besides Black Guinea with a black face;

wearing "such a polish of seasoned grime" as to seem "fresh coal," it recalls the accusation that Black Guinea's face was only painted black. This accusation was made by the cynical cripple, who had then cried, "I'm just in the humor for having him found, and leaving the streaks of these fingers on his paint, as the lion leaves the streaks of his nails on a Caffre." The boy leaves "with the air of a young Caffre." Black Guinea himself is, despite his "black fleece" and "bushy wool," as much a steer as a lamb. A drover calls him "old boy" as he puts his hand on Black Guinea's head "as if it were the curled forehead of a black steer," and Black Guinea has a "leather stump" which he uses as a foot. The mysterious boy "scraped back his hard foot . . . much as a mischievous steer in May scrapes back his horny hoof in the pasture." Of the forty-some-odd characters in *The Confidence-Man,* we are pointedly told that two have no assigned place to sleep. These two are the boy, who is the last character introduced, and the lamb-like man, who is the first character introduced. Because he has only a "deck-passage," the lamb-like man, although he seems to have "long been without the solace of a bed," is forced to sleep on the deck. The boy conducts his suspicious midnight activities because he has "no allotted sleeping-place." The boy is appropriately attired in the "fragment of an old linen coat, bedraggled and yellow," which seems to be all that is left of the lamb-like man's cream-colored clothes. Attention is drawn to the history and significance of his coat by a dialogue that is most significantly ambiguous in language and syntax:

"You seem pretty wise, my lad," said the cosmopolitan; "why don't you sell your wisdom, and buy a coat?"

"*Faith,*" said the boy, "that's what I did to-day, and this is the coat that the price of my wisdom bought. But won't you trade?" [Italics mine.]

The boy's yellow coat, which may once have belonged to the lamb-like man, leads us directly to the list of all the Confidence Man's disguises.

b) Black Guinea's List of Avatars

Black Guinea's list of "ge'mmen" has long been recognized as a list of all the Confidence Man's avatars. Nevertheless, each critic who has tried to explain the list has been left puzzled by some parts of it. Elizabeth Foster, the editor of the new standard edition of *The Confidence-Man,* has provided the most extensive explanation to date. Her analysis is important both for what she explains and for what she cannot explain:

> The crippled Negro had listed his friends in this order: a man with a weed, a man in a gray coat and white tie, a man with a big book, a herb doctor, a man in a yellow vest, a man with a brass plate, a man in a violet robe, and a soldier. There are two discrepancies between this list and the Confidence Men who appear. The only soldier or pseudo-soldier in the novel is the Soldier of Fortune, the cripple who appears while the herb-doctor is on board and who pretends to be a veteran of the Mexican War; he qualifies perhaps as a confidence man when he collects money under slightly false pretenses, but he is a victim rather than an accomplice of the herb-doctor and hardly seems an appropriate inclusion in the Negro's list. The other missing "friend" is the man in the yellow vest. None such appears at any time; but the operator, Charles Arnold Noble, has a "violet vest, sending up sunset hues to a countenance betokening a kind of bilious habit." The significant thing about the appearance of the bilious man is the fine and glowing quality of his clothes or outside, and the mean, sour quality of the man himself; whatever Melville had in mind about the yellow vest may have been well enough represented by the "sunset hues" and the bilious face. Although indeed a confidence man, like the soldier he appears in the wrong order and is a victim rather than an accomplice of the " 'metaphysical scamps.' " It seems most likely that Melville changed or forgot his earlier intention regarding some of the subordinate arrangements of the story. It will be remembered that Melville did not see this novel through the press. Ill and sorely troubled with his eyes, perhaps he did not even read through the whole manuscript before or after Augusta copied it.
>
> The cosmopolitan is most probably the man in the violet robe of the Negro's list; for, although his crimson garment is not the proper shade, no one else in the novel wears a violet robe, and the idea of color and extravagant oddity suggested by the term is best embodied in the strange garb of the cosmopolitan.[4]

If we assume that violet is not crimson, then we count not "two discrepancies" but three—three out of a list of eight. When it becomes necessary, in order to confirm an interpretation of an otherwise most precisely ordered work, to postulate that almost forty per cent of the most important passage is inaccurate and that this passage alone of all the passages in the book was victimized by the author's weak eyes and weaker memory, one would do well to re-examine the interpretation. Professor Foster's reading of both the passage and the book assumes the demonstrably untenable position that the lamb-like man is clearly not the Confidence Man: "At any rate, Melville clearly differentiates between him and the Confidence Men: he is innocent of fraud; he is unequivocal; he is not on the Negro's list of Confidence Men."[5] Since the lamb-like man's message prepares the flock of fools for many later fleecings, he is at the very least an unwitting accomplice to fraud, and "unequivocal" hardly describes this mysterious figure. And is it safe to say that he does not appear on the list which Professor Foster elsewhere finds so defective?

One of the discrepancies which Professor Foster notes is the non-appearance of what she calls "a man in a yellow vest," what Black Guinea calls "a ge'mman in a yaller west." Professor Foster apparently assumes that vest must mean waistcoat. But "vest," from the Latin *vestis,* traditionally meant any garment, particularly an outer garment, a robe, or coat.[6] Thus, both the lamb-like man, in his cream-colored suit, and the wandering boy, in his bedraggled yellow coat, wear a yellow vest. If the boy and the man, as has been hinted, wear the same yellow vestment, then the word "ge'mman" is all that remains to say who is more probably the Confidence Man. If "ge'mman" is taken to mean, as it apparently does in the rest of Black Guinea's list, "gentleman," then the cream-colored man is being described. But if "ge'mman" is here taken to mean "gamin," then it accurately describes the juvenile "marchand."[7] But we do not have to choose between the mysterious man and the mysterious boy, because the man appears with the sun on April Fools' Day and the boy appears shortly after the midnight which ends April Fools' Day. Perhaps the last scene reveals the realities behind the All Fools' Day masks, and the boy is the man unmasked. But what, then, is the Cosmopolitan, who is apparently an avatar of the Confidence Man, who is the central character of the second half of the book, and yet who appears in one scene with the boy? This question is the central mystery of *The Confidence-Man.* To begin to answer it, we must check off one by one and with great care the candidates for Black Guinea's list.

Black Guinea's list *seems* to be a list of the Confidence Man's disguises in the order of their appearance. But this appearance becomes systematically more and more equivocal. The first four and the sixth seeem to appear as described and in the proper order; for the fifth and seventh disguises there are several candidates appearing in different parts of the book; there are innumerable possibilities for the eighth. The ninth and last listing (which Professor Foster does not discuss) is the most ambiguous: "and ever so many good, kind, honest ge'mmen more abord what knows me and will speak for me, God bress 'em; yes, and what knows me as well as dis poor old darkie knows hisself, God bress him!" This last listing is at least as important as any of the others. It states as clearly as can be expected in the world of *The Confidence-Man* that there are considerably more than eight shapes of the Confidence Man in the world.

When Black Guinea asserts that there are "ever so many" who know him as well as he "knows hisself," he explicitly extends the suspicions (or faith) cast by his list to all on board the *Fidèle.* But even without this explicit extension, the list itself spreads a universal suspicion (or faith). Black Guinea's list suggests that we are to determine who the Confidence Man is by examining the colors each man wears, the physical objects each man bears, and the role each man plays. That is, we are to behave like the passengers on the *Fidèle,* who judge each other by what they wear (see the discussion between the good merchant and the President of the Black Rapids Coal Company on the "decorously dressed" card players and the card players wearing "colored cravats"), by what they bear (notice for instance the importance of various books—the big transfer book of the Black Rapids Coal Company, the small vellum-bound volume of Tacitus, the pocket-volume of Akenside, the big Bible), and of course by the roles they play. That is, we are to behave as we usually do, judging by appearances. We are to do what Black Guinea—in all probability an avatar of the Confidence Man—wants us to do.

Thus in order to read *The Confidence-Man* perceptively, it seems that we must begin by following the words of an avatar of the Confidence Man. This is one big joke. Another big joke is that all these very important and equivocal words are spoken by the Confidence Man in a dialect. We are thus invited to look for linguistic equivoques. Before we can guess whom these words indicate we must guess what they mean. And although it sometimes seems obvious who is wearing Black Guinea's masks, we must never overlook the less obvious possibilities. Let us now look carefully at the first eight references given by Black Guinea, the passenger list of the *Fidèle,* and a few dictionaries.

No. 1. "A werry nice, good ge'mman wid a weed." John Ringman, the "man with the weed" in the title of Chapter 5, apparently seems to be behind this mask. But if we take "weed" to mean tobacco, then the cigar scene of Charles Arnold Noble, the riverboat operator, and Frank Goodman, the Cosmopolitan, assumes added significance. And if we take "weed" to mean what Richardson's *Dictionary* (1844) says it means, "A covering; that which covers, spreads over vest or vestment, clothing or garment," then the first of Black Guinea's listings becomes as full of equivocal meanings as the last.

No. 2. "A ge'mman in a gray coat and white tie." "A man in a gray coat and white tie," the agent for the Seminole Widow and Orphan Society, is the obvious appearance. But by no means unsuspect is the Methodist minister who champions Black Guinea a few sentences after Black Guinea calls off his list. When he assaults the cynical cripple, a voice cries out, "The white cravat against the world!"

No. 3. "A ge'mman wid a big book, too." The president and transfer agent of the Black Rapids Coal Company, carrying the ledger-like transfer book under his arm, is the obvious appearance.[8] But the hypocritical old man, who, like the mysterious boy, first appears after April Fools' Day is over, who is the last character mentioned in *The Confidence-Man,* and who is first discovered reading a big book—the Bible—offers his candidacy. The Cosmopolitan tells him "in Providence, as in man, you and I equally put trust."

No. 4 and No. 6. "A yarb doctor" and "a ge'mman wid a brass

plate." These are the only two disguises of the Confidence Man apparently not shared at least in part by more than one passenger.

No. 5. "A ge'mman in a yaller west" and No. 7. "A ge'mman in
a wiolet robe." No passenger on the *Fidèle* wears either a yellow
waistcoat or a violet robe. Either the man in cream colors or the boy
in the old yellow coat, or both, as we have seen, may be "a ge'mman
in a yaller west." Only one other passenger, the herb doctor, wears
a yellowish garment; he is several times pointedly identified as the
man in the snuff-colored surtout. Two passengers wear garments
which might look something like violet, the "gentleman in a ruby-
colored velvet vest" and the Cosmopolitan, who "sported a *vest*ure
barred with various hues, that of the cochineal predominating"
[italics mine]. Charles Arnold Noble, the apparently mundane
riverboat confidence man, combines elements from both the apparently missing disguises by wearing a "violet vest." One other gentleman in a robe appears in the fateful final scene: he is the symbolic
"robed man" on the ground glass of the symbolic solar lamp.

No. 8. "A ge'mman as is a sodjer." Four passengers play the role
of playing the role of soldier on the *Fidèle*. The lamb-like man moves
through the crowd "shield-like bearing his slate before him." "Apparently a non-resistant," he perhaps resembles the "soldier-like Methodist" minister, who, while assaulting the cynical cripple, cries out,
"You took me for a non-combatant did you—thought, seedy coward
that you are, that you could abuse a Christian with impunity. You
find your mistake." This soldier-like Methodist is "a tall, muscular,
martial-looking man . . . who in the Mexican war had been volunteer chaplain to a volunteer rifle-regiment." The third "ge'mman"
who is as a "sodjer" is the man with the bandaged nose who, while
a woman sobs for the herb doctor's proffered alms, shufflingly rises,
and, with a pace that seems "the lingering memento of the lock-step
of convicts," offers himself as a "duly qualified claimant": " 'Poor
wounded huzzar!' sighed the herb-doctor, and dropping the money
into the man's clam-shell of a hand turned and departed." The next
chapter, entitled "A Soldier of Fortune," introduces a beggar who,
while claiming to the herb doctor to have been crippled by civil in-

justice, pretends to have been crippled in military combat in order to get alms.

> . . . arranging his tattered regimentals the best he could, off he went stumping among the passengers, . . . saying with a jovial kind of air: "Sir, a shilling for Happy Tom, who fought at Buena Vista. Lady, something for General Scott's soldier, crippled in both pins at glorious Contreras." (P. 110)

Described as a hyena clawing the herb doctor and displaying an hysterical cynicism, he recalls the cynical crippled "discharged customhouse officer" who wished to claw Black Guinea as a lion claws a Caffre. A "prim-looking stranger" accuses him of belonging to "the Devil's regiment"; the herb doctor then mysteriously intimidates the stranger. All of these "soldiers" seem to be "coming the old soldier," which means "to trick one by false representations, such as are made by a rogue who pretends to be an old soldier."[9]

These four passengers that are as soldiers by no means exhaust the possible significances of Black Guinea's penultimate listing. A real soldier, Colonel John Moredock, though not physically aboard the *Fidèle,* is one of its most important metaphysical passengers, incarnating the "metaphysics of Indian-hating." The very word soldier— derived from *soldus* and literally meaning one who receives pay— might include almost all the *Fidèle*'s passengers, making Black Guinea's penultimate listing as ambiguous as his ultimate. But "sodjer" does not necessarily mean "soldier." Some nautical usages of "sodger" or "sodjer" or "sojer" or "soger" offer even more curious possibilities. Melville, a recognized authority on nautical language,[10] had in *Redburn* used "soger" to mean a deceptive shirker of duty; he knew that "to call a sailor a *sojer* . . . was to start a fight."[11] He undoubtedly also knew that "a red herring . . . sailors usually designate . . . as a sodger."[12]

No. 9. "And ever so many good, kind, honest ge'mmen." This is the meat of *The Confidence-Man,* the meat upon which the Satanic Confidence Man feeds. Diabolical as he is, whether as the Black Man or a White Devil, the Confidence Man can hardly be distinguished among the *Fidèle*'s passengers. We think we know who the Confidence Man is when he appears as "a werry nice, good ge'mman wid a weed," as "a ge'mman in a gray coat and white tie," as "a ge'mman wid a big book," as "a yarb-doctor," and as "a ge'mman wid a brass plate."

But at the end of Chapter 23, which marks the exact center of the forty-five chapters in *The Confidence-Man,* there is a "cordial slap on the shoulder," and a voice "sweet as a seraph's" begins to turn our assurances upside down. From this point on, not one of Black Guinea's "ge'mmen" appears as described.

The sweet voice belongs to the Cosmopolitan, whose appearance divides *The Confidence-Man* precisely into distinct halves. In each of the Cosmopolitan's encounters a real question arises as to who is the greater confidence man, the apparently supernatural and possibly satanic Cosmopolitan or the mundane confidence men of this world. And there are many hints that those who confront the Cosmopolitan are the shape-shifting Confidence Man of the title. They assume not only each other's physical as well as metaphysical positions, but sometimes even each other's names.

After Pitch, who bridges the two halves of the book, retires, the first to greet the Cosmopolitan is an indisputable confidence man, an authentic, conventional riverboat operator. His first words measure the distance between the two halves of the book: "Queer 'coon your friend. Had a little skrimmage with him myself." Since Pitch had one little skrimmage with the herb doctor and another little skrimmage with the man with the brass plate, the riverboat confidence man's remark more than implies that he may be the Confidence Man.

Of course the Cosmopolitan himself is probably the last avatar of the Confidence Man. But in many ways he is different from the avatars of the Confidence Man in the first half of the book. He does not exactly fit any of Black Guinea's listings. He gives away two shillings and receives no money from anyone (although he does, perhaps, bilk the barber for a shave). He directly confronts the out-and-out Mississippi riverboat confidence man. He steadily grows in stature. He is the main character of half the book.

There are many hints that the Cosmopolitan may be a true savior who appears after a series of false saviors. Or, to put it in the metaphor which he himself uses, he may be a true sun dawning just after false suns: "For the Satanic press, by its coappearance with the apostolic, is no more an aspersion to that, than to the true sun is the coappearance of the mock one. For all the baleful-looking parhelion, god Apollo dispenses the day." The final chapter begins with a description of "a solar lamp" which had not been extinguished because "the commands of the captain required it to be kept burning till the natural light of day should come to relieve it." The Cosmopolitan then enters the scene "seeming to dispense a sort of morning through the night." Before he leaves he puts out the artificial solar lamp.

c) *How to Unmask a Confidence Man: Two Related Examples*

The lamb-like man would have us think no evil and believe all things. His mute scripture is of equivocal value on board the *Fidèle,* and if we readers listen to it we will not understand what is going on.

One obvious time when we must be suspicious and incredulous is while listening to the herb doctor's financial finagling. Although he says that he is "pledged to the one-price system," he juggles his prices to make them fit what the market can bear. This is of course not unconventional in American business practices, but he has one trick which even Madison Avenue is not allowed to use: "Well, if two dollars a box seems too much, take a dozen boxes at twenty dollars; and that will be getting four boxes for nothing, and you need use none but those four, the rest you can retail out at a premium, and so cure your cough, and make money by it."

So it is easy enough to find out that the herb doctor is a confidence man. But when the herb doctor says, "I took yonder clergyman" for the President of the Black Rapids Coal Company, he points to a more subtle and complicated disguise of a confidence man. By investigating this disguise, we can discover that the difference between the two halves of the book is more quantitative than qualitative; the second half simply amplifies the quieter but nevertheless pervasive equivocations of the first. We can thus discover that the difference between the Confidence Man and other men is more quantitative than qualitative. That is, contrary to what the lamb-like man would have us believe, none of the *Fidèle*'s passengers is beyond suspicion.

I cannot here demonstrate the ubiquity of suspicious acts and specious rhetoric, of role-playing and shape-shifting. But I can show how easily even the slightest credulity can be beguiled into thinking *The Confidence-Man* far more Christian than it is. Elizabeth Foster singles out for us what seems the most truly Christian Christian in the book:

Another theme, the most obvious of the novel, is the failure of Christians to be Christian. The Methodist minister, goaded into anger by the cynic, seized him and shook him "till his timber-toe clattered on the deck like a ninepin." But Melville's satire on the unchristian leaders of Christ's people is tempered by an honest tribute to the few who carry the Gospels into their acts. The Episcopal minister was steadfast in his kindness and charity—and was duped for his pains. (P. liii)

But the Episcopal minister is in reality a shape-shifting confidence man.

We have already seen that the "soldier-like" Methodist minister's assault on the cripple is defined by a voice as "The white cravat against the world!" and that indeed his white tie and his soldierly characteristics constitute a twofold eligibility for Black Guinea's list. The Episcopal clergyman—apparently a contrast to the Methodist minister, just as the lamb-like man is apparently a contrast to Black Guinea—is defined, obscurely but carefully, as another shape of the Methodist minister. The Methodist minister chronologically follows the Episcopalian just as Methodism chronologically followed the Episcopal establishment. After the Episcopal leaves in search of higher authority, the Methodist tries and fails to settle all issues on a personal basis. Three chapters later, someone identified only as "the young clergyman, before introduced," returns. We then think that we discover that this is the Episcopal clergyman when, in highly suspicious rhetoric, he tells the man in gray of what Professor Foster calls his steadfast kindness and charity:

"You see, shortly after leaving St. Louis, he [Black Guinea] was on the forecastle, and there, with many others, I saw him, and put trust in him;

so much so, that, to convince those who did not, I, at his entreaty, went in search of you, you being one of several individuals he mentioned . . . But, after diligent search, not finding you, and catching no glimpse of any of the others he had enumerated, doubts were at last suggested; but doubts indirectly originating, as I can but think, from prior distrust unfeelingly proclaimed by another." (P. 32)

This young clergyman continues these protestations throughout the chapter, reasserting that "with me at the time" the cynical cripple's "ill words went for nothing." But a careful reading of the chapter discloses who this clergyman is and provides an essential insight into the narrative techniques of *The Confidence-Man.* When he is asked who was the cynical cripple, the young clergyman betrays himself:

"He who I mentioned to you as having boasted his suspicion of the negro," replied the young clergyman, recovering from disturbance, "in short, the person to whom I ascribe the origin of my own distrust; he maintained that Guinea was some white scoundrel, betwisted and painted up for a decoy. Yes, these were his very words, I think." (P. 34)

" 'Impossible!' " is the next word, and impossible it is that the young Episcopal clergyman could know the cripple's very words, the very words to which he ascribes the origin of his distrust. For the cripple, after making his accusation, "was forced to retire." The young Episcopal clergyman had first appeared *after the cripple was gone,* and he was then pointedly introduced as "a person newly arrived from another part of the boat." His first words were not words of trust but an absurd request for witnesses to Guinea's goodness. When Guinea answered with his list of "ge'mmen," the Episcopal clergyman showed that his request was neither trustful nor sincere, and *he immediately departed:* " 'Where are we to find them?' half-rebukefully echoed the young Episcopal clergyman. 'I will go find one to begin with,' he quickly added, and, with kind haste suiting the action to the word, away he went." Immediately the cynical cripple returned and spoke the "very words" upon which the young clergyman now blames his distrust: " 'Wild goose chase!' croaked he with the wooden leg, *now again drawing nigh* [italics mine] . . . . 'He's some white operator, betwisted and painted up for a decoy. He and his friends are all humbugs.' " To this accusation (which might not be totally inapplicable to Black Guinea's latest friend) a new voice had responded: " 'Have you no charity, friend?' here in self-subdued tones, singularly contrasted with his unsubdued person, said a Methodist minister, advancing."

The role of the shape-shifting Christian clergyman becomes explicit just after his self-betrayal. When the man in a gray coat and white tie argues with the cynical cripple about the clergyman, both sides of their argument reveal his role: "Does all the world act?" asks the man in the gray coat and white tie; "Am *I*, for instance, an actor? Is my reverend friend here, too, a performer?" And the cynical cripple answers, "Yes, don't you both perform acts? To do, is to act; so all doers are actors." So that in the world of *The Confidence-Man,* even the most cynical are unaware of the profound depth of their accusations, and even a reader as familiar with the book as its editor can be unaware of many of its acts. Perhaps this explains why the minister is called a "kind gentleman," why a voice says that "we shall wait here til Christmas" for his return, and why, in the chapter entitled "Reappearance of One Who May Be Remembered," the herb doctor, ostensibly looking for the President of the Black Rapids Coal Company, says, "Another mistake. Surprising resemblance. I took yonder clergyman for him."

THE SETTING: A HINDU MASQUERADE

All the acts in *The Confidence-Man,* with the exception of those in the last chapter, take place on the first day of April. The significance of this fact cannot be overstated. On the most obvious level, it equivocates all actions and all words. On another, but explicit, level it reads into the assumed foolishness of April Fools' Day a general and ominous meaning. A conventional nineteenth-century understanding of the significance of the holiday can be found in Charles Lamb's little essay, "All Fools' Day." Lamb sermonizes on the sensibleness of foolishness, the senseless foolishness of the "wise-acre," the trustworthiness of the fool, and cries out, "Beshrew the man who on such a day as this, the *general festival,* should affect to stand aloof."[13]

The Cosmopolitan affects the same language and sentiments: " 'Life is a pic-nic *en costume*; one must take a part, assume a character, stand ready in a sensible way to play the fool. To come in plain clothes, with a long face, as a wiseacre, only makes one a discomfort to himself, and a blot upon the scene.' " But at the same time that Lamb was being whimsical about All Fools' Day, the comparative mythologists were discovering in this festival some disturbing significances.

The pioneers of Indian studies writing for *Asiatick Researches* discovered several apparent sources for the rituals which take place on the first of April. J. D. Patterson, for instance, pointed out that the "*Romans* celebrated the *Hilaria* at the vernal Equinox"[14] and that the festival lasted until the Calends of April. He suggested that in the Hilaria "it was the Earth, under the name of CYBELE, which was worshipped at the commencement of that genial season, when she receives from the Sun those vivifying rays, which are so adapted to the production of fruits and flowers."[15] As the Cosmopolitan obliquely suggests, this may be the time when "the true sun" extinguishes "the mock one." But Patterson's description of the Hilaria suggests another possibility: "the attending crowds assumed to themselves whatever rank, character, or dress, their fancy led them to prefer: it was a kind of masquerade, full of mirth and frolick."[16]

Moving to the East, Patterson finds in India a strikingly similar vernal celebration: "The *Hindus* have likewise their masquerading processions, in which Gods and Goddesses, Rajas and Ranis, are represented; and the ceremonies are concluded, by burning the past or deceased year, and welcoming the renovation of nature."[17] These Hindu masquerades, as we shall see, are most helpful in understanding the Confidence Man's masquerade.

When the Indian Huli was compared with the Roman Hilaria, when these festivals were compared with other European and Asiatic folk festivals, and when all these festivals were compared with Passover and Easter, there arose a growing conviction that some archetypal vernal celebration was the source of them all. The skeptics and apologists established their usual lines of battle around this discovery. Besides the rather weak suggestion that the almost universal festivals were mere coincidence, three principal explanations emerged: the

apologists argued that the pagan festivals were geographically diffused perversions of the Hebrew Passover and therefore of the Christian Easter (the Last Supper was, of course, the eating of the paschal
lamb); some skeptics argued that the rites of spring were simply
celebrations of the resurrection of the sun (the vernal equinox) or
of the resultant rebirth of nature itself; other skeptics argued that
Passover and Easter were geographically diffused versions of the
Hindu Huli.

Thomas Maurice as usual held to a geographical diffusionism line
and tried to conquer the impious astronomical and psychological the-
orists with their own weapons. He not only admitted all the similarities pointed out by the heretics but added to them a mass of similar
details which he insisted were *too* similar and *too* manifold to have
independent psychological origins. If first the universality of a vernal
celebration could be accepted—nay, embraced—and then the origin
of this universal practice could be moved from the Far East and the
West to the Near East, he could put the heretics back where they
started. So in *Indian Antiquities* he first relates April Fools' Day
back to Druidic rites and next traces these Druidic rites back to Hindu
rites. In a section entitled "The First of April or the Ancient Feast
of the Vernal Equinox, Equally Observed in India and Britain," he
begins by describing the great Druidic vernal festival: "The first of
April was anciently observed in Britain as a high and general festival,
in which an unbounded hilarity reigned through every order of its
inhabitants." He admits that "the sun at that period of the year entering into the sign of Aries, the new year, and with it the season of
rural sports and vernal delight, was then supposed to have commenced." But he asserts that the "proof of the great antiquity of the
observance of this annual festival, as well as the probability of its
original establishment in an Asiatic region . . . shall presently be
adduced."[18] With one possible exception, his account of the Druidic
rituals contains little that is relevant to *The Confidence-Man*. That
exception is the fact that "the Arch-Druid" on "the first of April"
leads a procession "to gather the sacred, wonder-working, *all-healing*
MISTLETOE from its parent oak; under the expansive shade of whose

branches the victims were sacrificed, and the festive rites commenced [italics Maurice's]."[19] This may, perhaps, show something about what Melville calls "the true character of the Herb-Doctor." The herb doctor dispenses what he claims to be the all-healing Omni-Balsamic Reinvigorator and Samaritan Pain Dissuader; he, like the Druids, goes directly to Nature for his cure-alls, eschewing "science, that forbidden tree"; he first approaches the sick man who is "visited, but not warmed, by the sun—a plant whose hour seems over, while buds are blowing and seeds are astir"; despite his claimed league with Nature, he is assaulted by the Titanic figure from the forest whose "walking-stick of swamp-oak" attracts the herb doctor's eye.

When Maurice turns to what he considers the origin of the Druidic rituals, he provides a great deal more information about the Confidence Man's rituals. Maurice directly confronts the paper which had started all the trouble for the apologists, and it is this paper which explains part of the Confidence Man's jokes:

[Of the still-preserved sports] none of the least remarkable or ludicrous is that . . . practice of making APRIL FOOLS, as it is called, on the first day of that month; but this Colonel Pearce, in a paper published in the second volume of the Asiatic Researches, has proved to have been an immemorial custom among the Hindoos, at a celebrated festival holden about the same period in India, which is called the Huli festival. I shall insert the account in the Colonel's own words: "During the Huli, when mirth and festivity reign among Hindoos of every class, one subject of diversion is to send people on errands and expeditions, that are to end in disappointment, and raise a laugh at the expense of the person sent. . . . the laugh is always in proportion to the trouble given."[20]

Maurice's immediate objection explains another part of the Confidence Man's jokes:

The least inquiry into the ancient customs of Persia, or the minutest acquaintance with the general astronomical mythology of Asia, would have taught Colonel Pearce, that the boundless hilarity and jocund sports prevalent on the first day of April in England, and during the HULI festival of India, have their origin in the ancient practice of celebrating with festival rites the period of the vernal equinox, or the day when the new year of Persia anciently began.[21]

Little are the passengers on the *Fidèle* aware of the traditions of the day on which they are sailing. They do not know that it is the great vernal festival day, "the birth-day of the Persian monarch," or that they are to await the arrival not only of "the new-born Sun," but also of "the son of the Sun, and his representative on earth."[22]

Maurice tried to move the archetypal vernal festival from India to Persia. He was immediately fired upon from another direction. Godfrey Higgins asserted that Maurice in this chapter had unwittingly proved that all these festivals were the vernal rites of the Bull and the Phallus:

The reader will observe in the whole of the above quotations from Mr. Maurice the style of the Christian apologist, who is endeavouring to account for a disagreeable circumstance which he cannot deny, and to shew that it is not inconsistent with his religious system. He will see that it is the evidence of an unwilling witness, and on this account evidence of the greatest importance. The learning and talent of Mr. Maurice are unquestionable, and it cannot for a moment be doubted, that he would have denied the fact if he could have done it honestly. But in the teeth of the most clear evidence of its existence *that* was absolutely impossible. . . . The reality, close connexion, and object, of the Tauric and Phallic worship, have been so clearly and fully proved by D'Ancarville, Payne Knight, Maurice, Parkhurst in his Hebrew Lexicon, Bryant, Faber, Dupuis, Drummond, and many others, that there is no room left for a moment's doubt.[28]

Higgins used Maurice and other authorities on spring, phallic, Tauric, and astronomical festivals and rites to relate April Fools' Day to the precession of equinoxes from Taurus to Aries:

After the equinox . . . ceased to be in Taurus, and took place in Aries, the equinoctial festivals were changed to the first of April, and were celebrated on that day equally in England and India: in the former, every thing but the practice of making April fools has ceased; but in the latter, the festival is observed as well as the custom of making April fools; that is, the custom of sending persons upon ridiculous and false errands to create sport and merriment, is one part of the rites of the festival.[24]

Like Higgins (and like Nathaniel Hawthorne, who had twenty-one years before discussed the Hindu April Fools' Day),[25] Melville centers attention upon the surviving Western and Eastern April Fools'

Day celebrations. The lamb-like man and steer-like Black Guinea begin the *Fidèle*'s Hindu masquerade.

To help celebrate the great spring festival day on which *The Confidence-Man* takes place, an assortment of Hindu figures comes aboard. As we shall see in the next section, some of these figures are Hindu gods, and Hindu theology and mythology provide the central structure of *The Confidence-Man*. With these figures come so many things from India that sometimes it seems as if the *Fidèle* were steaming down the Ganges, not the Mississippi.

Several enigmatic and suspicious remarks about "the East" alert us to watch for things Indian. Thus we can easily explain the brass plate worn by the man who sells boys, for the article on India in the 1832 American edition of the *Edinburgh Encyclopedia* tells us that "in cases of adoption, the child is placed on a large brass plate."[26] The same article provides more help. It includes a comparison of the Huli with All Fools' Day and gives a standard account of Hindu mythology and theology. It also gives another hint about the appropriateness of India, as conceived of by the West, to the world of *The Confidence-Man*: "especially among the Brahmins, there is frequently displayed a very extraordinary degree of urbanity, proceeding, not from feeling, or even politeness, so much as from hypocrisy. Their command of temper and countenance is indeed astonishing."[27]

Pitch claims that he had employed a boy "Thug." A comparison of *The Confidence-Man* with Edward Thornton's *Illustrations of the History and Practice of the Thugs* (London, 1837) hints that Thugs, translated by Thornton as "deceivers," perhaps lie in wait for the *Fidèle*'s travelers much as they did for all travelers in India:

Different parties frequently act in concert, apprising one another of the approach of travellers whose destruction promises a valuable booty. They assume the appearance of ordinary inoffensive travellers. . . . They are often accompanied by children of ten years of age and upwards; who, while they perform menial offices, are gradually initiated into the horrid practices of Thuggee, and contribute to prevent suspicion of their real character. Skilled in the arts of deception, they enter into conversation, and insinuate themselves by obsequious attentions into the confidence of travellers of all descriptions . . .

[On river Thugs:] Those who do the work of the boatmen are dressed like other boatmen; but those who are to take a part in the operations are dressed like travellers of great respectability; and there are no boats on the river kept so clean and inviting for travellers. When going up the river, they always pretend to be men of some consideration, going on pilgrimage to some sacred place, as Benares, Allahabad, &c.

. . .

It is a bad omen to meet, on the first day of an expedition, any person who has lost a limb; and happily for the maimed, it is equally bad to murder them.[28]

Appropriately, it is the shape-shifting Christian clergyman who laments "that but one man, and he with one leg, should have such ill power given him." The Thugs were motivated primarily not by their booty but by their religion. They faithfully served Kali, the goddess of destruction, the consort of Siva the Destroyer.

THE DIVINE MASKERS

While the apologists were defending their religion from the implications drawn from the dates of its festivals, they were also attempting to distinguish meaningfully their savior god from the mysterious savior god of every other religion. The mysterious beings who came to teach, guide, and redeem the Egyptians, the Hebrews, the Hindus, the Incas, the Aztecs, the Romans, the Greeks, the Persians, the Welsh, and the Polynesians were, for the orthodox, embarrassingly similar. Again, Hindu studies proved particularly troublesome, providing in Krishna, an avatar of Vishnu, an obvious counterpart to Christ. Spelling his name Chrishna or Cristna, the skeptics listed at length the events of his life. What made these events so disturbing is shown in Maurice's grateful acceptance of the apologist theory promulgated by Sir William Jones's "On the Gods of Greece, Italy, and India":

To return to the more particular consideration of those parts of the life of Creeshna which are above alluded to by Sir William Jones, which have been paralleled with some of the leading events in the life of Christ, and are, in fact, considered by him as interpolations from the spurious Gospels; I mean more particularly his miraculous birth at midnight; the chorus of Devatas that saluted with hymns the divine infant as soon as born; his being cradled among shepherds, to whom were first made known those stupendous feats that stamped his character with divinity; his being carried away by night and concealed in a region remote from the scene of his birth, from fear of the tyrant Cansa, whose destroyer it was predicted he would prove, and who, therefore, ordered all the male children born at that period to be slain; his battle, in his infancy, with the dire envenomed serpent Calija, and crushing his head with his foot; his miracles in succeeding life; his raising the dead; his descending to Hades, and his return to Vaicontha, the proper paradise of Veeshnu; all these circumstances of similarity are certainly very surprising, and, upon any other hypothesis than that offered by Sir William Jones, at first sight, seem very difficult to be solved. [Other difficulties include] the name of *Crishna,* and the general outline of his story, confessedly anterior to the birth of Christ, and probably as old as Homer, as well as the apparent reluctance of the haughty self-conceited Brahmin to borrow any part of his creed, or rituals, or legends, from foreigners visiting India.[29]

Jones's theory, that the Hindus had tacked an earlier story onto the wide-traveling spurious Gospels and embellished it grotesquely with their Oriental imagination, met difficulties from another part of the world. While the apologists were denouncing the skeptics and heretics for identifying Krishna with Christ, students of Peruvian mythology were quietly identifying Krishna with Manco Capac, one of those mysterious American redeemers who "make their appearance without any indication of the place of their birth . . . bearing the title of high-priests, of legislators, of the friends of peace, and the arts."[30] This identification could douse the wide-traveling spurious-Gospels theory in the deep, wide waters of the Pacific Ocean. One way out of the difficulties was the way taken by the official Mardian chronicles:

Alma, it seems, was an illustrious prophet, and teacher divine; who, ages ago, at long intervals, and in various islands, had appeared to the Mardians under the different titles of Brami, Manko, and Alma. Many thousands of moons had elapsed since his last and most memorable avatar, as Alma on the isle of Maramma. Each of his advents had taken place in a comparatively dark and benighted age. Hence, it was devoutly believed, that he came to redeem the Mardians from their heathenish thrall; to instruct them in the ways of truth, virtue, and happiness; to allure them to good by promises of beatitude hereafter; and to restrain them from evil by denunciations of woe. Separated from the impurities and corruptions, which in a long series of centuries had become attached to every thing originally uttered by the prophet, the maxims, which as Brami he had taught, seemed similar to those inculcated by Manko. But as Alma, adapting his lessons to the improved condition of humanity, the divine prophet had more completely unfolded his scheme; as Alma, he had made his last revelation. (*Mardi,* II, 38–39)

This, we may recall, was also the way which Jones and Maurice claimed the Hindus took: " '[The Hindus believe] that the Deity *has appeared* innumerable times, and by innumerable Avatars, in many parts, not only of this world, but of all worlds, for the salvation of his creatures; and that both Christians and Hindoos adore the *same God,* under *different forms.*' "[31] This was also the way of some of the strange heretics of the late eighteenth and early nineteenth centuries, who referred, for instance, to "the new, the tenth, and the last Messiah or Avatar, patronised by the Pope of Rome."[32] It is also the way later taken by Melville's Rolfe when he asks " 'whither hast fled, thou deity/So genial? In thy last and best/Best avatar.' "[33] But although the Mardian Pope, the pontiff of Maramma, patronizes Alma as an avatar, Alma as avatar is ultimately transcended by the religion of the heart; the psychological truth of Alma makes the historical truth of Mohi's chronicles and Maramma's dogmas of no consequence whatsoever.

The identity of "Brami, Manko, and Alma" appears again in *The Confidence-Man,* and again the psychological truth of the avatars provides something other than their historical truth. In *The Confidence-Man,* the psychological truth of the avatars' teachings leads to ruin, and the historical truth of the avatars makes this ruin a joke.

As we have seen, the pseudo-avatar is central to *Mardi, Moby-Dick,* and *Pierre.* The narrator of *Mardi* first passes himself off as Taji, "an Avatar," and, when he comes to believe his own fraud, he commits himself to destruction and damnation. Ahab assumes the role of the beneficent Osiris and commits himself utterly to a "supernatural revenge" which leads to destruction and damnation. Pierre seeks through a "pious imposture" to play the role of Christ; he ends imprisoned as a stony Enceladus in a granite hell. Taji, Ahab, and Pierre end in tragedy because they are not gods. But the Confidence Man appears a god to the readers and not to the characters, and that is the central joke of *The Confidence-Man*. It resembles the central joke of *Bartleby,* except that Bartleby himself is not the joker. It grows out of the tragi-comic game of follow-the-leader dramatized in *Benito Cereno*; but here the original leader has boarded the confidence ship. Apparently himself truly a god, the Confidence Man apparently deceives men into destruction and damnation.

When the good merchant (Mr. Roberts) in true charity puts his faith in Black Guinea, with the best intentions he paves the way for being fleeced twice and for having his name recorded in the transfer book of the Black Rapids Coal Company. If this were the transfer book of an earthly coal company, there would be no joke. And if the Confidence Man were merely the devil, the joke, although appalling, would not be entirely unconventional. One thing makes this joke exclusively and peculiarly a *Confidence-Man* joke: the lamb-like man, whose teachings are being put into practice by Mr. Roberts, and the President of the Black Rapids Coal Company, who is apparently registering Mr. Roberts for damnation, are apparently avatars of the same supernatural being. Christ and Satan are the shape-shifting joker known as the Confidence Man.

The concept of the avatar is the central structural principle of *The Confidence-Man*. Modern criticism of the book has partly recognized this fact by making "avatar" the conventional word to describe each of the Confidence Man's appearances. But no one has pointed out that "avatar" is a word and concept from Hindu theology, and that it is fully and peculiarly relevant to *The Confidence-Man*.

In *Mardi,* the redeeming avatar appears as three Mardian savior gods who correspond to three of the world's savior gods: Alma is Mardian for Christ; Manko is Manco Capac; and Brami is Brahma or Brahm. Manko, of course, is the only exact correspondence. Alma, the heart or soul, is a good name for a god of the religion of the heart, the religion of Serenia. Brami is equally suitable for an amphibian deity—half god, half idea. For Brahm (or Brahme, according to many mythologists) is an absolute, impersonal, and philosophically conceived divinity, the ineffable essence of the sacred, whereas Brahma is the personified Brahm conceived as a god. In the later Hindu theology, Brahma had become a distinct part of a trinity, the Creator in combination with Vishnu the Preserver and Siva the Destroyer. Since Mohi's chronicles describe an historical god in a world which needs an ineffable Brahm, the name Brami may be taken as symbolic of tensions between earthly and celestial conceptions, between the theology of Maramma and the religion of Serenia. *Moby-Dick* demonstrates that Melville was not ignorant of the stricter—in fact most strict—Hindu usage of the term *avatar*, and *Pierre* makes a joke about Millthorpe's unknowledgeable use of "avatar." In the strictest sense, *avatar* means a descent of Vishnu, and each of Vishnu's *avatāra* has its own significance. In Melville's parody of comparative mythology in two chapters of *Moby-Dick*, he evinces a detailed knowledge of the first of Vishnu's ten principal avatars, the *Matse* or Fish. *The Confidence-Man* demonstrates a detailed knowledge of all the principal avatars and of the significance of the minor avatars. To comprehend *The Confidence-Man*, one must share part of this knowledge. For Vishnu's avatars coherently order the ambiguities of Black Guinea's list of avatars.

Each of the three Mardian exemplars of the redeeming avatar sails on the *Fidèle*. *The Confidence-Man's* subject is the Christ, the Alma of *Mardi*. *The Confidence-Man's* first sentence compares Christ's embodiment, the lamb-like man, to Manco Capac, the Manko of *Mardi*. Vishnu, the incarnate Brami of *Mardi*, forms the structure of *The Confidence-Man* and provides the figure of the apparently redeeming avatar.

The "advent" of the lamb-like man comes suddenly and appropriately as the sun rises on April first, the day when the sun's northward equatorial crossing is celebrated variously in the various parts of the world. The book begins: "At sunrise on a first of April, there appeared, suddenly as Manco Capac at the lake Titicaca, a man in creamcolors, at the water-side in the city of St. Louis." As the sun passes from Pisces to Aries, while the Jews are eating the paschal lamb and waiting for the Messiah's herald, while the Christians are celebrating the Resurrection of the paschal Lamb, the Messiah, and while the

French are crying "poisson d'avril" at the victims of harmless little jokes, one of the passengers assembled on the "cross-wise balcony" of the *Fidèle* looks down at the sleeping lamb-like man and exclaims "Odd fish!" As *Moby-Dick* tells us, the first avatar of Vishnu was as a fish.

The second avatar was as a tortoise. The message of the "odd fish" sets up the good merchant for the tortoise-like Black Guinea; Black Guinea then sets up the good merchant for the next avatar by "shuffling a pace nigher" in order to cover the merchant's business card with "his one advanced leather stump." Black Guinea lists eight other major avatars of himself and "ever so many" minor avatars; after the fish and the tortoise there are eight major avatars of Vishnu and innumerable minor avatars.[34]

We have already seen how *The Confidence-Man* hints of many avatars, how Black Guinea's list equivocates and is equivocated by the blending, fading, and shape-shifting of the *Fidèle*'s passengers as "these varieties of mortals blended their varieties of visage and garb."[35] Krishna, whose name means "black," the antepenultimate and most popular avatar of Vishnu, in a special revelation in the *Bhagavad-Gita* shows his real nature, which is usually unseen by the eyes of man, to his companion: "Behold, O *Arjoon,* my million forms divine, of various species, and diverse shapes and colours."[36] Krishna explains, in fact, that he is omnipresent. Vishnu as Krishna also explains the occasions and purposes of his avatars:

"Although I am not in my nature subject to birth or decay, and am the lord of all created beings; yet, having command over my own nature, I am made evident by my own power; and as often as there is a decline of virtue, and an insurrection of vice and injustice, in the world, I make myself evident; and thus I appear, from age to age, for the preservation of the just, the destruction of the wicked, and the establishment of virtue."[37]

The salvation offered to the just by Krishna in the *Bhagavad-Gita* is an escape from the continual cycles of metempsychosis, an absorption into the godhead instead of a rebirth into the world. As Krishna explains to his disciple, those "whose confidence is in him . . . go from whence they shall never return."[38] *The Confidence-Man* ends when the Cosmopolitan, after citing to the old man the Scriptural "Jehovah shall be thy confidence," leads the old man away into the night.

The Christian Trinity, although it distinguishes to a certain extent different attributes of God, defines no physical conflict among these attributes and leaves the human mind capable ultimately of only a metaphysical and mystical conception of its nature. English literature has been by and large unsuccessful in dramatizing the Christian Trinity; the attempts of Bunyan and Milton show the strain. But the Hindu Trimurti is dramatically visual. Vishnu and Siva, whether embodiments of metaphysical principles in physical conflict or merely representations of different attributes of Brahm, do clearly set beneficence against maleficence, preservation against destruction, the forces in nature and God that are friendly to man against the forces that are inimical. Most of the mythologists read by Melville tended to conceive of the periodic avatars of these conflicting principles in Manichean terms, comparing them most often to Ormuzd and Ahriman of the Zoroastrians and Osiris and Typhon of the Egyptians. *The Confidence-Man* also sets forth periodic avatars of two conflicting principles. From the moment that the cream-colored man's shield-like message of charity is held up against the background of William Cream's "No Trust" sign until the Cosmopolitan confronts Cream's distrust with a pledge of confidence, two sets of avatars confront each other. From their conflict of opposite principles is spun the narrative of the masquerade. In the final confrontation, after midnight ends the masquerade, the Cosmopolitan's confidence confronts the winking cynicism of the mysterious boy.

The patterned conflict between the avatars may be studied conveniently in the animals associated with them. The first lamb-like avatar is called a "Moon-calf." When Black Guinea replaces him, the lamb becomes a "black sheep" and the moon-calf becomes a "black steer." These animal transformations may perhaps be hints of the zodiacal revolution, but their more obvious significances are of greater importance. They establish the identity of the lamb-like man and Black Guinea, they constitute the first of the many metempsychoses in *The Confidence-Man*, and they define the kind of animals at first associated with the Confidence Man—domestic or tamed animals. Black Guinea is also likened to an elephant opening his mouth for "tossed apples at a menagerie" and he calls himself, most meaningfully, "der dog widout massa." After he is compared to "a half-frozen black sheep nudging itself a cozy berth in the heart of the white flock," this flock is defined as a "flock of fools" by the first wild animal of *The Confidence-Man,* the first cynical cripple. When the cripple is called a wolf, a vulture, and a porcupine, and when he likens himself to a lion, the antagonistic counter-principle to the Confidence Man first becomes embodied. This counter-principle reappears as other wild animals. When the second cynical cripple appears—in manner, morals, and metaphysics indistinguishable from the first—as a hyena he claws the herb doctor. Before and after the second cynical cripple's appearance, the "poor, old rat" in an "old moleskin coat" blinking his "ferret eyes" twice engages the Confidence Man. This old miser is replaced by the wildest of all the Confidence Man's antagonists, the "ursine" Pitch, a "queer 'coon" who vacillates between being "all raccoon," "half wild-cat," and a "snapping turtle" as he badgers the Confidence Man.

As the first half of the book moves toward its close, the tameness of the Confidence Man becomes gradually more equivocal. When the mysterious Titan calls the herb doctor a "snake," a wild animal for the first time is associated with the Confidence Man. Then Pitch, identifying himself as a "coon," calls the herb doctor a "fox." Finally, the fawning doglike mannerisms of the PIO man, which recall the fawning mannerisms of Black Guinea, become in the mind of Pitch metamorphosed into the "undulating flunkyism . . . of the flunky beast that windeth his way on his belly." It is exactly at this point that the hand of the Cosmopolitan slaps Pitch's shoulder and the narrative moves into its doubly ambiguous second half. The snake who has just gone ashore, or has at least said that he was going ashore, at the Devil's Joke landing seems to reappear in several forms. After Indians are likened to snakes, both the riverboat confidence man and the Cosmopolitan seem to be metamorphosed into snakes. The animal transformations in the "wild goose chase" culminate in the figure of the mysterious boy, at once leopard-like, steer-like, and ("what sharp ears you have!") like the wolf who ate Little Red Riding Hood's grandmother.

The boy, embodying and uniting physical characteristics of the most important avatars of the Confidence Man, is also the last avatar of the Confidence Man's antagonist, the No Trust Man. He foreshadows the apocalyptic embodied union of the conflicting principles of preservation and destruction, of sympathy with man and antipathy to man, of confidence and distrust. For he is Muhakalu, an avatar of Siva, who "destroys all, or . . . absorbs all essences into himself at last," and who appears "clothed in red raiment," as "a smoke-coloured boy" whose "teeth are as large as an ogre's."[39]

All pointed and fluttering, the rags of the little fellow's red-flannel shirt, mixed with those of his yellow coat, flamed about him like the painted flames in the robes of the victim in *auto-da-fé*. His face, too, wore such a polish of seasoned grime, that his sloe-eyes sparkled from out it like lustrous sparks in fresh coal. (P. 277)

When the boy laughs "through his grime," he discloses "leopard-like teeth." He is the only avatar of the Confidence Man's antagonist who seems to be a party to the Confidence Man's joke. Just before leaving, the boy turns to the Cosmopolitan and says, "look a lie and find the truth; don't care about a Counterfeit Detector, do ye? or is the wind East, d'ye think?" The mysterious impostor from the East placarded on the first page of *The Confidence-Man* stands revealed, after midnight, in his last avatar.

According to contemporaneous mythologists, the ninth avatar of Vishnu was deemed by most orthodox Buddhists and most orthodox Hindus to be Buddha. But about this orthodoxy there was even less agreement than about most religious orthodoxies. There were other Eastern and Western theological and mythological explanations: Buddha was an earthly savior; Buddha was an earthly impostor; Buddha was not Vishnu but was the divine Savior (distinguished from what was deemed the orthodox Buddhist explanation, that Buddha was the last and greatest avatar of Vishnu as savior). And Maurice advanced still another explanation, which tried to resolve the puzzling contradictions posed by these others. He postulated two Buddhas, the first being the benevolent ninth avatar of Vishnu and the second an impious heretic who became the Chinese Fo.[40] This second Buddha, revered as a god, destroyed faith by saying at his death:

"Whatsoever I have hitherto told you concerning spiritual affairs, and a future scene of existence, is nothing more than an ingenious allegory. There are neither rewards or punishments after life. The principle of all things is an immense *Vacuum*; and human existence terminates in annihilation."[41]

Except for Maurice's finer points, these explanations offer nothing extraordinary. They are, in fact, the same controversial theories held about all the world's savior gods. We are most familiar with their application to Jesus Christ, elsewhere labeled by Melville the Western counterpart of Buddha.[42] All the orthodoxies, heterodoxies, and blasphemies of the Christian world begin by defining Jesus as either the divine Saviour, one of the incarnations of God, a great but mortal teacher, or a dangerous impostor—insane, wicked, or merely deluded. Any of these theories might possibly be argued about the Cosmopolitan, perhaps or perhaps not the last avatar of the Confidence Man, perhaps an earthly or divine savior, perhaps an earthly impostor.

But what was considered the orthodox Hindu explanation of Buddha is quite unfamiliar to Western theology and atheism alike, for neither theologians nor atheists explain Jesus as God incarnate in order to deceive man. According to contemporaneous mythologists, this was how the Hindus explained Buddha: Vishnu descended to earth as a delusive avatar, Buddha, to lead his enemies into beliefs which would destroy them; Buddha was Vishnu incarnate as a deceiver.[43] This conception of the ninth avatar of Vishnu explains the Cosmopolitan, apparently the last avatar of the Confidence Man. It also explains how the Confidence Man represents all the world's savior gods.

The Hindu concept of mystical absorption into the omnipresent godhead may seem to our dull Western minds an annihilation masked by what we might call its pantheistic formulation. But Buddha, deemed the ninth avatar of Vishnu, taught a mystical absorption which to any mind might be annihilation. To the minds of the mid-nineteenth-century comparative mythologists, Nirvana meant not only annihilation but also an unbelievable kind of atheistic urge toward self-destruction. In the 1850's masses of commentary on Buddhism appeared in both books and magazines.[44] The writers were usually puzzled by Buddha's nature and almost always shocked by the nature of his teachings.* They translated *nirvana* with amazed horror as "cessation of existence," and, when this translation seemed incomprehensible, they offered "the extinguishing of a flame or lamp" as a literal translation and visual explanation.[45] The punning substitution of various Christian abstractions for flame or lamp then became a cliché of the Christian magazinists. By 1856, the year before *The Confidence-Man* was published, these puns had become so familiar that a popular magazine article which never made the literal translation ended with these touching words of sympathy to the poor deluded Buddhists: "thy lamp has gone out in the sad hope of an everlasting sleep."[46] An explanation which appeared in at least two popular magazines the year after *The Confidence-Man* shows what sort of thing Melville's audience was reading about the etymology and significance of Nirvana:

The original meaning of the word Nirvana is, "a blowing out," like the extinguishing [of] the flame of a candle. No other word could have been invented more expressive of extinction and annihilation; yet it has been denied that this is really the belief of Buddhism—and that chiefly on the score of the discrepancy that exists between such a view and its supposed logical consequences, and the observed practice, of Buddhists. The dispute as to the meaning of Nirvana is, as Professor Max Müller has shown, not new; and he has successfully proved that, in the theory of Buddhism, extinction or annihilation is the end proposed.[47]

---

* Melville could hardly have shared the incredulity of most of his contemporaries. In the unfinished sketch "Rammon," which he apparently wrote years after *The Confidence-Man,* the title character axiomatically assumes that "cessation of being was the desired event" even before he hears "reports of Buddha and the Buddhistic belief." And in the poem "Buddha," published in the last year of his life, Melville suggests a comparison between Buddha's quest for Nirvana and James the Apostle's description of life as a vapor that passeth away.

Another source, a popular travel book which appeared in English two years before *The Confidence-Man,* tells us that Buddha, looked upon by his worshipers as " 'The Saviour of Men,' " "also substituted for his own name that of Gotamâ, that is, 'He who extinguishes and kills the senses' (*go,* senses, and *tamá,* darkness)."[48] The extinguishing of the solar lamp by the Cosmopolitan is, of course, the symbolic act toward which *The Confidence-Man* moves; the extinguishing of the solar lamp naturally concludes the Confidence Man's teachings.

The temples of Vishnu, according to Maurice, were filled with "the stench of lamps kept continually burning," which symbolized "his GLORY, by horns, imitative of the solar ray."[49] In the "gentlemen's cabin" [ge'mmen's cabin?] in which the last scene of *The Confidence-Man* is played, "burned a solar lamp," which the steward said the captain had commanded "to be kept burning till the natural light of day should come to relieve it." The lamp's "shade of ground glass was all round fancifully variegated, in transparency, with the image of a horned altar, from which flames rose, alternate with the figure of a robed man, his head encircled by a halo." This figure is, as we have seen, the only candidate for Black Guinea's "ge'mman in a wiolet robe" who wears what is actually called a robe. Yet the solar lamp and its ground-glass shade symbolize heavenly truth and the solar god who brings that truth to earth. It is the "last survivor of many," burning on "inwardly blessed by those in some berths, and inwardly execrated by those in others": "here and there, true to their place, but not to their function, swung other lamps, barren planets, which had either gone out from exhaustion, or been extinguished by such occupants of berths as the light annoyed, or who wanted to sleep, not see." The Cosmopolitan says—partly of the solar lamp, partly of the portable water closet which he has given to the old man for a life-preserver, partly of Providence—"Pah! what a smell, too." Then "for the good of all lungs" he extinguishes the lamp before leading the old man away. If the Cosmopolitan is the last avatar of the solar deity—Brami, Manko, Alma, the Confidence Man—then why does he extinguish the robed man, the horned altar, the solar lamp, solar god, and solar truth which symbolize himself?

Hinduism, at least as it was understood by the contemporaneous mythologists, answers the question. The last avatar of Vishnu, who according to the Buddhists purged corruptions from the sacred Vedas, according to the Hindus willfully obscured the Vedas in order to destroy all who followed his teachings. For them, Vishnu as Buddha extinguished the light of Vishnu. This may seem a preposterous theological trick to us and it may have seemed preposterous to Melville, but perhaps not too preposterous to use for dramatizing, in comic terms, the tragic preposterousness of the teachings of his inherited solar Saviour.

The extinguishing of the solar lamp, the natural conclusion to the Confidence Man's teachings, signalizes an ominous sequel, perhaps an apocalyptic sequel. And the last words of *The Confidence-Man* are: "Something more may follow of this Masquerade." It needs no information external to the last chapter of *The Confidence-Man* and the last book of the New Testament to suggest that what may follow may be apocalyptic in every sense.[50] But information found neither in *The Confidence-Man* nor in the book of St. John the Divine may meaningfully explicate Melville's relation of the two books.

The last major avatar listed by Black Guinea is the "ge'mman as is a sodjer," for which we found many not entirely satisfactory candidates among the passengers of the *Fidèle*. The last major avatar of Vishnu is that which is to come, Kalki the Destroyer, armed, leading a white horse. The comparative mythologists were startled by the similarities between Kalki and the white horseman, the armed Logos of Revelation 19, between the Christian and Hindu final comings.

Buddha, the last avatar so far, is the only avatar to appear in this fourth and final age of man, the Cali ("Time") Yug. But at the end of this Yug, Vishnu will descend for the last time, assuming the attributes of Siva the Destroyer, his counter-principle in the Trimurti.[51] At this time, "scarcely any vestiges of justice or piety will remain among mankind, who, degraded equally in stature as intellectual vigour, are considered at the end of that period [the Cali Yug] as ripe for the scythe that is doomed to mow them down."[52]

In an earlier chapter I suggested the following as one of Melville's possible reasons for not choosing the Hindu rather than the Egyptian myth for the structure of *Moby-Dick*: since the cosmic struggle between Vishnu and Siva is ultimately resolved into the unity of the Trimurti, this struggle could not support *Moby-Dick*'s tragic conception. For this very reason, because Vishnu and Siva are ultimately one, their struggle could very well support *The Confidence-Man*'s comic conception. Melville made the shape-shifting struggles and the ultimate identity of Vishnu and Siva into the central structural fact of *The Confidence-Man*. Confidence and distrust, tame animals and wild animals, love and hate—all become indistinguishable in a universe in which black is only another appearance of white.

In this universe man's Savior—Manco Capac, Vishnu, Christ, Apollo, the Buddhists' Buddha—is embodied by the Confidence Man, who is also man's Destroyer—Satan, Siva, the Hindus' Buddha. Melville's mythology converts all gods into the Confidence Man.

CHAPTER 7

BILLY BUDD; OR, BILI-BUDD
The Last Avatar

> *He has also the name of* Budd, Victory, *and* Buddugre, *the* "god of victory, the king who rises in light, and ascends the sky."
>
> SIR EDWARD DAVIES, *The Mythology and Rites of the British Druids*

> *They call their God Budd, the God of Victory, the king who rises in light and ascends the sky.*
>
> GODFREY HIGGINS, *Anacalypsis*

> . . . Bili Buada *or Bile of Victory, whose name possibly meant victorious Death.*
>
> JOHN RHYS, *Lectures on the Origin and Growth of Religion as Illustrated by Celtic Heathendom*

Billy Budd is Melville's last word on the myths of man. In it he describes the making of an idol, a god, and a myth—Billy Budd, who is a man and a god created by man.

Billy Budd opens and closes with the image of a being worshiped by sailors. In the beginning, the black African Handsome Sailor, worshiped like the grand sculptured bull of the Assyrians, fades out and Billy Budd, the blond English Handsome Sailor, appears. In the end, other sailors create of Billy Budd a deity which transcends the Handsome Sailor idol of a single ship; Budd becomes their Christ. Explicit narrative statements label the sailors who adulate the African and English Handsome Sailors and the sailors who finally deify Budd as the ignorant, superstitious sailors who abounded in the time before steamships, that is, they belong to that group of primitives who created the myth of the White Whale. But the myth which the sailors in *Billy Budd* make does not destroy, but saves, them.

Billy Budd, the incarnation of innocent and affable though potent meekness, contrasts in almost every way with Taji, Ahab, and Pierre. He is neither questor nor rebel, hunter nor outlaw. He is innocent of all sin, most especially of pride, the impetus of Melville's Titanic sinners. Taji, Ahab, and Pierre doom themselves with their over-intellection; Budd is almost incapable of intellection. They reject all forms; he accepts all forms. They are wild; he is tame. They are transcendently turbulent; he is transcendently placid. Although as primitive man Budd shows some similarities to other primitive men in the earlier works (such as Queequeg, Dagoo, Tashtego, the natives of Typee and Tahiti, and perhaps the crippled Titan who strikes the herb doctor), he is essentially most similar to two other earlier figures: Bartleby and the first avatar of the Confidence Man.

Bartleby, the lamb-like man, and Billy Budd share the following characteristics:

1. All are inarticulate. Bartleby is called "the silent man"; the lamb-like man is a deaf mute; Billy Budd stammers and even becomes a mute under emotional stress.

2. All have mysterious origins. Rumor is the last word on Bartleby's origin; the lamb-like man is "in the extremest sense of the word, a stranger"; Billy Budd, a foundling, must answer, "No, Sir," when asked, "Do you know anything about your beginning?"

3. All are meek and peaceful. Bartleby is "quite serene and harmless in all his ways"; the lamb-like man is a "non-resistant" who holds up the scriptural call for charity; Billy Budd is the "peacemaker" of the *Rights-of-Man*.

4. Nevertheless, each is victimized by the world. Bartleby is sent to prison on a charge of vagrancy precisely because he refuses to become a vagrant; the "singularly innocent" lamb-like man receives "jeers," "pushes," and "punches"; though Billy Budd's accuser calls him "an angel of God," he hangs him.

5. The images used to describe them are strikingly similar. Be-

sides such details as the comparison of both Billy Budd and the lamb-like man to the mysterious Caspar Hauser or the fact that all three seem to be dead men while still alive, the most significantly similar image is the appearance of each just before he leaves the scene.

Billy's appearance in the darbies is essentially like the final appearance of both Bartleby and the lamb-like man. He seems "a patch of discolored snow in early April," and "in effect he is already in his shroud."[1] The minister who visits him there finds that he "had no consolation to proffer which could result in a peace transcending that which he beheld." "Without movement, he lay as in a trance."

Strangely huddled at the base of the wall, his knees drawn up, and lying on his side, his head touching the cold stones, I saw the wasted Bartleby. But nothing stirred. I paused; then went close up to him; stooped over, and saw that his dim eyes were open; otherwise he seemed profoundly sleeping. (*Bartleby,* pp. 45–46)

His aspect was at once gentle and jaded, and, from the moment of seating himself, increasing in tired abstraction and dreaminess. Gradually overtaken by slumber, his flaxen head drooped, his whole lamb-like figure relaxed, and, half reclining against the ladder's foot, lay motionless, as some sugar-snow in March, which, softly stealing down over night, with its white placidity startles the brown farmer peering out from his threshold at daybreak. (*The Confidence-Man,* p. 5)

6. Each in his way represents Christ. We have already seen how Bartleby and the lamb-like man represent Christ. We shall see how Budd represents Christ.

Bartleby, the lamb-like man, and Billy Budd are all Christ-like beings who play similar roles. It is extremely important to notice, however, that these roles are also different. Whereas it is essential to *Bartleby* and *The Confidence-Man* that no character recognize the true nature of Bartleby and the lamb-like man, *Billy Budd* dramatizes the full recognition of Budd. And, perhaps most important, Bartleby and Billy Budd are innocent, but the lamb-like man is apparently an avatar of malevolence.

Since Budd is certainly innocent and the later avatars of the Confidence Man are probably malevolent, the apparent symbolic identity of Budd with the lamb-like man again raises the question: is the apparently innocent lamb-like man really the first avatar of the apparently malevolent Confidence Man? *Billy Budd,* if anything, reinforces the affirmative answer to this question. First, in the man-of-war world of *Billy Budd,* innocence becomes, if not a great sin, at least a great crime against society, a crime for which society decrees death. The state, the church, and the people combine to enact the ritual punishment of this crime. Second, Billy Budd is surrounded not only by images which recall the lamb-like man but also by some of the very images which cluster around all the avatars of the Confidence Man. Domestic and tame animals, particularly dogs, are frequently associated with both the Confidence Man and Budd. The comparisons of Budd, a "bully boy," to "a heifer," "a young horse," dogs, and other animals recall the animal descriptions of the Confidence Man. As one example, the first image used to describe Black Guinea compares him to a "Newfoundland dog" with his "good-natured, honest black face rubbing against the upper part of people's thighs." Budd's self-consciousness is likened to that of "a dog of St. Bernard's breed," and his face assumes "a look in its dumb expressiveness not unlike that which a dog of generous breed might turn upon his master, seeking in his face some elucidation of a previous gesture ambiguous to the canine intelligence." But similar details of imagery are tenuous and inconclusive. Far more important is the basic structural similarity between the opening of *The Confidence-Man* and the opening of *Billy Budd.* In the same way that the cream-colored lamb-like man fades out and is replaced by the steer-like Black Guinea, the Black Handsome Sailor fades out and is replaced by his symbolic equivalent, Billy Budd, the White Handsome Sailor. This alone refutes those who argue that the contrasting colors of the lamb-like man and Black Guinea must indicate a moral contrast. More important, it hints at what later becomes clear—Billy Budd's divinity. *Bartleby* is the story of a man who *may* be a god, but Melville's last two major works of fiction center upon men who *are* gods.

Billy Budd is the only one of Melville's protagonists who actually bears the name of a god. Curiously, he bears at one time the name of two gods. As Walter Sutton has pointed out in "Melville and the Great God Budd," elements of Buddhistic thought serve important functions in *Billy Budd*.* But the Eastern god Budd is not Billy Budd's primary namesake: both his first name and his last name are names of a particular Western god upon whose mythology and rites Melville constructed *Billy Budd*. This god is the god known as "the Celtic Apollo."

Astronomical conflicts between the true sun-god and mock sun-gods result in much of the imagery in *Mardi*; the opposition between Ahab, the would-be sun-god, and the nature of the true sun and the true sun-god creates some of the cosmic tensions in *Moby-Dick*; the Cosmopolitan equivocally suggests that he may or may not be the true sun and the true Apollo. As might be expected, the myth of the sun-god partly shapes Billy Budd's divinity. The sun-god myth was, of course, the myth upon which the heretical mythologists said that the story of Christ was founded, the myth which the apologists attempted to contrast with the Christ story. Greek mythology preserves this myth most coherently in Apollo, and, to a lesser degree, in Hyperion and Hercules. Billy Budd is compared explicitly to three gods, all Greek—Hyperion, Hercules, and Apollo. Of these three, Apollo is by far the most important. Hyperion yielded his dominion to Apollo; Hercules seems more man than god. Many mythologists therefore resolved all three into one god, represented by Apollo, "the perfection of united manly strength and beauty."[2] Budd, the "angel of God" who strikes down Claggart, appropriately resembles Apollo, to whose darts were ascribed all sudden deaths of men, particularly the sudden deaths of evil men.[3] And Apollo, like Budd, slays the serpent.

The mythologists found that killing the serpent was a central act in the sun-god myth. The apologists struggled with the prophecy

---

* Many nineteenth-century comparative mythologists used "Budd" as a spelling of the name of the Buddhist god. According to Howard Vincent's reading of the text of "Rammon," Melville twice spells the name "Budda" (*Collected Poems*, pp. 412, 413).

about Krishna, Christ's antecedent, and often called "the Indian Apollo," that he would bruise the serpent's head. The skeptics played games like the one Rolfe plays in *Clarel,* I, xxxi, when he telescopes Osiris, Christ, and Apollo into a single myth, even substituting Python, Apollo's reptilian foe, for Typhon-Set, the dismemberer of Osiris. As Maurice puts it, everywhere throughout Asia "was to be seen a god contending with his adversary, an envenomed serpent; Osiris, Hercules, Creeshna, and Apollo, are beheld alternately to aim at the slimy monster the victorious javelin, or wield a destroying club."[4]

The central act of *Billy Budd* comes when Budd slays the serpent. Earlier hints have implied that Claggart is the serpent of Eden. When he accuses Budd, Claggart becomes the reptilian incarnation of evil, the gliding demon hunted by Ahab:

Meanwhile the accuser's eyes, removing not as yet from the blue dilated ones, underwent a phenomenal change, their wonted rich violet color blurring into a muddy purple. Those lights of human intelligence, losing human expression, were gelidly protruding like the alien eyes of certain uncatalogued creatures of the deep. The first mesmeristic glance was one of serpent fascination; the last was as the paralyzing lurch of the torpedo fish. (P. 98)

Unlike Ahab, Budd can and does slay the demon. Claggart's dead body reveals his living nature: "The spare form flexibly acquiesced, but inertly. It was like handling a dead snake." Ahab is slain by the monster which he assails; in futilely trying to purge the seas of life of its gliding great demon, he destroys himself and his crew. Budd succeeds in slaying the monster, and he is therefore destroyed by man. But Budd attains not only victory over the serpent but also victory through his sacrifice over his destruction. And that is why he is named Budd, the "*god of victory,*" "the Celtic Apollo."[5]

Billy Budd is a story about Britain and its navy, and about the values they symbolize. Billy Budd himself is a living embodiment of an elemental kind of Britishness. We most clearly see the essence of Budd's ancient and primitive Britishness in the passage which explains why "the good chaplain" cannot impress "the young barbarian" with Christian notions of death and why he cannot "bring home to him the thought of salvation and a Savior":

Not that like children Billy was incapable of conceiving what death really is. No, but he was wholly without irrational fear of it, a fear more prevalent in highly civilized communities than those so-called barbarous ones which in all respects stand nearer to unadulterate Nature. And, as elsewhere said, a barbarian Billy radically was—as much so, for all the costume, as his countrymen the British captives, living trophies, made to march in the Roman triumph of Germanicus. Quite as much so as those later barbarians, young men probably, and picked specimens among the earlier British converts to Christianity, at least nominally such, taken to Rome (as today converts from lesser isles of the sea may be taken to London), of whom the Pope of that time, admiring the strangeness of their personal beauty so unlike the Italian stamp, their clear ruddy complexion and curled flaxen locks, exclaimed, "Angles" (meaning *English,* the modern derivative) "Angles, do you call them? And is it because they look so like angels?" (P. 120)

In describing these primitive and almost symbolic qualities of the ancient Britons, embodied by Billy Budd, Melville draws upon Polynesia, where he had seen "barbarism" and Christianity in conflict. The chaplain is received by Budd as "the primer of Christianity, full of transcendent miracles, was received long ago on tropic isles by any superior *savage,* so called—a Tahitian, say, of Captain Cook's time or shortly after that time." Billy Budd combines the ultimately primitive sailor, who is like the primitive Polynesian, with the ultimately primitive Briton, both Celtic and Teutonic, who is also like the primitive Polynesian. It should come as no surprise that in this context Melville, who thought of the Druids when he saw the stone ruins of the Typee valley, should think again of the Druids. And it was to Druidism that he went in quest of mythological and religious symbols appropriate to *Billy Budd*. The mythology and rites of the British Druids in large part define both the action and the symbolism of *Billy Budd*.

It is virtually impossible to pinpoint Melville's sources of information on the Druids. The Druids were discussed in detail by such ancient writers as Caesar, Pliny, Horace, Ammianus Marcellinus, Diodorus, Strabo, Lucan, Diogenes Laërtius, and Lucretius; English and Irish antiquarians had been publishing notes, articles, and books on the Druids for over two hundred years before *Billy Budd* was written.[6] There is, however, one source which Melville must have known at least indirectly. This is Sir Edward Davies's *The Mythology and Rites of the British Druids*. Melville read one account of Davies's works in Matthew Arnold's *On the Study of Celtic Literature* (1867), and references to them and the information they contained appeared often throughout nineteenth-century comparative mythology. According to Davies, the most important Celtic god was Hu, the "Celtic Apollo," known also as Beli and Budd.[7]

This British god was, in Davies's view, one source of the Greek gods to whom Budd is likened—Hyperion, Apollo, and Hercules. Davies claims that the Greek gods "are all plainly resolvable into one deity, *the sun*" (and, of course, are "no other than the *great patriarch*").[8] Since "the mythology of the Britons was of a character somewhat more antique than that of the Greeks and Romans . . . the Helio-Arkite god of the Britons comprehended, in his own person, most of the gods which pertained to their superstition."[9]

The god known as Hu, Beli, and Budd was seen "as the *greatest God,* and viewed as *riding on the sunbeams,* or personified in the great luminary, and operating in the clouds and meteors of heaven."[10] He is "expressly identified with Apollo, the solar divinity . . . He has also the name of *Budd, Victory,* and *Buddugre,* the '*god of victory, the king who rises in light, and ascends the sky.*' "[11] When Billy Budd is hanged, the ancient and modern British religions become one:

. . . the last signal, a preconcerted dumb one, was given. At the same moment it chanced that the vapory fleece hanging low in the East was shot through with a soft glory as of the fleece of the Lamb of God seen in mystical vision, and simultaneously therewith, watched by the wedged mass of upturned faces, Billy ascended; and, ascending, took the full rose of the dawn. (P. 124)

Billy Budd consistently symbolizes harmony, tranquillity, and peace, and these symbolic values are often expressed in Christian terms. The captain of the *Rights-of-Man* tells the lieutenant of the *Bellipotent,* who is about to impress Budd, that peace on the merchant ship, which only Budd has succeeded in bringing, will leave with him; and he begs him not "to take away my peacemaker!" The lieutenant's reply, an ironic rephrasing of a passage from the Sermon on the Mount, points up the central tension of *Billy Budd*: "well, blessed are the peacemakers, especially the fighting peacemakers." Just as the Sermon on the Mount supplies words to the officer whose actions mock it, Christianity itself can do no more in this man-of-war world than supply good chaplains for its men-of-war:

Bluntly put, a chaplain is the minister of the Prince of Peace serving in the host of the God of War—Mars. As such, he is as incongruous as a musket would be on the altar at Christmas. Why, then, is he there? Because he indirectly subserves the purpose attested by the cannon; because too he lends the sanction of the religion of the meek to that which practically is the abrogation of everything but brute Force. (P. 122)

Like the modern Budd, the ancient British god was also a symbol of peace; but his peace was the peace which comes from victory. A city's civilization lies within "the established inclosure of the band of the harmonious BUDD."[12] The harmony of Budd derives from slaughter: "And this connexion between the British divinities of *slaughter* and *victory,* is marked in the character of Merdin, who is styled—*Allwedd byddin Budd Ner—the ḳey,* or *interpreter of the army of the god of victory.*"[13] Vere speaks for Budd when he, like a dumb animal or mute god, cannot. Like Merlin (Merdin), Vere marks the connection between slaughter and harmonious victory. In the sacrifice of Billy Budd, Vere consecrates this connection, and dedicates himself and the world he commands to a harmony deriving from slaughter.

The first Handsome Sailor to appear in *Billy Budd* is worshiped like the grand sculptured bull of the Assyrian priests. The old British god Hu, Budd, or Beli—possibly the Celtic equivalent of Baal or Bel—was also often represented by a sacred bull.[14] Davies prints and twice translates a poem which describes a killing of the sacred bull, a killing which Davies says could be either an accident or a mystic ritual:

"It was my earnest wish that thou mightest live, O thou of victorious energy! Alas, thou BULL, wrongfully oppressed, thy death I deplore. Thou has been a friend of tranquility!

In view of the sea, in the front of the assembled men, and near the pit of conflict, the raven has pierced thee in wrath!"[15]

The similarities between the slaying of this sacred bull and the slaying of Billy Budd hardly need statement. Not a soul on the *Bellipotent* but earnestly wishes that Budd might live, Budd of victorious energy. Budd is indeed wrongfully oppressed, and his death is deplored by all. He has been the greatest friend of tranquillity. In view of the sea, in the front of the assembled men, and near the site of fatal conflict, Budd is ritually sacrificed, sacrificed because he has been pierced by the inscrutable wrath beneath Claggart's "silken jet curls."

Of course it was not for their sacrifice of bulls that the Druids were notorious. From Caesar's account on, the human sacrifices of the Druids had many chroniclers and commentators. One of the most widely known authorities was William Borlase, whose eighteenth-century research on the Druids was defended, attacked, and quoted throughout most of the nineteenth century. In a chapter entitled "Of the Druid Worship," Borlase briefly mentions that the Druids "used to sacrifice bulls" and carry "to war with them the image of a bull," but his central concern is with their human sacrifice. He points out that these sacrifices were particularly important in time of war: "For the redemption of the life of Man, they held, that nothing but the life of Man could be accepted by the Gods; and the consequence of this was, that those who implored safety from the dangers of war . . . immediately sacrificed some human creature."[16] To secure for his world safety from the dangers of war, Captain Vere sacrifices Budd.

According to Borlase's account of the Druids' choice of sacrificial victims, Billy Budd would seem to have been an ideal selection:

Their human sacrifice generally consisted of such criminals as were convicted of theft, or any capital crime; . . . but when such malefactors were not at hand, the innocent took their place. They held, that Man was the most precious, and therefore the most grateful victim which they could offer to their Gods; and the more dear and beloved was the person, the more acceptable they thought the offering of him would be accounted. Hence, not only beautiful captives and strangers; but Princes and the first-born of their own children, were, upon great and interesting occasions, offered upon their Altars.[17]

Billy Budd, sacrificed upon a great and interesting occasion, is a criminal convicted of a capital crime; he is innocent; he is dear and beloved by all; he is a beautiful captive; he is a stranger.

If there seem to be any contradictions between Billy Budd's role as sacrifice and his role as god, the next part of Borlase's account of Druidic sacrifice should partially resolve them:

In order to satisfy the scrupulous of the innocence of such barbarous sacrifices, and reconcile the devoted victim to his fate, the Druids held, that the souls of those who served as victims to their Gods in this life, were deified . . . and the remains of those who died in sacrifice, were accounted most holy, and honoured before any other dead bodies.[18]

And there are other partial resolutions.

While Melville was in the early stages of composing *Billy Budd,* John Rhys published a notable work on the Celtic religions. Rhys construed the Welsh Beli to be the Irish Bili or Bile, and he translated Beli, Bili, and Bile as Death.[19] It is easy to understand what Melville meant by the name which he finally decided to give to Billy Budd's ship.[20] The first half of *Bellipotent* is a complicated pun combining a Latin word for war, several of the names of Billy Budd's divine Celtic prototype, and the apparent meaning of these names; the second half suggests that this combination may triumph. Thus the name of the ship is a variant of Billy Budd's own name. For the last page of Rhys's work unites Bili with Buada, the Irish equivalent of Budd, translates these united names, and thus displays one meaning of Billy Budd and his ritual sacrifice: "Bili Buada or Bile of Victory, whose name possibly meant victorious Death."

As a sacrificial offering, Budd plays the role of both the ancient and the modern British god. Many have noticed that Christian terms and images accumulate more and more thickly around Billy Budd as he passes from sailor idol and blessed peacemaker to ritual sacrifice to sailor God. Even the change, "for special reasons," of the yardarm from which Budd is to hang accentuates his image as a Christ: instead of being hanged from the customary foreyard he is hanged from the mainyard, the yard which forms a cross with the central and highest mast.[21] But this crucifix is not merely Christian: "the cross was also used by the Druids as a sacred symbol." "The Druids seek studiously for an oak tree, large and handsome, growing up with two principal arms, *in the form of a cross,* beside the main stem, upright. If the two horizontal arms are not sufficiently adapted to the figure, they fasten a cross-beam to it."[22] Long after Budd's Christ-like and Budd-like ascension into the fleecy sky, the sailors regard the spar from which he was hanged as the true Cross:

The spar from which the foretopman was suspended was for some few years kept trace of by the bluejackets. Their knowledges followed it from ship to dockyard and again from dockyard to ship, still pursuing it even when at last reduced to a mere dockyard boom. To them a chip of it was as a piece of the Cross. (P. 131)

In this man-of-war world, man creates a god by hanging an idolized man from a warship's mainyard, and the mainyard becomes, to the commoners of this world, a true Cross to worship. The Christian terms and symbols piled upon Billy Budd thus have complicated but clearly defined functions. Obviously they exalt and extend Budd's symbolic values. The ancient British god for which Billy Budd is named certainly cannot make his ritual sacrifice as meaningful to modern readers as can the modern sacrificial god, the principal god of the Western world, the only god acknowledged by most of Melville's readers. But since Billy Budd unites the ancient and modern sacrificial gods in one body and one ritual, he embodies a comparison of the two myths. When we realize that Budd's myth is a myth consciously created by his captain, we realize that Budd also dramatizes a statement about all men's gods and shows how and why the Christian god may also have been created by man.

The mythic creation of *Billy Budd* is defined by a triangle which has for its apexes Starry Vere, Billy Budd, and Horatio Nelson. Each pair defines a line of meaning of which the third does not partake. Nelson and Budd die ritual deaths; Nelson and Vere consciously maintain the ritual around these deaths; Vere and Budd perform different parts in the same ritual. Vere does not die a ritual death; Budd is not conscious of the ritual significance; Nelson's ritual is quite different from that of Budd and Vere. Since Nelson performs the dual role of priest and sacrificial victim, his actions can be evaluated only ambiguously. Because "a sort of priestly motive" led him to adorn "*himself* for the altar and the sacrifice," his acts may be mere "vainglory." But what if the priest were not the ritual victim, the sacrificer not the hero? What if the slayer were less willing and more knowledgeable than Nelson, and the slain as willing and less knowledgeable? These are the questions propounded by the sacrifice of Billy Budd.[23]

Unlike Nelson, Vere fights not for the glory of war but against the permanence of war. His solitary reading and thought lead him calmly to define his foe. "Captain Vere disinterestedly opposed" the revolutionary tides not alone "because they seemed to him incapable of embodiment in lasting institutions, but at war with the peace of the world and the true welfare of mankind." He seeks to impose order on disorder. He interprets myth in terms of his dedication to order, and he sees that only the order dramatized by mythic ritual can prevail. Vere is the true priest of the man-of-war world which he commands and of the martial religion which orders this world.[24] With Budd's cooperation, he can maintain the rituals and myths upon which that religion depends.

Vere dissipates the last disorder of *Billy Budd* by calling for the drumbeat to quarters "at an hour prior to the customary one." "The drumbeat dissolved the multitude" because "true martial discipline long continued superinduces in average man a sort of impulse whose operation at the official word of command much resembles in its promptitude the effect of an instinct." Vere explicates the meaning of this ritual:

"With mankind," he would say, "forms, measured forms, are everything; and that is the import couched in the story of Orpheus with his lyre spellbinding the wild denizens of the wood." And this he once applied to the disruption of forms going on across the Channel and the consequences thereof. (P. 128)

The wild denizens of Vere's wood are the men he commands, whose quick response to martial discipline is almost instinctive. Billy Budd, that tame but potent animal, is the perfect sacrifice to these measured forms. The final ritual which follows the hanging and burial of Billy Budd shows how Vere uses these forms to spellbind his wild animals:

> At this unwonted muster at quarters, all proceeded as at the regular hour. The band on the quarter-deck played a sacred air, after which the chaplain went through the customary morning service. That done, the drum beat the retreat; and toned by music and religious rites subserving the discipline and purpose of war, the men in their wonted orderly manner dispersed to the places allotted them when not at the guns. (P. 128)

After the demonstration of the subservience of music and religion to war and the restoration of the order in which all men are allotted places when not at their guns, comes the last paragraph of Billy Budd's story:

> And now it was full day. The fleece of low-hanging vapor had vanished, licked up by the sun that late had so glorified it. And the circumambient air in the clearness of its serenity was like smooth white marble in the polished block not yet removed from the marble-dealer's yard.
> (P. 128)

The ordered forms of the warship's world create a serenity symbolized by a cut and polished, but unsculptured block. This block replaces the glorious fleece.

But the end of Billy Budd's story is not the end of *Billy Budd*: "But though properly the story ends with his life, something in way of sequel will not be amiss. Three brief chapters will suffice." These three brief chapters define the ultimate significance of Vere's religion and the sacrifice of Billy Budd.

In order, they show the effect of Budd's death on the obscure death of Vere, the lies which constitute the official account of Budd's death, and the myth which the sailors make of Budd's death. After the sacrifice of Billy Budd, the *Bellipotent,* "by rare good fortune," subdues and captures "the *Athée* (the *Atheist*)." This is the symbolic triumph of a religion over atheism; the religion which triumphs is a religion of war, of death, of ancient and modern sacrificial gods. Vere, mortally wounded in this symbolic battle, gives up command and later dies ashore, murmuring "Billy Budd, Billy Budd," in what seem "not the accents of remorse." Vere, perhaps the true savior, the preserver of society, could pass to the next commander an ordered command, the ordered command which defeats the *Athée*. Thus, Vere's preservation of martial order leads to the symbolic defeat of chaos, but this chaos kills him. And his death is not the death of a Nelson or a Budd. The second chapter of the sequel quotes the only account "that hitherto has stood in human record," an account which "appeared in a naval chronicle of the time, an authorized weekly publication." This account pictures Claggart the alien serpent as the British hero and Budd the primitive British innocent as the foreign villain. Thus, not only does the martial order decree death to the destroyer of evil, but also the official understanding confuses evil and good. In the final chapter comes the bluejackets' mythical version, a version in ballad form of a truth incomprehensible to the official publication and perhaps unknown even to Vere. Vere's intellectual truth and the sailors' mythical truth enclose the official lies, and transcend, each in its way, the official order.

In *Moby-Dick* the myth created by the superstitious sailors became Ahab's myth, and he futilely tried to slay the demon of the seas of life. Billy Budd slays the serpent with inadvertent ease, and therefore man himself slays Billy Budd. An incarnate metaphysical evil destroyed Ahab. Billy Budd, immune to this evil, is destroyed by the nature of man and man's society. Vere interprets this nature and sustains the military forms which regulate and which decree Budd's death. The sailors turn these "forms, measured forms" into the ballad myth of Billy Budd. These forms and the myth which accepts them mirror a society dependent both on forms and on their mythologized statement. Myth, destructive in the worlds of *Mardi, Moby-Dick,* and *Pierre,* preserves the world of *Billy Budd*. Ahab destroyed all but one through a myth; Vere saves all but one through a myth. But a world in which perfect innocence must be ritually sacrificed in order to create the measured forms upon which society survives is, perhaps, quite as appalling as the world of *The Confidence-Man*.

CHAPTER 8

THE WAKE OF THE GODS

Melville's major works, taken together, provide a coherent and extremely valuable exploration of myth. Like any other study of mythology, they examine and compare particular myths of the world, theorize about the mythmaking process, and ask what meanings, dangers, and values reside in myth. But they do some things which no formal study of mythology can do: they use some of the world's myths as means of ordering and defining action; they dramatize the mythmaking process in action; they dramatically display the meanings, dangers, and values of myth by showing myth itself in action.

At first Melville's mythology differed very little from that found in contemporaneous travel books. The two semi-autobiographical South Sea adventure stories use rather conventional, although unorthodox, formulas to explore the relations between Western, civilized, Christian myths and values and Polynesian, primitive, pagan myths and values. The transmutation of the raw materials began in *Mardi,* his first major work.

Mardi not only compares many of the world's myths, but also portrays the institutions, poetry, philosophy, and theology of the world as a collection of Polynesian myths. By dramatizing contemporaneous theories of mythmaking, *Mardi* tries to discover what myth means. By dramatizing the products of myth, *Mardi* tries to show what myths can do. Central to all the Mardian myths are the various myths of the savior. *Mardi* portrays all savior myths, whether embodied by the Hindu "Brami," the Incan "Manko," or the Christian "Alma," as dangerous deceptions. But it also sees in the teachings of these saviors —stripped of their dangerous mythic trappings—a possible salvation. Yet the safety of a nonmythic religion of the heart cannot keep the would-be god Taji from his suicidal romantic quest.

Moby-Dick drops the Polynesian metaphor and consummates much that began in *Mardi*. Like *Mardi,* it discusses, compares, evaluates, and parodies particular myths of the world and dramatizes the mythmaking process. *Moby-Dick* also appropriates one of the world's myths—the struggle between Osiris and Typhon—to arrange its own action and reveal much of what that action means. The would-be god in *Moby-Dick* is not, like Taji, a runaway sailor chasing a pretty girl. He pursues a real, unbelievably large and destructive dragon, which represents to him what the dragon has represented to many of the nations of the world. *Moby-Dick* presents the Egyptian myth of the savior and the Leviathan he hunts as a prototype or source of many myths, and suggests itself as a more accurate version of all these myths. Osiris and Typhon represent a kind of mythical truth transcended only by the mythical truth which Ahab represents. The myth of the savior, dramatized in terms of the Egyptian and Nantucket hunter of the great demon, becomes as glorious as it is dangerous. In his dragon hunt, Ahab becomes as a god and perishes because he is not a god.

In *Pierre* comparative mythology becomes of less importance, while the ethical values of myth become more important. The narrator of *Mardi* had assumed the name of a god at first merely to protect himself in Polynesia (just like Captain Cook). Ahab had played act by act the role of a god in a godlike but ungodly madness. Both sacrificed everything to their search for the divine. Pierre, however, begins by simply wanting to do the right thing, to do right by everybody. His very selflessness and enthusiastic devotion to what he thinks is his duty leads him into his ever deepening imitation of divinity. The first of these demigods is a fraud; the second is godlike in his impiety; the third stumbles into a "pious imposture." But pious as his imposture may seem to be, it leads him into a Druidic ritual which in turn carries him toward incest, murder, and a hell in which he plays the role of the heaven-defying Greek Titan Enceladus.

After the three audacious would-be gods—Taji, Ahab, and Pierre —meet similar fates, whelmed by the elements, Melville creates quite a different kind of figure. Their bold and loudly articulate assaults on the Absolute are replaced by a meek, inarticulate, and mysterious being who often seems to embody the Absolute. The three principal incarnations of this being are Bartleby the Scrivener, the lamb-like man in *The Confidence-Man,* and Billy Budd. Each incarnation defines and redefines the meaning of god to man.

All the would-be gods of *Mardi, Moby-Dick,* and *Pierre,* the possible god of *Bartleby,* the apparent god of *Benito Cereno,* and the real gods of *The Confidence-Man* and *Billy Budd* have one thing in common: they are all, no matter whether they are modeled on Polynesian, Egyptian, Greek, Hindu, Buddhist, or Druidic myths, similar to and different from Christ. One of Melville's purposes in exploring other myths is always to evaluate the myth of Christ.

"Alma," the Christ of the religion of the heart, defines the central tensions of *Mardi*; Taji misses divine religion in his imitation of mythic divinity. Ahab takes the next step; wholly ignoring the Christian morality for which Starbuck speaks, he commits himself to the role of Christ's predecessor and possible prototype—Osiris, the Egyptian hunter of the demon. Pierre takes the final step; in his moral imitation of Christ he attains the crucifixion and apotheosis of a Christ. And in becoming Christ, he unwittingly destroys all whom he is trying to save. Don Alexandro Aranda follows Christ and induces Benito Cereno to have confidence. As a result, naked evil, defined metaphorically as the Catholic Church, makes of both Aranda and Cereno symbolic Christs to follow to destruction. The implication for Melville was clear: if man, in becoming Christ, becomes an unwitting destroyer, then perhaps Christ, in becoming man, becomes the Confidence Man.

In the first three major works, the characters create their gods: *Mardi* is a book almost entirely about mythmaking; the central struggle of *Moby-Dick* derives from a myth created by Ahab and the whalemen's imagination; Pierre, after his hereditary persuasions are destroyed, constructs from the pieces a god to imitate. But with *Bartleby* a figure appears who is perhaps a god, and *The Confidence-Man* depends for its central joke on the Confidence Man's being in fact a god. The joke is that the *Fidèle's* passengers are being fleeced by a real god, a god not only uncreated by them but totally unrecognized by them. Only the readers of *The Confidence-Man* know that a god prowls the *Fidèle's* decks; they alone recognize him, and they alone can define him.

Billy Budd returns to the central theme of mythmaking, but the mythic god created by Vere and his sailors is as much a god as the Confidence Man. *Billy Budd* shows step by step the creation of a myth, complete with the rituals and ethics of a particular primitive mythology. Melville's mythology has thus come full circle.

Man in the world of *Mardi* creates many gods and can be saved without any god. In *Moby-Dick*, man invents a god to attack, and this god utterly destroys him. In *Pierre,* the gods become meaningless, the conflict between the relativism of earth and the apparent absolutes of heaven becomes mortal, and man, in following what seems heavenly truth, finds none to strike, no salvation—only self-destruction. *Bartleby* and *Benito Cereno* pick up the possibilities of self-destruction, show how all forms of monasticism lead not only out of the world but also into the earth, and prove all the savior gods to be beyond man's creation. Thus sails the *Fidèle,* on which the Confidence Man, an uncreated god, enters the world to gull man with the earthly lie of heavenly truth.

But in *Billy Budd* man can again create his god. Man creates a god and then decrees, performs, and witnesses his ritual slaughter. The god is a man. His religion is a myth which saves man from himself.

Notes

NOTES

CHAPTER I

1. See Frank E. Manuel's *The Eighteenth Century Confronts the Gods* (Cambridge, Mass., 1959) for a superb full-length picture of eighteenth-century mythology, its psychological theories, and its notion of a primitive mind.

2. For a general account see Howard Key, "The Influence of Travel Literature upon Melville's Fictional Technique" (unpublished Ph.D. dissertation, Stanford University, 1952). For a detailed account of Melville's use of Near Eastern travel literature see Dorothée Finkelstein, *Melville's Orienda* (New Haven, Conn., 1961), particularly Chapter 4.

3. Amasa Delano, *Narrative of Voyages and Travels* (Boston, 1817), p. 219.

4. Bayle's influence on Melville, who bought his own set of the *Dictionary* in 1849, has been widely discussed. See, particularly, Millicent Bell's "Pierre Bayle and *Moby-Dick*," *PMLA*, LXVI (1951), 626–48. Melville's use of Maurice's *Indian Antiquities* and *History of Hindostan* was first suggested by Howard Vincent in *The Trying-Out of Moby-Dick* (Boston, 1949), pp. 278–80.

5. See Arthur Christy's *The Orient in American Transcendentalism* (New York, 1932).

6. *Melville in the South Seas* (New York, 1939), pp. 120, 168.

7. *Ibid.,* p. 168.

8. *Typee,* in *Selected Writings of Herman Melville* (New York: Modern Library, 1952), p. 657. (Subsequent references to this edition and to other editions of Melville's works will be given in parentheses in the text.) In viewing Stonehenge as the work of the Druids, Melville shares the usual nineteenth-century opinion, which is now generally discredited.

9. *Clarel,* ed. Walter E. Bezanson (New York: Hendricks House, Inc., 1960), III, vi, 81–90.

10. *Collected Poems of Herman Melville,* ed. Howard P. Vincent (Chicago: Packard and Co. and Hendricks House, 1947), p. 226.

11. In *Selected Writings of Herman Melville,* p. 155.

CHAPTER 2

1. *Mardi: and A Voyage Thither,* 2 vols. (New York: Harper & Bros., 1849), I, 204. Because *Mardi,* Melville's first major work, has been out of print more than a dozen years and because there has never been an adequate modern edition, I use the first American edition. I have taken the liberty of correcting only those errors in spelling and punctuation which are disconcerting and which are obviously errors.

2. "Comparative Mythology," *Oxford Essays* (1856), p. 86.

3. See *Typee,* p. 744, and *Moby-Dick,* end of the chapter "The Praire."

4. *Asiatick Researches,* 5th ed. (London, 1806), I, 221–22.

5. *Journal of a Visit to Europe and the Levant,* ed. Howard C. Horsford (Princeton, N.J., 1955), p. 118.

6. 4 vols. (London, 1831), I, 115ff.

7. *Ibid.,* p. 115.

8. See *Melville's "Mardi": A Chartless Voyage* (New Haven, Conn., 1952), pp. 67–70.

9. William Whiston, *Astronomical Principles of Religion* (London, 1725), pp. 155–56.

10. *An Account of a Surprising Meteor etc.* (London, 1716), p. 63.

11. Edward Davies, *Celtic Researches on the . . . Ancient Britons* (London, 1804), p. 522, observes that "Apo" is Hebrew for viper; Sir J. Gardner Wilkinson, *A Second Series of the Ancient Egyptians,* 2 vols. (London, 1841), I, 435, says that "Apop, which in Egyptian signifies a '*giant*,' was the name given to the Serpent" or "Evil Being."

CHAPTER 3

1. *Moby-Dick: or, The Whale,* ed. Luther S. Mansfield and Howard P. Vincent (New York: Hendricks House, 1952), p. 180. All quotations have been checked against the first American edition.

2. David Hume, *The Natural History of Religion,* ed. H. E. Root (London, 1956), p. 30.

3. Henry David Thoreau, *A Week on the Concord and Merrimack Rivers* (Boston, 1899), p. 76. This was first published in 1849; Melville borrowed Evert Duyckinck's copy in 1850 (No. 524 in Merton M. Sealts, Jr., *Melville's Reading: A Check-list of Books Owned and Borrowed,* offprint from *Harvard Library Bulletin,* 1948–50, Vols. II, III, IV).

4. To give all the references to Moby Dick as a god would be to cite most of the major and many of the minor studies of *Moby-Dick.* A short list of those made by the most disparate critics should suffice: William Braswell, *Melville's Religious Thought* (New York, 1959), p. 59; Richard

Chase, *Herman Melville: A Critical Study* (New York, 1949), p. 49;
Charles Olson, *Call Me Ishmael* (New York, 1947), p. 82; Lawrance
Thompson, *Melville's Quarrel with God* (Princeton, N.J., 1952), p. 204;
Yvor Winters, *In Defense of Reason* (New York, 1947), p. 214.

5. Howard Vincent has noticed Melville's parody of contemporaneous
comparative mythology in the chapter entitled "The Honor and Glory of
Whaling," in *The Trying-Out of Moby-Dick*, p. 276.

6. See Millicent Bell, "Pierre Bayle and *Moby-Dick*," pp. 626–48, and
Vincent, *The Trying-Out of Moby-Dick*, pp. 276, 283–86.

7. James Baird, *Ishmael* (Baltimore, 1956), p. 32.

8. Finkelstein, *Melville's Orienda*, p. 163. Dr. Finkelstein gives the
evidence for Rustam and the White Demon on pp. 162–64. Van Wyck
Brooks first suggested *Beowulf* in *Emerson and Others* (New York, 1927),
p. 205. Koh Kasegawa argues for Tiamat and Bel-Merodach in "*Moby-
Dick* as a Symbolic Myth," *Studies in English Literature* (Tokyo),
XXXVI (1960), 251–72.

9. One previous critic has related, rather enigmatically, the Osiris myth
to *Moby-Dick*. See Olson, *Call Me Ishmael*, pp. 83, 116.

10. See Dr. Finkelstein's section entitled "Belzoni and Ancient Egypt."

11. See "Asiatic Researches . . . Vol. IX," *Edinburgh Review*, XV
(1809), 185, and the review of J. C. Prichard's *An Analysis of the Egyptian
Mythology* (London, 1819) in *Monthly Review*, XCII (1820), 240.

12. Thomas Maurice, *Indian Antiquities*, 7 vols. (London, 1794–1800),
III, 257.

13. The classical sources of Egyptian religion are collected very conveniently, in the original languages, in *Fontes Historiae Religionis Aegyp-
tiacae*, ed. Theodore Hopfner, 2 vols. (Bonn, 1923).

14. Sealts No. 147.

15. *The Golden Bough*, 3d ed., 12 vols. (London, 1911), VI, 3. A useful comparison of mid-nineteenth-century knowledge with Plutarch's may
be found in Gustav Parthey's *Uber Isis und Osiris*, published in Berlin the
year before *Moby-Dick*.

16. *Indian Antiquities*, III, 228.

17. Thomas Maurice, *The History of Hindostan*, 2d ed., 3 vols. (London, 1819), I, 304.

18. *Ibid.*, p. 312.

19. *Ibid.*, p. 22.

20. *Ibid.*, p. 320.

21. Plutarch, "Isis and Osiris," *The Philosophie Commonly Called the
Morals*, trans. Philemon Holland (London, 1603), p. 1296. Holland's
translation is the one from which Melville quotes in the "Extracts."

22. *The Historical Library of Diodorus the Sicilian,* trans. G. Booth, 2 vols. (London, 1814), I, 18.

23. See Manuel, *The Eighteenth Century Confronts the Gods,* p. 190.

24. Hume, *The Natural History of Religion,* p. 57n.

25. See VIII (1823), 237. For a detailed account of Melville's interest in Denderah see Finkelstein, pp. 128–30. Dr. Finkelstein includes a plate of the Denderah Zodiac (facing p. 130).

26. Holland's translation, p. 1316.

27. *Indian Antiquities,* III, 243.

28. *History of Hindostan,* I, 22.

29. "Asiatic Researches . . . Vol. IX," *Edinburgh Review,* XV (1809), 186.

30. "Reuvens on the Egyptian Museum at Leyden," *ibid.,* LIII (1831), 379.

31. See *The Golden Bough,* VI, 16; W. W. How and J. Wells, *A Commentary on Herodotus,* 2 vols. (Oxford, 1957), I, 209; Herodotus, *History,* II, 86.

32. The awkwardness of this apology suggests that it was one of the last-minute revisions which seem to abound in *Moby-Dick.* Howard Vincent's chapter "The Breaching of *Moby-Dick*" sketches Melville's hectic transmutation of the book from simple nautical adventure into complicated symbolical adventure.

33. Maurice's preoccupation with finding trinities led him to collect in a separate volume some of the discoveries made in *Indian Antiquities.* See his *Dissertation on the Oriental Trinities: Extracted from the Fourth and Fifth Volumes of Indian Antiquities* (London, 1801).

34. "Isis and Osiris," pp. 1300–1301.

35. See Godfrey Higgins, *Anacalypsis,* 2 vols. (London, 1836), Vol. II, Chapter 2, particularly pp. 77 and 91.

36. Sir J. Gardner Wilkinson, *A Second Series of the Ancient Egyptians,* 2 vols. plus 1 vol. of plates (London, 1841), I, 339–40.

37. *Anacalypsis,* II, 98–100. A dozen years after *Moby-Dick,* Higgins's books were said to "contain so much strange and out-of-the-way knowledge . . . that they have served better even than the Anatomy of Melancholy as quarries of stone to literary builders; their frequent use for this purpose has been noticed in the reading-room of the British Museum." See John Hill Burton, "Druids and Bards," *Edinburgh Review,* CXVIII (1863), 49.

38. The Iron Crown of Lombardy. First pointed out by Stanley Geist, *Herman Melville: The Tragic Vision and the Heroic Ideal* (Harvard Honors Theses in English, No. 12; Cambridge, 1939), p. 47, and cited by

Braswell, *Melville's Religious Thought*, p. 66. Braswell also uses the passages I cite as evidence that Ahab "has taken upon himself the sufferings of mankind" and that he may "remind one of Jesus Christ."

39. Richard Chase's *Herman Melville: A Critical Study*.
40. *Indian Antiquities*, VI, 193.
41. *History of Hindostan*, I, 320.
42. "Pierre Bayle and *Moby-Dick*," pp. 626–48.
43. *Indian Antiquities*, VII, 580.
44. *Anacalypsis*, II, 77.

CHAPTER 4

1. *Pierre; or, The Ambiguities*, ed. Henry A. Murray (New York: Hendricks House—Farrar, Straus, 1957), p. 200. All quotations have been checked against the first American edition.

2. The stones and rocks in *Pierre* have been frequently discussed, most notably by Richard Chase in the chapter "The Ruined Tower" in *Herman Melville;* by Milton Stern in the chapter on *Pierre* in *The Fine-Hammered Steel of Herman Melville* (Urbana, Ill., 1957); and by Saburo Yamaya in "The Stone Image of Melville's 'Pierre,'" *Studies in English Literature*, XXXIV (1957), 31–58. My discussion at different points coincides and disagrees with each of these three.

3. Manuel, *The Eighteenth Century Confronts the Gods*, pp. 141, 175.
4. *Ibid.*, p. 156.
5. *Ibid.*, p. 174.
6. E. G. Squier, "Aboriginal Monuments of the State of New York," *Smithsonian Contributions to Knowledge* (Washington, D.C., 1851), II, 99–106, 132–57, 164, 196. This also appeared as *Antiquities of the State of New York* (Buffalo, 1851).
7. See, for example, Baird, *Ishmael*, pp. 365–66, and Finkelstein, *Melville's Orienda*, p. 140.
8. *Indian Antiquities*, VI, 132–33.
9. Thompson, *Melville's Quarrel with God*, p. 253.

CHAPTER 5

1. *Bartleby* in *Piazza Tales,* ed. Egbert Oliver (New York: Hendricks House, 1948), p. 28. All quotations from *Bartleby* and *Benito Cereno* have been taken from this edition and have been checked for significant variations against both the original magazine versions and the first American edition of the *Piazza Tales*.

2. See R. H. Fogle's comments on "the narrator-god" who "plays the role of fate" in *Melville's Shorter Tales* (Norman, Okla., 1960), p. 26. Fogle sees this as ironic, but his interpretations of the irony are quite different from mine.

3. Yamaya, "The Stone Image of Melville's 'Pierre,'" p. 38.

4. "Melville and the Great God Budd," *Prairie Schooner*, XXXIV (1960), 129.

5. *Indian Antiquities*, V, 221.

6. *Ibid.*

7. *Ibid.*, p. 246.

8. *Ibid.*, VII, 865.

9. *Ibid.*, V, 247.

10. *Ibid.*, pp. 259–60.

11. *Ibid.*, p. 253.

12. *Ibid.*, p. 256.

13. *Edinburgh Review*, CI (1855), 83.

14. Several critics have discussed the significance of Catholic symbols in *Benito Cereno*. In "'Follow Your Leader': Melville's 'Benito Cereno,'" *Virginia Quarterly Review*, XXIII (1948), 61–76, Stanley Williams maintains that the religious images and incidents in the story dramatize what Melville "believes concerning one of man's oldest institutions, the Catholic Church." Williams discusses the "themes of the fading glories of the Church and Spain" and argues that the cloister is a valid answer, in fact the only answer, for such as Benito Cereno. An interpretation closer to mine is Rosalie Feltenstein's "Melville's 'Benito Cereno,'" *Nineteenth-Century Fiction*, VI (1951), 245–55. Miss Feltenstein shows that the Inquisition is as important to the story as the peaceful cloister. (But see for a minor correction of this article Thomas E. Connoly's "A Note on Name-Symbolism in Melville, *American Literature*, XXV [1954], 489–90.) A recent article, Paul Smith's "*Benito Cereno* and the Spanish Inquisition," *Nineteenth-Century Fiction*, XVI (1962), 345–49, augments Miss Feltenstein's account.

15. William Stirling, *The Cloister Life of the Emperor Charles the Fifth*, 3d ed. (London, 1853), pp. 103–4, and variant, William Stirling, "The Cloister Life of the Emperor Charles V," *Fraser's Magazine*, XLIII (1851), 372. These works will be referred to respectively as *Charles* and "Charles."

16. *Charles*, pp. 104–5, 148, 321.

17. *Ibid.*, pp. 104, 152, and "Charles," p. 379.

18. *Charles*, p. 119.

19. *Ibid.*, p. 104, and "Charles," pp. 373, 375.

20. *Charles,* p. 320, and variant, "Charles," p. 373.

21. *Charles,* p. 80, and "Charles," p. 529.

22. *Charles,* p. 149.

23. *Ibid.,* p. 117, and "Charles," p. 375.

24. *Charles,* p. 5. The shoulder belongs to William of Orange, soon to be the nemesis of Spanish power. I doubt any relation to Babo.

25. "Charles," p. 534.

26. *Ibid.*

27. *Charles,* p. 94.

28. "Charles," p. 367, and variant, *Charles,* p. 27.

29. *Charles,* p. 243.

30. "Charles," p. 533, and variant, *Charles,* p. 185.

31. "Charles," p. 539, and variant, *Charles,* p. 273.

32. *Charles,* pp. xiii–xvii, 231, and "Charles," p. 535.

33. *Charles,* p. 247.

34. *Ibid.,* p. 278, and "Charles," p. 540.

35. For details see "El Emperador, Incorrupto," *ABC: Edicion Semanal Aerea* (Madrid), September 25, 1958.

36. "Charles," p. 540, and variant, *Charles,* p. 279.

37. *Charles,* p. 321.

38. Thomas Babington Macaulay, *The History of England,* 5 vols. (New York, 1849–61), I, 69. (Sealts Nos. 335–37.)

39. *Ibid.,* p. 64.

40. *Charles,* p. 261, and variant, "Charles," p. 544.

41. *Charles,* p. 206.

42. Both Stirling and Melville are drawing on a convention of the Gothic novel and nineteenth-century historiography. For an important discussion of this convention see David Levin, *History as Romantic Art* (Stanford, Calif., 1959), Chapter 5 ("Priestcraft and Catholicism").

43. "Charles," p. 529, and variant, *Charles,* pp. 79–80.

44. *Charles,* p. 14.

45. *Ibid.,* p. 242.

46. *Ibid.,* p. 186, and variant, "Charles," p. 376.

47. *Charles,* p. xxvi.

48. *Ibid.,* p. 317.

49. *Ibid.,* p. 188.

50. "Charles," p. 530.

51. William Paley, *The Evidences of Christianity,* Part II, Chapter 8, in *The Works of William Paley* (New York, n.d.), p. 203. Paley was, of course, required in most English and American schools, and Melville had early become acquainted and disgusted with what he was later to call "the

counting-room philosophy of Paley." See William Gilman, *Melville's Early Life and Redburn* (New York, 1951), p. 58.

52. Paley, p. 181.

CHAPTER 6

1. For the identification of Mark Winsome as Emerson see Egbert S. Oliver, "Melville's Picture of Emerson and Thoreau in *The Confidence-Man,*" *College English,* VIII (1946), 61–72. For the identification of Poe see Harrison Hayford, "Poe in *The Confidence-Man,*" *Nineteenth-Century Fiction,* XIV (1959), 207–18. Pitch is, of course, the modern Diogenes. In the chapter entitled "In the Polite Spirit of the Tusculan Disputations," Pitch has a philosophical discussion about innate knowledge and innate virtue with the man from the "Philosophical Intelligence Office." As my wife first pointed out to me, this modern philosophical dialogue is a carefully constructed parody of Plato's *Meno.* Melville apparently used Emerson's essay on Plato in *Representative Men* as the source for his picture of Socrates. Emerson describes Socrates' "hypocritical pretence of knowing nothing," his "imperturbable" temper, and the way in which, "so careless and ignorant, as to disarm the wariest," he draws them "in the pleasantest manner, into horrible doubts and confusion." There is much else in Emerson's essay which casts light on the character of the PIO man, the Cosmopolitan, and the ethical and metaphysical issues in *The Confidence-Man.*

2. See, for instances, Elizabeth Foster's introduction to the Hendricks House edition of *The Confidence-Man* (New York, 1954); James E. Miller, Jr., "*The Confidence-Man:* His Guises," *PMLA,* LXXIV (1959), 102–11; and John J. Gross, "Melville's *The Confidence-Man:* The Problem of Source and Meaning," *Neuphilologische Mitteilungen,* LX (1959), 299–310.

3. John Cawelti, "Some Notes on the Structure of *The Confidence Man,*" *American Literature,* XXIX (1957), 287.

4. *The Confidence-Man,* Hendricks House ed., pp. lxx–lxxi (this edition is used throughout). J. W. Schroeder, in "Sources and Symbols for Melville's *Confidence-Man,*" *PMLA,* LXVI (1951), 363–80, frankly admits his inability to explain important parts of Black Guinea's list.

5. P. lii. It is surprising that Professor Foster, who sees that the Confidence Man is Satan and suggests that he is a god or gods, should insist on exempting the lamb-like man from Black Guinea's list.

6. See the definitions in Webster's and Richardson's dictionaries, the two modern authorities Melville cited in "Etymology," *Moby-Dick.*

7. At least one modern critic uses the word "gamin" to refer to the boy. See Dan G. Hoffman, "Melville's 'Story of China Aster,' " *American Literature*, XXII (1950), 148.

8. The name of the company is, of course, comically ominous in context, but it resembles the Black Diamond and Anti Cinder Coal Company, for which poor, innocent Mr. Sedley is agent in *Vanity Fair*.

9. Albert Barrère and Charles G. Leland, *A Dictionary of Slang, Jargon, and Cant*, 2 vols. (London, 1897), "Soldier."

10. C. M. Babcock, the philologist who has made some interesting studies of Melville's language, shows that Melville was indeed an expert on nautical language, that "for some thirty individual items from *Moby-Dick* alone, Melville's usage is the first or only citation in the historical dictionaries (NED and DAE). Some whaling glossaries quote Melville directly in the definition of specific expressions." "The Language of Melville's Isolatoes," *Western Folklore*, X (1951), 286.

11. *Ibid*.

12. *OED*, "soldier." See also *Century Dictionary*. Barrère indicates that "coming the old soldier" may relate to "soldier" meaning "a red herring."

13. *"Elia": Essays Which Have Appeared Under That Signature in the London Magazine* (Philadelphia, 1828), pp. 84–90. The entire essay sheds a little light on facets of *The Confidence-Man*. See, for instance, Lamb's comments on "wise, melancholy, politic port." Melville owned Lamb's works (Sealts No. 316).

14. "Of the Origin of the Hindu Religion," *Asiatick Researches* (Calcutta, 1805), VIII, 77.

15. *Ibid.*, p. 78.

16. *Ibid.*, pp. 77–78.

17. *Ibid.*, p. 78.

18. *Indian Antiquities*, VI, 71.

19. *Ibid.*, pp. 84–85.

20. *Ibid.*, pp. 72–73.

21. *Ibid.*, pp. 73–74.

22. *Ibid.*, p. 79.

23. *Anacalypsis*, I, 25.

24. *Ibid.*

25. "April Fools," *American Magazine of Useful and Entertaining Knowledge*, II (Boston, 1836), 339–40.

26. See XI, 284.

27. *Ibid.*, p. 286.

28. Pp. 5–6, 31, 79–80.

29. *History of Hindostan*, II, 222–23.

30. Alexander Humboldt, *Researches Concerning the Institutions and Monuments of the Ancient Inhabitants of America*, trans. Helen Maria Williams, 2 vols. (London, 18—?), I, 29. Krishna is identified with Manco Capac on I, 213.

31. Quotation from "On the Gods of Greece, Italy, and India" cited in *History of Hindostan*, II, 245.

32. *Anacalypsis*, I, 677.

33. *Clarel*, II, xxi, 65–68.

34. Bulfinch's *Age of Fable*, which appeared in Boston two years before *The Confidence-Man*, enumerates only the Fish, the Tortoise, the Krishna, the Buddha, and the Kalki avatars, and indicates that there are ten major and numerous minor avatars; see pp. 427–28.

35. In *Clarel*, III, vi, 84–86, Derwent uses this plurality of gods in his psychological theory of religion, claiming that the imagination of "tropic India . . . breeds gods like seeds."

36. *The Bhagvat-Geeta*, translated, with notes, by Charles Wilkins, facsimile reproduction from the 1785 edition (Gainesville, Fla., 1959), p. 89. Wilkins's was the standard nineteenth-century edition.

37. *Bhagvat-Geeta*, pp. 51–52. Also quoted in *History of Hindostan*, I, 491.

38. *Bhagvat-Geeta*, p. 59.

39. "The Hindoo Pantheon," *Hogg's Instructor*, V (1850), 349.

40. *History of Hindostan*, I, 368–70.

41. *Ibid.*, p. 370.

42. See *Clarel*, I, v, 204–5, and "Rammon," ll. 88–89 in Eleanor Tilton's variorum edition, "Melville's 'Rammon': A Text and Commentary," *Harvard Library Bulletin*, XIII (1959), 50–91. As Professor Tilton says, Melville chose Buddha as "a religious teacher who in character and doctrine would correspond to Christ, a correspondence he did not intend his readers to miss" (p. 91).

43. For a learned account see Vans Kennedy, *Researches into the Nature and Affinity of Ancient and Hindu Mythology* (London, 1831), pp. 262ff. For a popular account see Thomas Bulfinch, *The Age of Fable* (Boston, 1855), p. 427.

44. The year before *The Confidence-Man* appeared, the *Westminster Review* in one article, "Buddhism: Mythical and Historical," reviewed six works (LXVI [1856], 296–331). The year after *The Confidence-Man*, the *London Quarterly Review* in one article, "Buddhism," reviewed seven works (X [1858], 513–44). Within a few months of the publication of *The Confidence-Man* other major articles on Buddhism appeared in the

Eclectic Review (1857), the *Southern Literary Messenger* (three numbers in 1857), the *Christian Observer* (1858), the *Mercersberg Review* (1858), the *Christian Remembrancer* (1858), and *Littell's Living Age* (1858).

45. These translations often come directly from Spence Hardy's influential *Eastern Monachism* (London, 1850).

46. "Buddhism: Mythical and Historical," p. 331.

47. Review of Rowland Williams's *Paraméswara-jnyana-goshthi: A Dialogue . . . in which Are Compared the Claims of Christianity and Hinduism* (Cambridge, 1856), in *Littell's Living Age*, LVII (1858), 377 (reprinted from the *Christian Remembrancer*).

48. Abbé Evariste Régis Huc, *A Journey Through the Chinese Empire*, trans. from the French; 2 vols. (New York, 1855), II, 182.

49. *Indian Antiquities*, V, 85.

50. See Schroeder, "Sources and Symbols for Melville's *Confidence-Man*," p. 374 for a relation between the lamp, robe, and altar of *The Confidence-Man* and those of the book of St. John the Divine.

51. See *Asiatick Researches*, VIII, 53.

52. *History of Hindostan*, III, 121.

CHAPTER 7

1. *Billy Budd: Sailor (An Inside Narrative)*, ed. Harrison Hayford and Merton M. Sealts, Jr. (Chicago, 1962), pp. 118–19. For additional commentary on the similarities between Billy Budd and the lamb-like man, see pp. 140, 144, and 300. The editors point out that in a canceled passage Melville actually refers to Billy Budd as "the young mute" (pp. 144, 376).

2. Charles Anthon, *A Classical Dictionary* (New York, 1854), "Apollo."

3. See, for instance, Anthon's account.

4. *History of Hindostan*, II, 228.

5. Edward Davies, *The Mythology and Rites of the British Druids* (London, 1809), pp. 116, 120, 468, 584, 627; *Anacalypsis*, I, 154.

6. To gain some idea of the mass of work on the Druids, see *Druids and Druidism: A List of References*, compiled by George F. Black (New York, 1920), and the *Catalogue of the Books in the Celtic Department* of the Aberdeen University Library (Aberdeen, 1897).

7. Davies, *Mythology*, pp. 116ff.

8. *Ibid.*, p. 124.

9. *Ibid.*, p. 123.

10. *Ibid.*, p. 112.

11. *Ibid.,* p. 116; see also *Anacalypsis,* I, 154: "they call their God Budd, the God of Victory, the king who rises in light and ascends the sky."

12. Davies, *Mythology,* p. 364.

13. *Ibid.,* p. 468.

14. *Ibid.,* p. 135.

15. *Ibid.,* p. 577; also, slightly variant, pp. 172–73.

16. *Antiquities, Historical and Monumental, of the County of Cornwall. Consisting of Several Essays on the First Inhabitants, Druid-Superstition, Customs, and Remains of the most Remote Antiquity in Britain and the British Isles* (London, 1769), pp. 126–27.

17. *Ibid.,* p. 126.

18. *Ibid.*

19. John Rhys, *Lectures on the Origin and Growth of Religion as Illustrated by Celtic Heathendom: Hibbert Lectures, 1886* (London, 1888), pp. 91, 643, 678.

20. See pp. 20–21 of the Introduction to the Hayford-Sealts edition for the evidence that the *Bellipotent,* not the *Indomitable,* was Melville's final choice for the name of the ship.

21. Vincent Freimarck, "Mainmast as Crucifix in *Billy Budd,*" *Modern Language Notes,* LXXII (1957), 496–97.

22. These two quotations come from E. I. Sears, "The Celtic Druids," *National Quarterly Review,* XI (1865), 1–26, a review of several eighteenth- and nineteenth-century works on the Druids, including one work by Davies and one by Godfrey Higgins. Several pages later, Sears quotes in full Borlase's account of Druidic sacrifice.

23. For three different treatments of Budd's death as ritual sacrifice see Tyrus Hillway, *"Billy Budd:* Melville's Human Sacrifice," *Pacific Spectator,* VI (1952), 342–47; Ray B. West, Jr., "The Unity of *Billy Budd,*" *Hudson Review,* V (1952), 120–28; and R. H. Fogle, *"Billy Budd:* The Order of the Fall," *Nineteenth-Century Fiction,* XV (1960), 189–206.

24. For another type of modern-day Druid, see the sketch Melville wrote at about this time and variously entitled "Asaph Blood," "Daniel Orme," and "Daniel Druid." (Hayford and Sealts correct the long-standing misimpression that this sketch was at one time part of *Billy Budd.*) It is interesting to note that Daniel Orme's counterpart on the *Bellipotent* is the Dansker, who is merely an "old Merlin" with limited oracular powers and no priestly functions. The presence of a fully developed bluejacket Druid on Vere's ship would have mitigated his priesthood of the modern Budd's religion. Vere can command at will the rituals of the "good chaplain" as he could not command a bluejacket priest.

Indexes

A SELECTED INDEX OF
NON-JUDAIC-CHRISTIAN GODS, MYTHS,
AND RELIGIONS IN MELVILLE'S WORKS

The principles of selection used in preparing this Index may be best illustrated by some examples of what have and have not been included. Fabulous beasts such as basilisks, griffins, hippogriffs, and unicorns have not been indexed, but fabulous beasts such as Python and the Kraken have been; Tartarus is not indexed, but Valhalla and Morven are: Lethe is not indexed, but Phlegethon is; nymphs and satyrs, Fate and the Muses have not been indexed. In other words, I have tried to exclude mere literary commonplaces.

The Index omits almost all the countless references to Judaic-Christian mythology and worship. But references to the following are included: Anak, Beelzebub, Belial, Leviathan, and Mammon; uncanonical Rabbinical myths; a few unorthodox sects such as the Gnostics, the Marcionites, and the Mormons.

References to *Clarel, Collected Poems, The Confidence-Man, Moby-Dick,* and *Pierre* are to the Hendricks House editions; references to *Mardi* are to the first American edition; references to *Typee* and the short fiction (*Bartleby, The Encantadas,* "The Two Temples," "Poor Man's Pudding and Rich Man's Crumbs," "The Paradise of Bachelors and the Tartarus of Maids," "The Lightning-Rod Man," "The Happy Failure," "Jimmy Rose," *Benito Cereno,* "The Bell-Tower," "I and My Chimney," "The Apple-Tree Table," and "The Piazza") are to the Modern Library Giant, *Selected Fiction of Herman Melville*; references to *Billy Budd* are to the Hayford-Sealts variorum edition; references to the *Journal* of 1849–50 are to Howard C. Horsford's edition; references to the *Journal* of 1856–57 are to Eleanor Melville Metcalf's edition; references to Melville's lectures ("Statues in Rome" and "The South Seas") are to Merton M. Sealts, Jr., *Melville as Lecturer*; references to *Israel Potter, Omoo, Redburn,* and *White-Jacket* are by chapter only. The sketches and fragments in Volume XIII of the Constable edition are referred to by title only.

The following abbreviated titles are used:

GENERAL INDEX

Melville's characters and the like are identified by the titles of the works in which they appear. The abbreviations used are listed on p. 224.